MW01131042

PRAISE FOR THE POWER OF A PLANT

"This is how change happens, one person at a time, one community at a time. Green Bronx Machine is changing the way children eat, learn, and live!"
—*Reverend Al Sharpton*, PoliticsNation, *MSNBC*

"Stephen Ritz's gift to Dubai has been his passion, his humility, and his belief that when we nurture our roots, beautiful blossoms will grow. Through relationships like these, we will be able to create an alliance of friendships that serve the greater global good and enable our children to live with peace of mind, happiness of heart, and unique bow ties."
—*Dr. Abdulla Al Karam, director general of Knowledge and Human Development Authority (KHDA), government of Dubai*

"Stephen Ritz is the ultimate food superhero. In addition to overcoming his own challenges like losing more than 100 pounds, he has used his knowledge, energy, passion, and spirit to educate youth and thousands of people across the world about healthy and sustainable eating. After talking to him or hearing him speak, you feel inspired and realize that the solutions to alleviate hunger, poverty, obesity, conflict, and other environmental and social problems are not only out there, but they are possible and doable."
—*Danielle Nierenberg, president of Food Tank: The Food Think Tank*

"To know Stephen Ritz is to understand the soul of a true educator and visionary. *The Power of a Plant* traces his journey to create a learning environment that empowers students to take ownership of their own destiny with the knowledge and skills of what it takes to be healthy and happy. Stephen's commitment and compassion to serve the least among us transformed not only the lives of his students but his own life."
—*Jennifer Seydel, PhD, executive director of Green Schools National Network*

"Fertile seeds of change are being planted and nurtured in one of America's most barren neighborhoods, and the resulting bounty is transforming the minds, bodies, and communities of a generation of forgotten youth. There is no more inspiring, hopeful story than that of Stephen Ritz and his Green Bronx Machine and his intrepid efforts to grow a better world, literally. His story feeds my mind, heart, and soul, and will yours, too."
—*Joel Makower, chairman and executive editor of GreenBiz Group; coauthor of* The New Grand Strategy: Restoring America's Prosperity, Security, and Sustainability in the 21st Century

"Over our days embedded in CS-55, the school where Stephen voluntarily spends most of his life, my unique perspective allowed witness to a man fully present in his life's mission—to nurture his students with love and respect. It moved me to tears more than once as I savored every moment of joy and energy radiating from them in response. Those are the days I will remember above all others.

It only takes a moment after meeting Stephen to know that this is a man devoted to changing the lives of his students. Through passion, patience, and the power of a plant that produces real food, Stephen Ritz is building healthy minds and bodies and empowering thousands of children to discover and exploit the potential they never knew they had. *The Power of a Plant* is the extraordinary story of Stephen Ritz—indeed one of the world's most genuine heroes and important role models of our time."

—*Joe Lamp'l, creator, executive producer, and host of* Growing a Greener World

"Just like the amazing plants growing in his South Bronx classroom, possibility grows everywhere he plants the seeds of inspiration. Stephen has a true gift; he inspires all he meets: 5th graders in the Bronx in the morning, a head of state over lunch, and a room full of executives that same evening. And I can report this firsthand. This book is evidence that one man's passion and purpose can truly change the world."

—*Mitchell M. Roschelle, PwC partner; NY Business Development Leader; trustee of PwC Charitable Foundation, Inc.*

"Thanks to people like my good friend Stephen Ritz, we are telling a new Bronx story!"

—*Ruben Diaz Jr., Bronx borough president*

"We live in an economic culture which has chosen to exploit its own children as profit centers for unhealthy food industries, violence, debt, and a myriad of electronic gizmos rather than nurture those same children as the creative agents of a healthy, sane, peaceful, sustainable future. How do we change? It's simple, really. We turn that nurturing over to the kids themselves, taught and guided by Stephen Ritz. Stephen Ritz combines compassion, wisdom, joy, and humor with an urgent, prophetic zeal to teach kids to grow their way into a healthy world. At this time there is no more essential message and no more essential man."

—*Robert Shetterly, artist of "Americans Who Tell the Truth"*

"When Steve Ritz takes the stage to give a talk, he creates an experience that always ends with a standing ovation. His work with and dedication to students in the South Bronx—the poorest congressional district in the country—leaves you laughing, crying, and so inspired you want to jump in and help. He's one man on a mission to not just change lives, but to save them as well—all through growing and educating children with food."

—*Diane Hatz, founder and executive director of Change Food*

"Steve Ritz and I both believe in the powerful ability of projects to drive policy, not the other way around. Our careers followed parallel paths built on trial and error, progress, and results over rhetoric. His book is the culmination of real-world experiences and can add value to whatever you are trying to accomplish."

—*Majora Carter, entrepreneur, real estate developer, urban revitalization strategist*

"Kudos to Stephen Ritz, whose energy and passion were destined to plant a seed that would grow into a forest! His students and followers have been enormously blessed to have him as a leader. And now, with *The Power of a Plant*, his work will have even greater reach and impact."

—*Rae Pica, education consultant and author of* What If Everybody Understood Child Development?

"This green-fingered teacher became one of the top 10 finalist teachers of our US $1m Global Teacher Prize in its inaugural year—a competition that attracted over 5,000 nominations and 1,300 final applications from 127 countries. Since then, both the prize and Stephen's remarkable life-giving program have spread their influence even further around the world. In his new book, *The Power of a Plant*, Stephen shares his incredible journey together with what he has learned so that we can all have food for thought as we search for the simple and elegant solutions needed to make a better world."
—*Vikas Pota, CEO of the Varkey Foundation*

"Stephen Ritz inspires, delights, and provokes. Because of his boundless energy and optimism, he helped me grow as an educational leader. Most importantly, he never loses sight of the ultimate goal—making school a better place for all students."
—*David Ross, CEO of Partnership for 21st Century Learning*

"Collaborating with Stephen Ritz has been one of the most rewarding experiences of my life in education; he is a bastion of hope, inspiration, and positivity. I'm proud to support his effort to extend his incredible influence on the world. Once you read this uplifting book, you will know why!"
—*Walid Abushakra, superintendent and chairman of Esol Education*

"In *The Power of a Plant*, Stephen Ritz, an extraordinarily creative and effective teacher, reflects on his craft and journey, explaining how he ignites the imagination of his students and nurtures their love for learning, around growing food, all while contributing to the need for healthy food of the students and their families. This book is essential reading for anyone who seeks understanding of the immense potential of our public schools and of the conditions that help our best teachers realize that potential for our students."
—*Fernando M. Reimers, PhD, Ford Foundation Professor of the Practice of International Education; Harvard University, Graduate School of Education*

"Stephen Ritz could quite possibly be *the* most inspirational person I have ever had the opportunity to meet and work alongside; he is a true role model for me and thousands of others. His genuine belief in the beauty and power of the human spirit shows up moment by moment in his unwavering commitment and love to help students, adults, schools, and communities grow into their fullest potential. *The Power of a Plant* beautifully captures the essence of his character and power of his work, and the reader's inspiration will *grow* with each turn of the page."
—*Jenna Cramer, vice president of Transformation and Community, Green Building Alliance; and Green & Healthy Schools Academy*

"Stephen Ritz is not only teaching kids about the world, he's showing them—and all of us—how to create a better world together, not only through his holistic educational methods but also by being the person he wants his students to be. Having visited his school in the South Bronx, I was shocked by the conditions in which these children have to learn, but also uplifted by how Stephen involved the whole community in creating situations for children to learn and thrive. This book is required reading for everyone involved in educating our children for a better world."
—*Jelmer Evers, Global Teacher Prize finalist, teacher, and author of* Flip the System: Changing Education from the Ground Up

"Stephen Ritz has a magnetic personality and a green thumb, but the many students who are inspired to love their studies because of him are also motivated by the gardens he builds with them. They see a huge paradise of plants growing on the concrete outside their Bronx school, and it becomes a source of pride and a resolve to succeed. It is as if they are saying, 'If this garden can flourish year after year in this hard-edged neighborhood, then so can I.'"
—*Bill Yosses, White House executive pastry chef, 2007–2014*

"Challenging times call for innovative solutions and bold thinking, and no one does that quite like Steve Ritz. He is what happens when you take equal parts passion, creativity, and a commitment to change lives and top it off with a goofy cheese hat. Steve has been a constant inspiration during my time in public life, and I know that the lessons distilled in this book will inspire you as well. Go Green Bronx Machine!"
—*Honorable Gustavo Rivera, New York state senator*

"From serendipity to sense of purpose, Stephen Ritz's odyssey, imbued with grit and resilience, has magically transformed the lives of countless young people to passionately pursue their dreams. They enriched not only their own lives but also their communities—often those plagued by poverty, violence, addiction, and despair into ones shining with hope and a brighter future. A remarkable and spellbinding story that will inform and inspire the reader. "
—*Sanjiv Chopra, MD, professor of medicine, Harvard Medical School; author; and speaker*

"Stephen Ritz's Green Bronx Machine is an extraordinary combination of a skillful authentic education approach and innovative social entrepreneurship. His masterful teaching skills, dedication to service of students and community to transform schools into fertile learning environments has made a profound, positive impact on classrooms around the world. Stephen's message and model of learning via the 'power of the plant' transcends the walls of the classroom and steps successfully into the realm of a real-life learning phenomenon."
—*Steve Revington, pioneer of Authentic Learning; Canada's Prime Minister Award of Teaching Excellence; 2016 Global Teacher Prize Top 50 finalist*

"I am very hopeful for the future, and teaching kids at an early age that they can be 'makers' and 'doers' of things vs. just consumers of things is so very important. Stephen is empowering the next generation of makers in his classroom. He gets it. Feed them well, give them an environment where they can learn by doing, get hands on, and share with each other—this is a formula that can be replicated and one where everyone wins. His book, *The Power of a Plant,* shows us how!"
—*Sherry Huss, cofounder of Maker Faire*

"Stephen Ritz is on the forefront of a food justice revolution. Realizing that healthy food impacts learning and performance, he has taught many of our scholars at Community School 55 via Green Bronx Machine in the Bronx how to take their health and their future into their own hands. This book paves the way to grow a generation of citizens who think critically about the intersections of health, learning, and participating in the world around them. It's a must-read for anyone who cares about the future and #BuildingABetterBronx."
—*Honorable Michael Blake, New York state assemblyman, Democratic National Committee*

"*The Power of a Plant* gives readers a glimpse at Stephen Ritz's contagious enthusiasm about the importance of urban gardens in education and nurturing the potential of young people—particularly youth in low-income communities where economic and political forces have often limited educational opportunities. *The Power of a Plant* recounts the evolution of a program—Green Bronx Machine—that, through critical pedagogy and community building, has changed the lives of the youth that have participated in it. These perspectives will be important for educators in the immediate future and for years to come."
—*Kristin Reynolds, PhD, urban food systems researcher, New York, NY; adjunct faculty in environmental studies and food studies at The New School; coauthor of* Beyond the Kale: Urban Agriculture and Social Justice Activism in New York City

"Don't be distracted by the kale. It's a prop. Steve is a magician, a vegetable wizard, and he's growing engaged learners with an appetite for life and a hunger for knowledge. El Capitan Ritz is teaching a generation how to give, how to 'human' with all the grace and fierceness needed by a teacher in a Bronx classroom."
Mud Baron, teacher, Tweeter—@Cocoxochitl, candidate for Pasadena Unified School Board, California farmer—Muir Ranch

"Stephen Ritz and Suzie Boss have developed a great guidebook for project-based learning using gardening as a model."
—Larry Ferlazzo, teacher, author, and Education Week *teacher advice columnist*

"Stephen is so incredibly inspiring. He brings many of my favorite things—education, vegetables, empowerment—to the table with his work with students in the Bronx. We all need to be aware of the problems facing our country with access to healthy foods and the concerns of childhood obesity, and Stephen is an amazing activist finding solutions to these issues. As Stephen always says, 'Sí se puede!'"
—José Andrés, chef/owner of ThinkFoodGroup

"Stephen Ritz has discovered a living key to an engaged, happy, healthy student: Give a child a seed to plant and both the seed and the child will grow and flourish. His book will lead you on a beautiful journey to the excitement youth experience when they learn by caring for plants, their communities, and themselves and in the process transform their lives."
—Illène Pevec, PhD, author of Growing a Life: Teen Gardeners Harvest Food, Health, and Joy

"Stephen's infectious energy and insight to inspire youth to overcome social hardships and challenges using grassroots education and meaningful social values is a roadmap to community success . . . a must-read for every educator, policy maker, healthcare professional, and parent. His messages to youth are compelling, purposeful, and globally relevant. I wish every school had a Stephen Ritz . . . the world would be a better place! Want to build a healthier community? Read this book . . . grow a garden . . . relish the outcome . . . Stephen Ritz is a trailblazer for neighborhood success!"
—Greg Chang, DMD, founder and chairman of SuperChefs Cookery for Kids, creator of Westin Hotels Kids Eat Well Program, 2016 Practice Education Team Award UBC Health, Fellow of the American College of Dentists

" 'Give a man a fish and you feed him for a day; teach a man to fish and you feed him for a lifetime.' Give a child a seed, teach a child to grow food, create global food security together. My dear friend Stephen Ritz, founder of Green Bronx Machine, has done just that, motivating thousands of people in the most nontraditional ways to grow food at any age in some of the most challenging places on the planet—truly *The Power of a Plant*."
—Diana Dehm, host of Sustainability News & Entertainment Radio

"Stephen Ritz has learned how to grow the hardest-to-reach young people into full-fledged citizens, and in *The Power of a Plant*, he shares the secrets of his success. Ritz's highly personal account of Green Bronx Machine, a widely acclaimed school-based urban agriculture program that motivates, inspires, and educates kids, shows that the act of cultivating food can be the key to individual success and a source of community power. It is a must-read for teachers, parents, activists, and policy makers."
—Nevin Cohen, PhD, associate professor of health/food policy at CUNY School of Public Health; research director at CUNY Urban Food Policy Institute; coauthor of Beyond the Kale: Urban Agriculture and Social Justice Activism in New York City

"Father to many, hero to all, Stephen Ritz and *The Power of a Plant* are an inspiration for all—in the process, he has become the face of a movement and industry that is feeding people, nourishing souls, and healing the earth. With passion, purpose, and boundless optimism, Steve is cultivating humanity's best traits. His deep, genuine love for children and his community is the fertile ground hope for all of us grows from."

—*Farmer David Smiles, CEO of Uriah's Urban Farms*

"Learning about Stephen Ritz through his TEDx Talk and later visiting Green Bronx Machine took me back 50 years to my days as a child spending the summer in Belgium with my grandfather in his vegetable garden. It was all about the magical experience of planting a seed, watching it grow, cooking it in my grandmother's stock pot, and finally tasting, appreciating, and sharing what I grew. Through his teachings, Stephen gives his students this type of magical experience and inspiration and lets them know anything is possible. *The Power of a Plant* is a powerful message in showing us how plants and people can be a catalyst for bringing more peace to our world."

—*Alain Coumont, chef and founder of Le Pain Quotidien and Le Botaniste*

"I can think of no word more worthy of praise than teacher, and I know of no teacher more praiseworthy than Stephen Ritz."

—*Jay Martin, CEO of Juice Plus+*

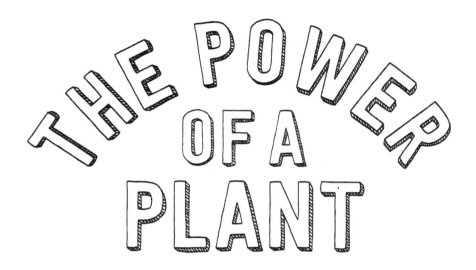

THE POWER OF A PLANT

A Teacher's Odyssey to Grow Healthy Minds and Schools

STEPHEN RITZ

FOUNDER OF GREEN BRONX MACHINE

WITH SUZIE BOSS

RODALE.

RODALE
wellness

Live happy. Be healthy. Get inspired.

Sign up today to get exclusive access to our authors, exclusive bonuses,
and the most authoritative, useful, and cutting-edge information on health,
wellness, fitness, and living your life to the fullest.

Visit us online at RodaleWellness.com
Join us at RodaleWellness.com/Join

Rodale books may be purchased for business or promotional use or for special sales.
For information, please write to:
Trade Books/Special Markets Department, Rodale Inc., 733 Third Avenue, New York, NY 10017

Printed in the United States of America
Rodale Inc. makes every effort to use acid-free ⊗, recycled paper ♲.

Photo, page 2: Fred W. McDarrah/Getty Images.
All other photos are courtesy of Stephen Ritz.

Book design by Yeon Kim

Library of Congress Cataloging-in-Publication Data is on file with the publisher

ISBN 978–1–62336–864–7

Distributed to the trade by Macmillan

2 4 6 8 10 9 7 5 3 1 hardcover

RODALE.

We inspire health, healing, happiness, and love in the world.
Starting with you.

For children,
communities, and
a world that needs more love
and
for all the unplanted seeds
waiting to blossom

My wish for you is that you continue. Continue to be who you are, to astonish a mean world with your acts of kindness.

—MAYA ANGELOU

CONTENTS

PREFACE

Five years ago, at the TimesCenter in New York City, I limped onto the stage and gave a short TEDx talk that I didn't think would get any attention. "I am not a farmer," I began. "I am a people farmer. My favorite crop is organically grown citizens."

To my amazement, those words before an unfamiliar audience on a huge Manhattan stage launched an outpouring of interest in the green classrooms and outdoor gardens that I have cultivated across the South Bronx. In the poorest congressional district in America, in the least healthy county in all of New York State, in neighborhoods that are densely packed with public housing, my students and I have transformed communities, schools, and lives into a luscious cornucopia that nourishes bodies, minds, and souls.

We grow indoors and outdoors, with big, burly teenagers and the most adorable little farmers you'll ever meet. We've planted flowers, shrubs, and trees to beautify our communities. We've grown enough produce to send fresh food home with hundreds of students and donate even more to shelters and kitchens serving our most vulnerable families. By connecting our green projects with the curriculum, the seeds we plant during the school day germinate academic results and open career paths that forever change the trajectory of my students' lives. I grow vegetables, but my vegetables grow students, schools, opportunities, and lives. Our results have attracted attention from the White House to the Vatican.

From all over the world, people ask about our award-winning program, which we proudly call Green Bronx Machine. How does the simple act of teaching children to plant seeds lead to better health, stronger academic performance, and more hopeful communities? How have we managed to grow so much goodness and opportunity in a community challenged by environmental degradation, high crime, chronic disease, and generational poverty? And just how fast can we bring this remarkable program to other communities that are desperately seeking solutions? I'm eager to share the answers and inspire others to fire up their own green machines.

This is my odyssey.

I'm a proud Bronx native who stumbled into teaching by happenstance, only to discover that I had a passion and knack for engaging the hardest-to-reach students. But it took a classroom accident, two decades into my teaching career, for me to discover the power of a plant to delight, nurture, and inspire curiosity in everyone from tattooed gang members to wide-eyed tots. Along the way, with passion, purpose, and hope, I've learned some critical lessons and a few handy metaphors about greening the classroom and growing something greater.

It all starts with soil. Our communities are our soil. If a plant is going to thrive, it needs to take root in a healthy growing medium. The same goes for students. The best soil for growing young minds and bodies is a thriving, supportive community. In the Bronx, like so many communities around the world, our soil needs to be respected, refreshed, replenished, watered, and tended.

Seeds come next. I tell my students that they are my seeds, and they are packed with genetic potential. My goal is to plant those seeds in the most fertile setting possible so that they all reach their full talents and genetic potential. I am determined to grow something greater with the greatest natural resource in the world: the untapped human potential in low-status communities.

Then comes the harvest. My students' efforts have yielded more than fifty thousand pounds of vegetables, along with improved attendance, reduced disciplinary issues, better academic results, increased health outcomes, and the immeasurable joy of sharing that bounty with others. We cook what we grow, too, in classrooms where the distance from farm to table is measured in footsteps. By following my own advice about healthier eating, I've lost more than a hundred pounds. I've even developed a taste for arugula and eggplant.

I'd be lying if I told you that I started with a grand plan to transform public education. None of this happened overnight. As you'll discover, my ultimate journey to create a living, thriving, green classroom took some time. In fact, I like to say I'm one big mistake! But my secret is, I keep falling *up* the ladder of success.

I'm going to take you back to the beginning, when my own Bronx boyhood cultivated deep connections to a community that others were all too ready to write off. When I started teaching as a young adult, I had no idea that I would go on to design an innovative program to inspire learning and community change. My outgoing personality was useful for engaging teenagers, but then what? To really reach the students who were not being well served by public schools, I had to do some serious learning myself. That took time, too, but I've leveraged everything I learned along the way to build what we now call Green Bronx Machine.

My story is full of surprising turns, setbacks, and heartbreak but also unexpected partnerships. I call these *collisions, connections, and co-learnings.* When I bump into interesting people or come across ideas that inspire new possibilities, I'm eager to learn together. That's how we create a multiplier effect. The innovations that you'll read about in the coming chapters, from our classroom Tower Gardens to our Green Bronx Machine Mobile Classroom Kitchen, are all the result of staying alert for opportunities and then adapting fresh ideas to work in our classroom.

I'm the first to admit that I don't always know what's going to work. I'm determined to find out, even if I have to fail a few times to get to good answers. That's the story of my life: shifting attitudes from impossible to *I'm possible*, changing mind-sets from opportunity is nowhere to opportunity is *now here.*

When I started teaching a lifetime ago, my goal was to be one person who could make a difference in the lives of young people. So I'm humbled by the accolades and attention that I have received. More profoundly, I am uplifted by the resilience and spirit of the young people you're about to meet. Vanessa, Calvin, Miguel, and so many more have grown up to be productive, contributing, and caring citizens. They make me Bronx proud.

Knowing how many other communities are hungry for solutions, I'm eager for readers to get inspired by my story, follow my lead, and plant new seeds to grow something greater. My odyssey is proof positive that if you show up, grow up, and are willing to work hard, amazing things can happen. Passion, purpose, and hope are my secret sauce, and these ingredients are free to all, no purchase required. Root your feet in the ground and extend your head to the sun. As we say daily, *Sí se puede*, and make epic happen!

PROLOGUE

all 2004—"Mr. Ritz, please come down to the main office."

When I heard this announcement blaring over the loudspeaker, I felt my anxiety ramp up. What could this be? I was just weeks into a new job as a science teacher at Walton High School. Surely I hadn't screwed up yet?

When I got to the office, the secretary was bubbling over with excitement.

"There's a package here. You and the students are going to love it!"

A gift? That made my day. She handed me a giant box from an association called New Yorkers for Parks. I was on a lot of lists after years of teaching science in the South Bronx, and sometimes we'd get donations or samples of equipment I could use in class.

"Thanks!" I called out, walking away with my treasure so I could get back to the classroom. What could it be? Sports equipment, science kits, robots? The box was large and heavy, I had big hopes, and I was desperate for any resources to make learning more engaging and interesting for my students. Curiosity got the better of me. I opened it right there in the main hall.

What I found inside turned my excitement to . . . huh?

Onions? What the hell was this?

I stared at this big box of onions and all I could see were projectiles. My new class was full of students with tattoos and piercings and mustaches who were not prone to talking things out politely. More than one physical fight had already broken out in class, with pencils and books flying across the room. Last thing I needed was to have this box open in class—the onions would be turned into baseballs immediately and possibly hurled at my head. So I quickly stashed them out of sight and forgot about them. I pushed the box under a huge old radiator in the classroom and got on with my day.

Six weeks later, another one of those fights broke out in class. This was so commonplace that we had a detailed protocol to follow, and that protocol was: Duck.

On that memorable October day, two students in my class pushed back their chairs and sprang to their feet. I made a beeline for the two of them, trying to keep the other students out of their reach. I was about to call for help when I saw the boy, a student named Gonzalo, reach under the radiator. That's when everything seemed to go into slow motion.

Please don't let him have a weapon under there, I thought.

He yanked something loose and out spilled . . . flowers.

Dozens of bright yellow flowers on long green stems that grew out of . . .

Holy crap. They weren't onions after all.

The class gasped as if Gonzalo had pulled a rabbit from a magician's hat. Those flowers were just as unexpected and incongruous under the fluorescent lights. Fists instantly stopped flying. The boys now clamored to give flowers to the girls. The girls wanted a stem or two to take home to their mothers. And the science teacher in me had to figure out what the hell had just happened.

I didn't even know that the flowers were daffodils, let alone how steam from the hissing radiator had forced them to bloom. Youth who lived in neighborhoods of concrete and barbed wire were equally clueless. This wasn't magic—it was nature. And it was amazing! Now we had a mystery to solve, a real experience with scientific inquiry. Turns out that was a teachable moment for all of us. Little did I know what we had secretly uncovered.

When people ask me where I got the idea to leverage a green curriculum to help students become healthier, more academically engaged, productive citizens, I often tell them about the daffodils. But it's far from the whole story.

Before I was able to recognize this as a teachable moment, I first had to become a capable educator. I had to put in the time to develop my philosophy of education and build a tool kit of strategies to engage the hardest-to-reach students. Before I could build the relationships that are so fundamental to learning, I had to really get to know my students and recognize the assets of the South Bronx community we all share. I also had to figure out how to introduce new ideas in an educational system that makes innovation a daily challenge, especially in schools serving children who are growing up in poverty.

There's one more piece to this story that I seldom talk about. The day of the daffodils came along just when I desperately needed to rekindle my own sense of hope. A series of personal tragedies had almost extinguished my natural optimism. But as I watched my students at Walton High School respond to those humble yellow flowers, I felt something stirring in me. Under the most inhospitable conditions, nature had found a way to engage, inspire, and delight us all. Here was hope made visible. Those surprising blooms opened my eyes to the power of a plant.

None of us in the room that day had a clue that we were about to turn a fleeting moment into a movement. To show you how this whole unlikely story unfolded, I need to go back to the beginning.

"WE WILL NEVER STOP STRUGGLING HERE IN THE BRONX, EVEN THOUGH THEY'VE DESTROYED IT AROUND US. WE WOULD PITCH TENTS IF WE HAVE TO RATHER THAN MOVE FROM HERE. WE WOULD FIGHT BACK, THERE IS NOTHING WE WOULD NOT DO. THEY WILL NEVER TAKE US AWAY FROM HERE. I FEEL VERY MUCH A PART OF THIS AND I'M NEVER GOING TO LEAVE. AND, AFTER ME, MY CHILDREN WILL BE HERE TO CARRY ON... I HAVE VERY STRONG CHILDREN AND VERY STRONG GRANDCHILDREN."

If you grow up in the South Bronx today or in South-Central Los Angeles or Pittsburgh or Philadelphia, you quickly come to understand that you have been set apart and there's no will in this society to bring you back into the mainstream. The kids have eyes and they can see, and they have ears and they can hear. Kids notice that no politicians talk about this. Nobody says we're going to make them less separate and more equal. Nobody says that.

—JONATHAN KOZOL

PART I

PREPARING THE SOIL

CHAPTER 1

THE ROOKIE

Summer 1984—I hobbled down the metal stairs of the Jackson Avenue subway stop in the South Bronx with my knee in a brace that ran from my thigh to my ankle. It was so hot, it felt like even the sidewalks were sweating. I was on my way to interview for my first teaching job and didn't want to be late.

Like so many young men in my neighborhood who came of age in the early 1980s, I dreamed of finding glory and fortune on the basketball courts. And why not? I was six foot three and wiry, with bottomless energy, a reliable three-point shot, twenty-eight-inch waist, and blue suede Puma sneakers. I could jump pretty well for a white guy, too. Four years of college had given me untold hours to work on my game and party as hard as the cast from *Animal House*. My goals in college were to spend as much time as possible on the basketball court, make art, and meet girls. It was as if I had been invited to a four-year happy hour. By graduation time, I knew happy very, very well. If I had scholarly classmates who sweated over tests and essays, our paths didn't intersect.

I didn't think about what came next until I graduated, and then I didn't have a clue. I tried playing pro ball during a postgraduation trip to Israel to visit my grandmother. That's where I tore up my knee. The long flight home to New York gave me time to ponder my next career move. My mother, a teacher herself, had told me about the massive shortages facing

New York City schools. At her urging, I had taken the test to get a temporary teaching certificate before I headed overseas. While I was away, she fielded calls from principals desperate to interview me.

So here I was, ready to give teaching a try. My flight home from Israel had arrived hours late. I had to go to the interview straight from JFK Airport. There was no time to change clothes, let alone stop at a barbershop and tame my mop of curly hair that had been growing all summer. From the neck up, I looked like Peter Frampton with a sunburn. But my legs were whiter than Larry Bird's. Dressed in high-tops and still in my extra-short basketball shorts, I made my way toward my interview as fast as my awkward knee immobilizer would allow.

The scene at street level stopped me cold. Underneath the elevated tracks on Westchester Avenue, every surface was covered in graffiti and gang tags. The trains rumbling overhead were like moving murals of spray-painted art. Across the street squatted a one-story, red brick post office with bulletproof windows. Delivery trucks idled in front of the meat warehouse on the opposite corner. Beyond that, what passed for community seemed to just . . . stop. The Bronx that I knew from my boyhood, a place I had romanticized in memory, was long gone. This Bronx might as well have been a scene from post–World War II Germany.

Lot after lot was abandoned. A fire hydrant spewed water onto the empty street. Piles of bricks, scorched mattresses, twisted metal, and other debris were the only remnants of the apartment buildings that had been burned and bulldozed. Others were simply left standing to rot. Waves of arson fires and vandalism had swept through this neighborhood a decade earlier, and the place still looked scorched and forgotten. Even though I grew up in the Bronx, I had been away long enough to see it with fresh eyes. The destruction felt so recent and so all pervasive, I could practically smell the smoke.

Looming on the horizon like a massive stage set, rising up and out of St. Ann's Avenue, was the five-story silhouette of South Bronx High School. It looked haunted. Except for one adjacent building, there was nothing much around it in an eight-block area except blue sky and charred remains. The distant Manhattan skyline could have been from another planet.

"Man, no way you want to teach at South Bronx," my friend T.C. had warned me when I told him about my interview.

"Why not?" I countered. "We both grew up in the Bronx." I left out one important detail. A decade earlier, my parents had fled the excitement of the Bronx for the suburban safety of Rockland County, New York.

"Not *South* Bronx," he reminded me.

Despite T.C.'s warnings, I wasn't worried. "You know me," I told him. "I can get along with anybody, anywhere." Knowing the crowd of characters I hung out with, he didn't disagree.

As I started making my way up St. Ann's Avenue, I replayed the warnings about the drugs and violence that I'd heard about this neighborhood. Heroin had ravaged the community in the 1960s, followed by a swift and unrelenting wave of cheap cocaine in the late 1970s. Now it was crack: the fast food of street drugs. Anybody with three bucks in his pocket could buy in and get insanely high, if only for ninety seconds.

St. Mary's Park, a few blocks on the other side of the train tracks, was designed a century earlier to be an urban paradise. Paths meandered gracefully through greenery, punctuated by big granite boulders. This former oasis had become an open-air drug bazaar. You couldn't walk through it now without hearing the crunch of crack vials under your shoes. Every day, garbage trucks were filled to the brim with nothing but discarded drug paraphernalia.

When I was a block away from the school, a movement on the top floor caught my eye. Without warning, a chair came flying out of an open window and made a silent and graceful arch toward the street before smacking the asphalt. It bounced and bounced and bounced until it came to rest. The whole scene looked surreal, like a movie in slow motion. The kid who hurled the chair pulled his head back indoors without a word. Nobody came outside to investigate. The only car on the street swerved around the broken chair without slowing down.

Maybe it was youthful bravado or maybe I just really needed a job, but those first impressions didn't scare me off. To the contrary, I figured this was the new normal. I simply continued inside the school, where I found the principal holed up in his office. Without ever looking up, he made a quick phone call and introduced me to my soon-to-be supervisor. When the supervisor and I got in the elevator to go up to the fifth floor for the interview, the elevator lurched and dropped dramatically. The doors opened on the bowels of the ancient building. The supervisor stepped out and, without a trace of irony, said, "Hmm, this doesn't look like the fifth floor."

Right then and there, I knew I couldn't go wrong here. The expectations were so low, any warm body would do. In 1984, at South Bronx High School, the bar for teacher competence was simply being able to move your time card from left to right. Punch in on time and that was it! When the supervisor asked me about my background in math and science, I told him I'd taken some science classes in high school. In fact, I had aced the Regents Exam in biology.

"Great!" he said. "You'll be wonderful."

On the spot, I accepted his offer to teach every subject to a self-contained class of special education students for something like $9,000 a year. I had no idea what I was getting into.

On the first day of class, the assistant principal stopped me just outside my classroom door. "Here's your room key, your key to the faculty bathroom, and your chalk," he said. He handed me five class rosters filled with names.

"Wait, how long is this supposed to last?" I asked him, peering into the flimsy box that held twenty pieces of chalk to use on my cracked blackboard.

"Best wishes—good luck!" he called out over his shoulder as he disappeared down the hall. That was it, Teaching 101. And so it began: no credentials, no specific degree needed, no special training, not even a workshop, pep session, or tutorial. All it took to get a teaching job in 1984 was a four-year degree in anything, a simple test requiring no preparation or content, and a heartbeat. For me, this seemed like a perfect fit.

While I was taking roll that first day, I paused to make eye contact with each student and did my best to memorize every name. At twenty-one, I was the same age as my oldest students who had been held back so many times, they were about to age out of public education while I was just aging in. Many of the boys had more facial hair than I did. The girls had way more attitude. Some students were brand-new immigrants to America, wide-eyed about the promise of public school. Others knew the system all too well; it had failed them for years.

When I called out Vanessa's name, I heard chuckles from the back of the room. "Is she here?" I asked, wondering if she was one of the students who appeared to be napping on their desks. "Do we need to wake her up?"

"Don't worry. We all know when Vanessa's here," promised a boy with a knowing look.

The first day Vanessa bothered to show up for class, I heard her coming before she arrived. Just outside my doorway, she shouted an angry promise down the hall and over her shoulder, "What the fuck, yo? I'll beat your ass."

I didn't see who she was yelling at, but I couldn't miss Vanessa. This big, belligerent voice came from a short, stocky body. Shaped like a whiskey barrel with arms, she overflowed with fury and aggression. And why? Because it was Tuesday. Because the sun was up. Vanessa didn't need a reason to be mad at the world. She caught me watching her and glared right back. She lifted one eyebrow slightly as if to ask, "You gonna fuck with me, too?"

Right away, she asked for a hall pass so she could go hang with her friends. Everybody, and especially the boys, watched to see what would happen next. We all knew the principal's ironclad rule: no hall passes during the first five minutes or last five minutes of class. Keeping kids in their seats was his weak solution to curtail fighting in the hallways and bathrooms. He was so insistent on this rule, he made me sign an agreement to abide by it. In fact, that was the only bit of teacher training I was given as preparation for my new job.

"Please take a seat," I suggested.

Vanessa gave me the hard stare that other teachers and even some of her classmates had come to fear. Anything might set her off. That morning, I held the match.

"Look," I started, "maybe that works with other teachers. But not with me. This is a two-way street. You give what you get and get what you give. You need to be in class."

"You don't know what I need," she shot back. "You can't understand me."

"I understand that if you want to learn anything, you have to put in the effort, and that starts with showing up."

"What do you know about what we go through? What do you know about Hispanics? About the Bronx? You don't know nothin'. You're here to get a paycheck. And you're just *white*. Gringo, go home!"

Although I could not argue with her about my skin color, I simply said, "You know what, you don't know me." Keeping my voice calmer than I felt, and looking her dead in the eye, I respectfully asked her to take a seat. This time she complied, and I thanked her.

Vanessa looked shocked when I found her outside at lunchtime and handed her half my sandwich. I didn't brown-bag or eat the slop in the school cafeteria. Instead, I had acquired a taste for the sandwiches made at a local deli. "Let's get to know each other," I suggested. "This is going to be a long-term relationship, not a drive-by."

"Are you serious, yo?" she said. "You're giving me half?" That made a deeper impression on her than the fact that I was using my own break time to sit down with her. In a neighborhood where children are lucky to get crumbs, half a Boar's Head ham and cheese with mayo—known as the "ghetto gold standard of sandwiches"—is a windfall.

Over many lunches in the weeks that followed, I learned more about her story. Her older brother, deep into drugs, consumed her mother's attention. Vanessa was determined to prove that she could be just as bad if that's what it took to get noticed. Behind that tough exterior, she was hiding superior coping, avoidance, and survival skills. She could be as mean as a pit bull or, when it suited her, as charming as a poodle.

Her sharp intellect came out in flashes, like when she would deliver a highly sophisticated, exuberantly profane analysis of why public housing sucked. She didn't hesitate to bully other students, smoke weed at recess, or frighten teachers with her temper. When she arrived in my classroom with sweet breath, acting goofy, I knew that she (like so many others) had stopped in the bathroom to guzzle a bottle of Calvin Cooler. This cheap and sugary wine cooler was marketed so heavily in the neighborhood that my students called it Ghetto Kool-Aid. Cheaper than milk or juice, and available in every color of the rainbow, it was often the breakfast beverage of choice that made school far more tolerable for students.

Vanessa had no intention of doing homework or following any rules unless they suited her. Most days, though, we managed to get along. On great days, she ran the class for me. A natural leader, Vanessa could quiet an unruly class with a look or get everyone focused on the lesson with an insightful question. When she wanted to learn, it was game on for all.

As a rookie teacher, I didn't know the meaning of pedagogy. My goal was to stay one lesson ahead of my students. It wasn't hard with the science textbooks I found in the basement. Many of them were written in the 1950s or 1960s. We were reading aloud in class one day when a student raised his hand and said, "It says here, 'One day, man will go to the moon.'"

Another student chimed in, "Yo, you think that's possible?" His question made me doubt my own memory for a moment. Was I imagining that moon landing or did it really happen?

When I told them about Neil Armstrong and his giant leap for mankind, they just shrugged. Michael Jackson was moonwalking his way across America—that was all the lunar knowledge my students understood. For them, a space suit was a black leather jacket with three zippers. For many, information came live and direct via MTV.

To compensate for my lack of training, limited supplies, and outdated materials, I trusted my instincts. Growing up in the Bronx in the 1960s and '70s had taught me to read the unwritten rules. In densely packed urban spaces, people are constantly sizing each other up. You figure out at a glance whom you can trust, who's willing to make eye contact, and who's hiding an attitude behind sunglasses. A handshake and a promise are as binding as a legal contract. Playing ball taught me more about the value of straight talk. You don't say you can dunk; you just do it. Actions count more than words. To win a bet about my athletic abilities, I had once jumped over a Yugo parked at a South Bronx curb. I collected my payoff and jumped back over it again.

I still lived by the same rules I'd learned as a boy. As seemingly lawless as the Bronx had become, here and now those rules still mattered. My classroom wasn't apart from the world my students inhabited; it was a part of the same living ecosystem.

Before my students realized I was an athlete, I made a bet with them. We all marched into the gym. I got out a ladder and lined the rim of the basketball hoop with books, balanced just so. Beyond required textbooks, the books I selected mattered to me and I instinctively knew they would interest and inspire my students as well. It was simply a matter of connecting them—a Herculean leap that far exceeded the ten-foot distance from floor to rim. "If I can jump up there and grab those books, you have to read them," I said. "Agreed?"

My students laughed. I might have been crouching down a little to make it look less feasible than it was.

"Go for it, Ritz," one of the boys said, feigning encouragement. But the look on their faces telegraphed what every kid was thinking: *no way.*

"Okay. I'm gonna give it my best shot. Wish me luck."

With a flair for the dramatic, I moved the ladder out of the way and rubbed my hands together while I eyed the net.

Two quick steps and *jump!* Wham! I snatched a book off the rim and delivered it straight into a student's hands.

"That one's yours!" I said.

Stunned, he looked at me with wide eyes, knowing that we now had a deal as solid as a signed contract.

I jogged over to my spot again.

Step, step, *jump!* Wham! Did it again.

A second book off the rim and into a student's hand. No longer an anomaly, I did this until every student had a book and a homework assignment to read it. And wouldn't you know? Every one of them read those books. We started to identify books and authors that resonated so much, we actually wanted to read them as a whole class. Students kept coming to class because they wanted to see what trick I'd come up with next.

I quickly realized that my students were curious about my life, my history, and any details related to my family. As I shared stories about my own life to connect with my students, they learned that education and hard work have always been part of my life and my family history. My students were fascinated to learn that I was the son of an immigrant. That made me different from most other teachers but gave me something in common with many of my students. While I often joked with them that I was a science experiment and found in a trash can, my students loved learning about the family that birthed and raised me. As we discovered what we had in common, students were starting to feel that we were all family. By extension, they were connected with what I loved. I used that to leverage points of entry for all lessons.

I often parented my students and, frankly, some of them attempted to parent me. I didn't have to tell them that I felt like a man-child, not even capable of growing a respectable mustache. Next to some of my students, I looked more like a middle schooler. Yet I had been given control over their destinies. When they called me "Mr. Ritz," I turned around and started looking for my father. Surely they didn't mean me? Students laughed at that and called me Mista (short for Mister) instead. Then they joked that my first name must be Yo, last name Ritz. In class and in the hallways, they would call out, "Yo Ritz," and I would answer with a smile.

Our relationship deepened when I took time to share my family's story. My father was born in Romania and came to New York as a boy by way of Israel. His family landed in lower Manhattan and soon moved to a nicer home in the Bronx. "The family legend is that, at twelve years old, my dad pushed his family's belongings in a wheelbarrow through Manhattan and up the Grand Concourse to a walk-up on Miriam Street and 196th."

"Wheelbarrow? No way!" my students said in a chorus, but I knew they were listening.

When my parents met, my dad was working in the mailroom at Brown Brothers Harriman, a big private bank in Manhattan. He didn't read very well. His teachers never realized that his literacy problems had to do with understanding Hebrew better than English. He was accustomed to reading a page from right to left, not the opposite.

"Teachers told his parents he was slow," I explained. I paused there to see a couple of my English language learners exchange meaningful glances. In school, it's too easy to forget that English is not the only language worth knowing in the world. My students were living their own version of this story.

My dad found a warmer welcome in the athletic department at Clinton High, then an all-boys school in the Bronx, where his natural talents and willingness to do whatever it took to win made him a top pick for any team. Basketball was his first love ("just like you, Mista," one of the boys interjected), but he could throw a football with accuracy all the way across the Grand Concourse to Valentine Avenue, a feat worthy of incredulous respect, even by professional standards. Sports skills and his team ethic earned him respect but didn't help him learn to read. When he landed the mailroom job, he struggled to get mail in the right slots by matching letters and symbols.

My mother worked for the same bank but in the accounting department. She didn't have a problem reading, but she couldn't add very well.

One day, my father found her in tears, absolutely inconsolable, as if tragedy had struck. She was crying because she couldn't get the numbers to add up. Making out words on a page still challenged him, but he could follow numbers up and down with ease. He saw that she had made a simple transposition error. In turn, she quickly figured out that he could use some help with reading and she could use some help with math, and together, they could help each other succeed as individuals and as a team.

"So that's how my parents met, over their difficulties with literacy and numeracy," I told the class.

"Awwww, sweet," one of the girls said. "They still together?"

I explained that my parents' relationship flourished, and my mother went on to become a special education teacher. "So that's how I wound up here with you," I told them. "Is it any wonder I became a teacher?"

Many of my students lived with only one parent or maybe a grandmother. I still lived at home, too, but the differences in our home lives were stark. I had a younger brother and two hardworking parents who loved me unconditionally. Both my grandmothers thought I could do no wrong. Love of and for grandma was another common denominator I had with my students, and for the same reason: unconditional love. Intergenerational love and respect resonated deep within me.

Many of my students' family units were in constant flux, some as seasonal as the weather. Most students walked to school from public housing, much of it riddled with rats and cockroaches. For others, there was a deeper and overarching sense of oppression and despair. Whether the issue was housing, mail delivery, basic public services, or even access to shopping, the sense of separate and unequal was systemic and pervasive. Without anyone to show them alternatives, many assumed they'd be stuck in the projects and in the same rut forever.

My official address was my parents' home in Rockland County. It was clean, safe, and supportive but definitely boring. I felt like a squatter. It represented a world I'd been struggling to come to terms with since leaving the Bronx at the end of sixth grade.

Sharing stories about my life helped me connect with students and kept them coming to class. That was connected to my bigger goal of keeping them out of trouble. I knew that young people who were hungry for quick money could find opportunities galore in this predatory economy as lookouts or spotters—the drug trade version of paid internships or much, much worse. I'd see students who were broke one week driving a BMW to school the next. Then a week later they were cuffed and hauled out by the cops, only to be back in school in another month ready to repeat the same cycle.

The real trick was to make school relevant to their lives. Was I a genius? Not at all. Was I highly credentialed? Even less so. But I cared enough about these children to find ways to engage them. Even as a rookie teacher, I understood that caring relationships are the strongest foundation for learning. Just as I promised Vanessa, you give what you get and get what you give.

CHAPTER 2

TEACHING WITH EVERYTHING BUT THE TEXTBOOK

Spring 1985—"Ladies and gentlemen, pencils out. Here's your DO NOW."

One of the only teaching tips I received from my supervisor was to start every class with a three-minute activity to focus students' attention. He called this a DO NOW. I took his advice but added my own spin. Students would walk into my class and hear the Beastie Boys blasting, "Hold it now!" They answered with a chorus of "Hit it!" and knew it was time to get out their math books.

Connecting with my students turned out to be easy. After all, we shared the same passions: basketball, hip-hop, and a desire for love. My daily commute from my parents' home in Rockland took fifty minutes with no traffic. I kept my windows rolled up until I got to the Cross Bronx Expressway, then cranked down to hear the Bronx reinventing itself. Hip-hop was bubbling up from the charred remains of these neighborhoods, and the whole world was listening. Run-DMC hit it big with their first gold record in 1984, the first rap album ever to be nominated for a Grammy, and other artists were poised to follow their lead. House parties with Grandmaster Flash on the turntables launched the next big neighborhood stars and signature dance moves, which quickly spread via MTV to cities and sub-urbs across the country. Seemingly overnight, and long before the Inter-net, it was as if the whole world fell in love with the Bronx through the power of hip-hop.

From one Bronx block to the next, you could catch the same songs blasting out of boom boxes and car speakers. The streets had a pulse all their own, as dramatic as a soundtrack. Corner to corner, bodega to bodega, even floor to floor within a building, you would hear the same music throbbing like a heartbeat. Radio deejays had the power to turn artists like Doug E. Fresh, the first human beatbox, into overnight sensations. For weeks, the only thing I heard anywhere was his song "The Show." I listened endlessly to Malcolm McLaren's "Buffalo Gals."

During lunch breaks and after school, I heard my students making their own beats, turning themselves into percussion machines and ampli-fying the rhythm of the streets. We all knew every lyric recorded by Big Daddy Kane, the Real Roxanne, the Fat Boys, and more. So naturally, I brought that music right into class.

Along with music, I used my big voice, bigger personality, and grab bag of nutty stories from my own Bronx adventures to grab students' attention. But then what? I was on my own to figure out the next move. How could I get students interested in content that they didn't care about learning? How could I convince them they had the capacity to learn, after years of being told they couldn't? None of us—students or teacher—had any support. Curriculum? Nope. Scope and sequence? Never heard of it. Oversight? Nonexistent. Accounta-*what*?

On an afternoon three days before Christmas during my first year of teaching, a white man named Bernhard Goetz shot four black teenagers aboard the No. 2 subway train in Manhattan. All four victims were from the Bronx. All four were unarmed. Two were shot in the back.

When we came back to school from the holiday break, I handed out new reading material: front-page newspaper stories about the Subway Vigilante.

The news couldn't have hit much closer to home. This shooting happened on the same train I often rode with my students. Just by sitting together, my students and I challenged the prevailing stereotypes. Other young people of color saw me as a stand-in for Bernhard Goetz and glowered at my students for even talking to me. Other white people saw my students as the threat and put as much space as they could fit between us and them. The city couldn't have been more polarized. Mayor Ed Koch's favorite line to New Yorkers was "How am I doing?" In our neighborhood, the overwhelming response to his question was "Pretty shitty."

So we talked about that.

In class, we talked about racism, about the self-perpetuating cycle of low expectations, about what it means to be afraid or hateful of people who are "others"—different from us.

Gathered in a circle where every single student knew that he or she would be heard, we talked about what we meant by "us."

One boy caught me by surprise when he said, "Yo Ritz, somehow you just belong with us. You don't seem white. You don't seem black. You're different from every other teacher. You don't act like an authority, but I feel like you've been sent to lead us somewhere."

"I'm not always sure where we're heading next," I admitted, "but I do know you have to show up to grow up. Bring your body, and your brain will follow."

As we read the news about events close to home, I challenged students to consider their next steps. "These stories are all about people demanding justice," I told them one day. "But if we want anything to really change, it's going to have to start with *just us*. What else and who else have we got?" That drew nods of agreement.

Exacerbating the tension was that an overwhelming majority of the leaders who held the power over these children's lives—be it teachers, the dean of students, guidance counselors, school administrators, government officials, or police—were predominantly, glaringly white. None of them lived in the neighborhood, nor could they speak to any aspect of it. "It's like they're making a living off us," one girl complained, and I couldn't argue.

We desperately needed great African American and Latino leaders in education in the same way that we needed them as characters in books and movies. Show a child that someone who looks like him or her can be powerful, can make a difference, can be a hero, and you have opened up that child's world forever. Children need to see it in order to be it. Instead, my students saw the people in charge as interlopers at best. These people came to the South Bronx to make a living, but the lives they built for themselves happened someplace else, and far, far, far away. Long before Spike Lee directed us to *Do the Right Thing* and Public Enemy screamed "Don't Believe the Hype," we understood separate and unequal, being apart from instead of a part of. After, we had anthems and mantras that would forever change the trajectory of our lives.

On a daily basis, my students and I were affected by decisions that were made far away, by authority figures we never met. To challenge that dynamic in my classroom, I tried to be as accessible as possible. One strategy was to build lessons around experiences we all shared.

On a rainy, miserable Monday, I arrived at school and discovered that those unseen authorities had assigned me to teach a new section of math. I walked into class and announced, "Ladies and gentlemen, I need your help. If I'm ever going to get my own apartment, I need a budget."

That's how I introduced a math project called "How to Make Your Money Last to the End of the Month." This wasn't a one-day lesson. It was a long-term, multilayered learning experience for all of us, and it wouldn't be completed until I had moved into my own place.

This wasn't make-believe. My students knew that I was eager to move out of my parents' home and into my own apartment. In fact, they were all rooting for me. They even upped the ante because they wanted me to afford a sweet spot, not some dump that I could get for cheap.

"You don't want an apartment in this neighborhood," Ramon advised me. "We can do better for you." My success would be their success. Their sense of passion, purpose, and hope for my life really touched me. We would scour daily newspapers and the *Village Voice* for rental apartments while reading interesting articles together along the way.

We started working out my monthly budget.

"Here's a copy of my last pay stub," I told them as I handed out the first assignment. "What do you notice?"

"That top number is a whole lot bigger than the bottom one," Angel said.

"Right. You have just pointed out the difference between salary and take-home pay," I said with a nod. "Everything in between is what gets taken out for taxes and other deductions."

"Taken out? Is that the same as subtraction?" asked Armond, making exactly the connection I was hoping for between math and real life.

"Yo, subtraction is a bitch," Angel said, drawing laughs. "It's like gettin' jacked—cut at the knees."

"Now I know why they call it taxes, yo," chimed in Manny.

Their goal was to work out how much I would need every month to save up for a deposit, pay rent, keep the lights on, and keep my stomach full. Oh, and there had to be enough left over to buy sneakers. On the pie charts my students sketched out for me, sneakers got their own slice. This was a lesson everybody found useful.

As I got to know my students better, I noticed that for all their attitude and academic difficulties, these children were natural problem solvers. If I put a real-life dilemma in front of them, they couldn't help but try to solve it. That's something tough neighborhoods teach you. Just navigating your way home can require negotiating circumstances beyond your control, like knowing which stairwells will get you jumped for pocket change.

My students hungered for problems within their grasp to solve. So while I created space for us to talk in class about daunting issues like social justice and racism, I also looked for problems that we could solve in a day. Help students solve a math problem that makes any sense in their lives, and bingo!

To understand timelines and estimation, we figured out the fastest way to get across the Bronx by subway. We took trips to the subway and learned positive and negative integers using the numbered stops. Uptown was positive, downtown negative. In math and in life, a double negative could be a positive. They started to see how simple operations can turn chaos into order. With math, you can cut through uncertainty and arrive at proof. How cool is that?

Vanessa turned out to be a math wizard. She could work out multistep problems in her head. She got everybody to understand what it means to equalize a variable when she said, "What you do to one side you do to the other. You call it equalizing a variable. I call it getting even. Like, you hit me, I'm gonna hit you back."

I didn't want to encourage violence, and certainly not from Vanessa, but her metaphor made perfect sense. Understanding math is sweet revenge indeed.

Left to my own devices as a new teacher, I figured out a few more things that worked, like rapping math. Our cracked blackboard and notebooks became our turntable and microphone.

> **What you do to one side, you do to the other**
> **That's how you solve the equation, brother**
> **You start on the left, you go to the right**
> **You make it fair and keep the numbers tight**

The rhymes might have been corny, but they got students' attention and introduced them to orders of operation in a language they understood. We freestyled our way to academic performance. Even cooler, these special ed students—sequestered from the mainstream and labeled academic failures— started passing the state exams.

To grasp exponents, students only had to think about fame and fortune that happened in the worlds of music and drugs. A guy who was selling his hip-hop CDs on the street corner could change his fate overnight by making one big television appearance. Exponential growth! But we also had firsthand knowledge of people making big money and then squandering it on drugs and getting shipped off to jail. Exponential loss! My students respected the limits of zero. In their lives, crossing into negative numbers meant you owed somebody. You were better off at zero. Long before Robert Downey Jr. catapulted into fame with *Less Than Zero*, we all knew it's good to be on neutral ground.

In the world we shared, hip-hop was more than music. It was fashion. It was attitude. It was everything. Musicians like Slick Rick set the standard with his Kangol beret, heavy gold chains, glittering medallions, and painted sneaks. Haute couture was no match for 149th Street or Fordham Road in the Bronx if you wanted fashion that reeked of tough street style. Even on public assistance, my students managed to come to school in shell toe Adidas and Puma Clydes with thick laces. My students relished the slogan of British Knights: *The shoe ain't nothin' without the BK button.* Swagger came as naturally to them as breathing. Southern Boulevard and Westchester Avenue became our promenade for Bronx Kings and Queens. Be seen there or be square.

I didn't question their spending habits. Far from it. I could have passed for a member of the Beastie Boys with my thick gold chains, street-smart demeanor, and red-and-black Pumas. By my second year of teaching, I was wearing my hair in Jheri curls like Michael Jackson. When I showed up for work in my first pair of Air Jordans, I was as proud as any of my students of my latest fashion investment. And when I scored a pair of Bernard King autographed sneakers the year he was the leading NBA scorer, I was the talk of the school and beyond. Parents and strangers I met on the street wanted to talk about my sneaks. They were the height of street cred, at least for the moment.

My teacher colleagues thought I was nuts. I was young and fearless, eager to embrace everything about the Bronx. Most of my fellow teachers were older, wearier, and eager to get out and go home at the end of the day. They came out of their locked classrooms only for a smoke break or to bitch and moan in the faculty lounge. They would teach last period in their winter coats, ready to bolt at the final bell.

To me, the Bronx wasn't burnt. It was fertile with untapped human potential, diversity, and style that got more extreme by the day. Even though I didn't know anything about compost yet, I could see how this was becoming the ideal growing medium for creativity, connectivity, and opportunity. Or as I like to say, collisions, connections, and co-learnings.

Bronx artists didn't need to buy canvases when they could tag train cars and spray buildings with their exuberant, furious designs. Bronx innovators weren't titans of technology; they were turntable geniuses who knew how to hook up an empty building to the power grid and create a place to party. Bronx dancers didn't give recitals or perform in concert halls; these B-boys and B-girls used their raw athleticism to invent fresh dance moves on street corners. My students were part of this *Beat Street* generation.

Long before the maker movement got its start, unleashing do-it-yourself creativity across the country, our borough and backyards were a tinkerer's paradise. It was a place where you could create something with only will, attitude, and scrap, otherwise known as passion, purpose, and hope. The Bronx might have looked like rubble, but it was teeming with life. And I was part of it.

It didn't take long for me to get drawn into the whole electrifying scene. I reconnected with my old friends and made dozens of new ones through our shared love of music, art, and partying. I had been earning money as a deejay since high school, when a buddy and I bought two turntables, a fog machine, and pole lamps that we rigged with disco lights. Back then we worked bar mitzvahs, weddings, and weekend parties. Now I stayed up all night to deejay at clubs and then headed off for a day of teaching. South Bronx High School by day, Roxy by night. Students marveled at the cavalcade of characters who would meet me outside school in the afternoon or drop me off in the morning.

"Mr. Ritz, you got mad swagger," announced Kelvin one morning. "I give you props!"

After a night out, my typical breakfast was a bag of salt-and-vinegar chips and a grape soda from the bodega uphill from school. All that salt and sugar was the perfect wake-up fuel, hyperstimulating and hypersensory. That was all I knew, loved, and thought I needed.

"Yo Ritz! Is that in your budget?" my students would call out when they spotted me at the counter, buying the same cheap crap they were loading up on to jump-start their day. None of us questioned why the bodegas didn't stock anything fresh to eat. None of us gave a damn what we were doing to our bodies. We all loved the same junk. If I had extra cash, I'd blow my budget on more snacks and sweets from the cornucopia of ghetto goodies. They would come in handy later in the day when I was ravenous again. I was only too happy to share with my students.

To make sure I got to school on time, I splurged on my first wristwatch. I picked out an analog version with a sweeping second hand, knowing that I could have some fun telling time the old-fashioned way with children who only knew digital watches. Knowing that my students would be there waiting, I finally had a reason to get to class on time.

Forsaking practicality for passion, my priorities shifted from getting an apartment (too long term) to a new, fancy car (all too immediate). I went from excited to committed and jumped right into a brand-new, two-tone blue Pontiac Grand Am with a sunroof and a booming, booming, booming sound system. It was as if I had a disco that came with a new car attached, complete with tinted windows and a miniature Magic 8 Ball hanging from the mirror. That was a noticeable upgrade from my parents' secondhand Honda Civic. The Civic was so worn out, you could pull up the floor mats and see asphalt underneath your feet.

"Mista Ritz, you are da bomb!" students shouted when I pulled up in my shiny new ride. They protected it as fiercely as if it was their own investment.

One afternoon, a girlfriend from college named Lizette came by after school to surprise me. My students spotted her out the classroom window before I did. Sitting on the hood of my Grand Am, she looked harmless—a tiny thing with glasses, flowered pants, and a mane of dark hair. But to my students, she was a potential vandal. They grabbed whatever was handy— big wooden protractors, yardsticks, scissors—and went after her.

I ran to catch up, yelling, "Hey, it's okay! She's my girlfriend! She can sit on my car!"

When the last school bell rang, I'd head to a buddy's place in the projects so I could grab a quick nap on his couch and get ready to do it all again. I never officially lived in the projects, but I had plenty of friends who did. I moved through the community with an ease that amazed my students. On the occasions when our paths would cross in an elevator or stairwell, they looked surprised.

"Yo Ritz! What are you doing here?"

To me, the Bronx felt like a perfect fit. My motto was give love, get love, keep it moving.

When I was a kid, I couldn't have told you the scientific definition of ecosystem or monoculture. I just knew that I struggled with the sameness of the suburbs. I missed the noise and the daily adrenaline rush of my boyhood streets as soon as we left the Bronx. That hyperstimulating environment fed my craving for excitement and kept my short attention on high alert.

My Bronx buddies and I had lived like an urban version of the Little Rascals, forever hatching schemes and plots. The school day was when we plotted our adventures. School mattered to us, but not for the reasons educators intended. It was the central hub of our social world. After school, we built tree houses out of lumber that we lifted from construction sites when nobody was looking. Tracey Towers, the tallest building in our part of the Bronx when it was built in the 1970s, was a favorite spot for finding scrap materials. We didn't think we were stealing, just being resourceful.

If we had questions about how to do something, we could approach the small business owners in our neighborhood. Their shops and storefronts—which were long gone by the time I started teaching—had been the epicenter of culture for kids like us. They could have been movie sets with names like Fat Arty's Dirty Deli, Milton's Candy Shop, Mr. Chin's Pet Shop, and Looey Lem's Chinese Hand Laundry. Every day, we interacted with characters like Giuseppe the Veggie Man; Max the Fish Man; Dave the Butcher; and Salvatore Nunzio the Barber, who cut our hair with a straight razor.

We were one secret door knock, handshake, or back room away from somebody who knew somebody who could do something for us. Early on, we learned the incredible value of any sentence that began, "I know a guy . . ."

Constantly in and out of each other's apartments, my buddies and I compared the contents of kitchen cupboards like amateur anthropologists. And what a diverse collection of friends I had. Their families were Irish (Billy Eichorn), Italian (Christopher Guadagnino), Puerto Rican (Rosario Rodriguez), Jewish (me), and black (Miles King), each with customs and traditions and foods that seemed exotic to everyone else. Charlton Davenport, with a name like a nobleman, was African American. So was Gary West, who by sixth grade had a mustache and hair under his arms. That made him a legend.

In the era before cell phones, beepers, or the World Wide Web, we relied on rumors, urban legends, and stories shared around the kitchen table for our information. Small pieces of paper with cryptic names, numbers, and secret codes were our sacred documents. This was a time when people mattered far more than things.

It didn't take much to keep us entertained. For a buck, we could buy two slices of pizza, a fountain soda, and an Italian ice and still have money left to play pinball. Thanks to our ingenuity, we only needed one quarter to pay pinball for hours. We convinced a guy with a drill press to punch a hole in our quarters. Insert a Duncan yo-yo string in the hole and you could yank the same quarter out of the machine over and over again. We didn't need lessons or specialized instructions to pull off our capers. There was no YouTube or Khan Academy to school us. This was straight-up trial and error. Years before Nike trademarked "Just Do It," those were the words we lived by, day to day and minute to minute.

My parents had our best interests at heart when they uprooted us and moved across the Tappan Zee Bridge. Daily headlines in the 1970s screamed one scare story after another: soaring murder rates, subway muggings, garbage strikes, cops getting pink slips, fire escape break-ins. Heroin was everywhere with a vengeance, robbing people of their lives and our neighborhood of its possessions. Overnight, the Vietnam War robbed my friends of their older brothers and cousins. By sixth grade, we felt like the oldest guys in the neighborhood.

Sometimes bad news struck closer to home. Shortly before we moved to the suburbs, a friend's older brother was stabbed to death over a bicycle, three blocks from our home. Confronted with crime, drugs, police tension, inflation, an oil crisis, and pervasive white flight, then mayor Abe Beame struggled to keep what was referred to as "Fear City" from going bankrupt during the 1970s. It was time to go. My folks were lured north by the promise of better schools, safer neighborhoods, homeownership, and enough other Jewish families heading in the same direction to fill a synagogue.

By the 1980s, my old haunts were mostly just memories. Being back in the Bronx felt more like an awakening than a homecoming.

The first open house night of my teaching career took place on a rainy fall evening. The earliest arrival was the grandmother and guardian of a boy named Darryl.

"I just have to meet Mr. Ritz. You are my grandson's favorite teacher," she told me.

Darryl had some developmental delays due to lead poisoning. He stood out in class for a number of reasons, starting with his size: six foot six, maybe 120 pounds soaking wet, with the biggest feet in the world. His classmates all knew that Darryl was slow, but they never picked on him. Far from it. They loved him.

Darryl's gift was that he took time to notice little things. He was kind, he was patient, and he never got frustrated. He lived for service and loved to contribute; he was a teacher's dream and a model employee in the making. That made him an asset for any task that required attention to detail.

"Darryl, you are hereby appointed Homework Captain," I told him early in the year. At the start of each class, he would meticulously check everyone's homework against an answer sheet. He even got the other students to write neatly and keep their math answers in tidy columns. They wouldn't do that for me. But for Darryl? No problem!

On his own, Darryl came up with an ingenious color-coding system. Now he wasn't just checking homework; he was doing data analysis to reveal his classmates' errors in understanding. His work—which I had intended as busywork—informed and improved my teaching. It was one thing to say an answer was wrong. It was another thing entirely to see why it was wrong and be able to correct misunderstandings. Long before I became fluent in data analysis, Darryl organized tables of the most common mistakes. He did it with pride and joy, and when his work helped drive other students' performance, his contributions became that much more critical. Darryl came to school early and stayed late. He became a celebrity, valued and loved by all of us.

"For once he's happy about coming to school. I want to thank you for that," his grandmother told me. "And did you know that he has perfect attendance so far this year?"

Of course I knew. I had pinned a perfect attendance badge on Darryl's shirt at the end of the first grading period. He had worn it every day since.

"You don't need to thank me," I said. "Darryl's a fine young man. I love having him in class. He's an important member of our team." I meant every word. In our classroom, Darryl had found passion, purpose, and hope. Those were the gifts I yearned to give every child. I dreamed of creating a classroom where every child had a sense of place and a sense of purpose, and where their individual talents and passions could be respected and integrated into a greater goal. I wanted to rebrand the stigma of special education into Unique Education.

To show her gratitude, Darryl's grandmother handed me a home-cooked meal. While we were saying our good-byes, I watched a huge cockroach crawl out of her overcoat pocket. I tried desperately not to recoil, even when she leaned in to give me a hug. It was terrifying, traumatic, and tragic, but I hugged her right back.

At our second conference a few months later, she arrived with a frying pan that had my name written on it. "Darryl told me some of the kids are giving you a hard time," this sweet grandmother said. "Nothing works better than a skillet upside the head. With this, you can scare the Jesus into them. That's what they need." I kept the skillet on my desk all year—as a paperweight. That year, Darryl and the whole class passed their state math exam.

On good days, my students' successes made me want to do this job forever. I volunteered for extra duty to take them on outings and to special events. We didn't have to travel far to find something interesting. They loved seeing where things were made, like a local bakery that produced ten thousand rolls a day or print shops that made handbills to advertise upcoming music shows. We sat together in the bleachers of Yankee home games, singing and cheering our hearts out. Right outside of school were doors waiting to be knocked on, elders waiting to tell stories, buildings that spoke of days gone by, and vacant lots sprouting dreams and hopes for a better future. All of it could be leveraged into classroom activity. While I was all about basic teaching—ABC's—I realized there was a new ABCD—asset-based community development—and I was determined to make my classroom the epicenter.

If you look around, there are lessons everywhere—naming the angles of a baseball diamond, computing how many rolls the baker needs to put on each tray to get to ten thousand a day, calculating the speed of the printing machines. Watching real things come off a production line let us get granular. What did it take to make something? What were the steps involved? How did you regulate manufacturing so that you produced just the right number each day? Teaching happens in school, but learning and application take place out in the real world.

And some of it was just for fun, because that was important, too. A lot of these children had never been to a live ball game, a museum, or a show. How did I get tickets? I knew a guy . . .

Between working extra jobs and deejaying at night, I started showing up early and staying extra late. The investment in that wristwatch was coming in handy. In fact, I was coming to realize that every moment mattered. If I wasn't saddled with the extra duties that a rookie teacher can't avoid, like cafeteria monitor, I would keep my classroom open at lunch so students would have a comfortable place to hang out. Two of my lunchtime regulars were twin sisters, Carmen and Julia. Deeply religious Pentecostals, they wore skirts down to their ankles. They weren't allowed to listen to pop music at home. But at lunchtime in my room, sitting with their buddy Maritza, they got to sample this secret pleasure. They brought me home-cooked meals because they worried about my health. Back then, I was still as skinny as a pencil. Over *pastelón* and *pernil* (plantain lasagna and pork), we practiced English and prepared for tests; it was heaven, without death or the Bible.

Meanwhile, I filled my class with comic books, music magazines, and anything else that might grab my students' attention. I listened to students analyze the characters from everybody's favorite movie, *Scarface*, figuring out who they wanted to emulate. Connecting with their interests was where my pedagogy began.

My motto: Culture eats strategy for breakfast.

It wasn't until decades later that I realized a business guru named Peter Drucker had made those very words famous. What I knew instinctively was that I couldn't expect students to learn anything unless I made them feel welcome, respected, and connected. I couldn't fix the broken school culture by myself, but I could create a safe space in my classroom where we all trusted each other. Give love, get love. That was more essential than any lesson plan. Passion, purpose, and hope became my mantra.

"Nothing is off-limits in this class," I told my students one afternoon. "Anything you want to tell me, you can tell me."

"It burns when I take a piss!" one boy called out to get a reaction.

"Okay, that's a parking lot talk," I responded. "If there's anything you want to talk about that the whole class might benefit from, then we can talk about it here."

There were a whole lot of both: parking lot talks about personal issues ("Mr. Ritz, I'm pregnant and I don't know what to do") and class discussions ("I'm tired of store owners looking at me like I'm about to steal something from the second I walk in the door"). There were days when it mattered more that we were talking about welfare checks and racism than about scientific theories. But really, one led to the other. When you let young people get out the things that need to come out, they can free up their minds to listen and learn whatever else you put in front of them.

A teenager known as "Transit" suggested a real-life math lesson that I could never, ever have imagined. Transit had earned his nickname by sucking subway tokens out of turnstiles—literally sucking them out with a deep breath and his lips pressed against the turnstile. His profession predated the era of Big Brother and video surveillance. In fact, it was rumored that he had inside connections at the station. Transit took his stolen tokens and sold them at fifty cents on the dollar to check-cashing stores, sometimes clearing as much as $1,000 a week. He was rooting for a proposed fare increase because he anticipated a pay raise. But he didn't know how to fig-ure out what his new cut should be.

"How do you round up when it's an odd number?" he asked one day, explaining his predicament. "I don't want to get cheated."

When the fares went up and Transit got a bigger cut, he showed up at school Monday morning with a four-finger gold and diamond name ring that spelled out TRANSIT. He bought the whole class a Carvel ice cream cake shaped like a subway token to boot. As always, food was central to the celebration.

To give ourselves a new challenge, we started an Academic Olympics team.

"Vanessa, we're making you captain," I announced before the whole class. It was a badge she wore with pride—when she bothered to show up. Her attendance was spotty, but she never missed an academic competition.

When my students won a citywide competition in math, people couldn't believe it. Things like that didn't happen at our school—or at any school in the South Bronx, and especially not with a team of special ed students.

I had quickly figured out that many of these children had no business in special education. In fact, placing students in special education *was* a business. They had been banished to my classroom because of behavior issues, poor English skills, poor advocacy, or lack of motivation caused by simple boredom. With each small win, we had a chance to celebrate their accomplishments. Some days I brought in pizza or wrangled free movie passes from a local theater. To this day, I say celebrate often.

My fellow teacher colleagues were baffled by the young upstart in the special ed room. "Why are you working so hard?" they'd ask me. "Look around you. Do you really think you can fix this mess?"

Many of them just wanted to do whatever it took to get through the day. Fridays and Mondays were the worst days for teacher absentees. The day before a vacation, we were lucky if 50 percent of the staff showed up. My own record was far from perfect. No one held me accountable, except my students. When I realized that they missed me if I didn't show, that motivated me to improve my attendance.

Even though students were accustomed to poor teacher attendance, they wondered why so many teachers went missing at once during certain times of the year. It was as if they just vanished. None of their teachers lived in the neighborhood, which only added to the resentment.

"It's the Jewish holidays," I explained. "You know anything about Passover?"

"I know there's a section at Pathmark that says 'Passover' on it, with, like, 'matzo balls' or some shit," one of the boys offered.

"What the fuck is a matzo?" asked Shante.

"Do you know why it's celebrated?" I asked.

No one did.

"It's a festival to thank God for putting an end to Jewish slavery in Egypt."

This had exactly the effect I thought it would: dead silence for a few seconds, followed by one brave soul calling out, "Jewish people were slaves? Like . . . *slaves*?"

There was just one logical thing to do: I planned a Passover Seder in my homeroom.

Rival gang members in yarmulkes played the part of the four sons, each responsible for asking a question. I designated another boy to lead us in reading the Haggadah. We called him Rabbi Wilfredo. Of course we sampled all the symbolic foods. For my students, this event turned into a powerful history lesson. Most were amazed to learn what Jewish people— my people—had gone through. "Mista, are you really sure you are Jewish?" was the most repeated question of the day!

The tables were turned. My students knew me as a white guy who celebrated their culture. They reveled in the fact that I loved hip-hop as much as they did. Now they were curious about my heritage. What did I celebrate?

Why? That opened the door for us to talk about what unites us as humans, despite our differences. "You brought us together, Mista," Wilfredo told me.

We went on to study the Holocaust, and for that, I wanted to attract some guest speakers. I knew just where to look: my grandmother's nursing home and my aunt's work with a respite program for Jewish seniors.

Holocaust survivors with thick accents came into our classroom and told the students what happened in those concentration camps. They heard about book burnings and neighborhoods burning, about families dying. They saw time-worn photographs of children's hollow faces.

Even tough kids were moved to tears, and so was I. We weren't just doing required reading; we were tapping into our common humanity. Old white people, young black people . . . they were all living a story of resilience.

The students would ask great—and sometimes shockingly honest—questions. "Why would you still want to live?" one of them asked, after learning that our guest's parents and sister died in gas chambers.

"Look what I would have missed," he responded. "I have had a lot of pain in my life, but I never gave up hope. I outlived our tormentors. I built a life and a successful printing career, and I had three kids and seven grandchildren who all live right here in New York City. No matter what, there is always hope that your life can turn around when you don't give up."

It was exactly what they needed to hear: Your circumstance doesn't have to be permanent.

Some teachers openly resented what I was achieving with students who had never been successful in school before. "You're making us look bad," a friendly colleague confided in me. The same teacher told me, "There's a rumor you're bribing kids to show up." With what, junk food? And on my crappy salary?

I learned early in my teaching career about being a tall poppy. You were going to get plucked, and not always for the right reasons. Stand out too much above the crowd and you risk getting cut down.

I also learned a thing or two about corruption. When my students won the Academic Olympics, Bronx Democratic leader Stanley Friedman, one of New York's most powerful politicians at the time, came for a photo op. He told me that he was impressed with what I was doing with these children.

Then he pulled me aside and added, "If you make a political contribution, you might even wind up being principal someday."

Was this how business was done? I was clueless. But I didn't contribute. Even if I had wanted to, I didn't have any extra cash. Less than a year later, Friedman was convicted of racketeering, conspiracy, and mail fraud in a federal case, and bribery in a state case. He ended up serving four years of a twelve-year sentence.

I didn't want to be a principal anyway. I didn't have a clue what a principal did. Did this person even work in the building? I never saw administrators in the halls or classrooms. I was still figuring out what it took to be a teacher.

Despite the occasional breakthroughs I had with students, I didn't kid myself that I had the answers. We were all swimming upstream against conditions beyond our control. That became crystal clear as I watched a change come over Vanessa. In a matter of days, she lost her fierce attitude. Instead of being pissed off or laughing at the curveballs that life threw at her, she seemed numb. All emotion had drained out of her. She was losing weight fast. Her skin looked sallow, as if the color was leaching out of her. She was edgy, nervous, restless, and craving sleep that never came. I knew what this was.

"Vanessa, stick around a minute?" I asked her at the end of class. She barely nodded but she didn't leave. When the room was empty, I sat beside her and said, "Look, you need help."

I cut to the chase without bothering to ask why. The reasons were all too obvious. I wanted to get to solutions. After seeing some of my own friends get caught up in drugs, I knew what crack use looked like. Her flat affect told me everything. This tough, smart kid who relished being in charge had given up control of her life. I feared for how she was financing her addiction. When she came down, she was as terrified as a little kid waking from a nightmare. Her face tugged at my heartstrings. At sixteen, she could look like an innocent six-year-old one minute, a hardened fifty-year-old the next.

"Ritz, I fucked up," she told me, her eyes welling over. "I don't know what to do. And the crack—it just keeps calling me."

"Just keep coming to school," I begged her. "I'll get you some help."

That was a promise I was determined to keep, even though I had no idea how hard it was going to be to access outpatient drug treatment for a juvenile. This was long before rehab was widely available. Vanessa's mother was struggling with too many issues of her own to manage her daughter's care. School provided a semblance of routine and was a necessity to keep the welfare checks coming to her family, but it offered nothing in the way of substance abuse counseling. So after school, Vanessa and I would set out in my Grand Am to visit treatment centers across the South Bronx.

While I drove, she talked. And she talked and she talked and she talked. Remarkably, I listened and took it all in. I felt like I had found a long-lost kid sister. She filled me in on the classroom dramas, rivalries, and romantic breakups that I had missed or misinterpreted. She took command of the radio, turning me on to hip-hop musicians that I hadn't heard yet. The girl had so much rhythm and street style, she could dance sitting down. She steered me to the most mouthwatering, cheesiest pizza in the neighborhood. I inhaled those slices with such gusto that she started calling me the Big Cheese.

As long as we kept talking, I knew that she wasn't using. Those daily drives bought her some time, but I could feel the clock ticking. On days when Vanessa didn't show up for class, I paced the halls and worried that I had lost her to the streets. Some nights I camped out on her doorstep, waiting for her to come home in the morning. Finally, we found an outpatient program that would take her. It was far from her apartment, but I was happy to be her ride.

"I don't know how I'll ever pay you back, Ritz," she said one afternoon when I stopped to fill up my gas tank.

"I don't want payback, Vanessa," I told her. "Pay it forward."

No one cautioned me not to get so involved in a student's personal life. In those days, nobody worried about rumors or false accusations. All I worried about was what might happen if I did nothing. I thought of the words of activist and journalist Dorothy Day: "The biggest mistake is sometimes to play things very safe in this life and end up being moral failures." I had no idea that my simple act of doing something for Vanessa would one day save dozens of other lives.

CHAPTER 3

GROWING INTO TEACHING

Spring 1986—As much as I cared about my students, and as much as I liked teaching, I was also a man-child barely out of my teens myself. My friends were still behaving like life was a continuation of *Animal House*. During my own college years, I had been asked to "graduate elsewhere"—a polite way of saying get lost—not once, but twice, before finally graduating from SUNY Purchase College.

While I could see the problems in Vanessa, I could not see them in myself. After all, I never partied until after school or on weekends. I convinced myself it was just a way to blow off steam. On Sunday mornings, if I was waking up on Orchard Beach after a late night out, I'd often bump into my students heading out to start their own adventures. "Yo Ritz! We knew we'd find you here!"

Even with my students' best efforts to keep me on a budget, my money never lasted until the end of the month. My active social life was expensive. When I had cash in my pocket, I was as impulsive as my students. Everything caught my eye. To expand my income, I started taking on extra jobs. It was easy money as long as you were willing to hustle and didn't ask too many questions.

The underground economy was huge. In all neighborhoods like the South Bronx, the underground *was* the economy. Back before cell phones were in everyone's pocket, street-smart entrepreneurs figured out that information is currency. They patched together their own ways to keep communications flowing. Beepers and coin-operated phones were the go-to technologies for anybody who needed quick communication—from the legitimate fashion industry and other local businesses to the underworld of betting, numbers, drug dealing, and more. With deregulation, coin-operated phones became the Wild West of the communications industry. Pay phones on the streets were still leased by the city, but indoor pay phones installed in restaurants, butcher shops, and bodegas offered new revenue sources for landlords and store owners who converted to them.

Who owned this new market didn't matter to me. All I needed to know was how to sell the phones. The rest could stay shrouded in secrecy. A guy like me, who liked talking to people and wasn't afraid of anybody, could sometimes make several hundred dollars a day selling coin phones and prepaid calling cards. I didn't need to know who owned the hardware, who made the calls, or what they talked about. Still, I had a nagging feeling that I was part of something I couldn't live with for long.

I quickly earned enough to rent my own little slice of heaven. My first apartment was on the top corner of a massive, six-story complex on 238th Street. The building had a planted courtyard. The street was gorgeous and lined with trees. Surely my students would be proud. I turned my apartment into a loft with exposed brick walls. An up-and-coming painter named Daniel Hauben lived around the corner and made art out of the jangled geometry of fire escapes, train trestles, and brick buildings. With a view of the city skyline, artists for neighbors, and house parties to deejay every night, I thought I was living the dream.

When my mother came to see my new place, she opened the refrigerator. Inside were fifty pairs of the latest and greatest sneakers. No food. I didn't own pots or pans, and I had another hundred pairs of never-worn sneakers stashed in the kitchen cupboards.

"Why do you have sneakers in your fridge?" she asked.

"Mom, they're like me," I told her. "Just chillin'."

The good times didn't last. That extra cash in my pocket paid for a whole lot of stupidity. I played the role of adult in the classroom, but I had a long way to go to get there in my personal life. Seemingly independent as I appeared, I was an impulsive adult child, a human pinball.

I was as confused as my students about the future. Whom did I want to become? I could make quick money in the hood, but at what cost? I thought I was bulletproof. I didn't yet understand what it meant to take responsibility for your actions. Career goals? Clueless. I liked teaching, but after two years on the job, I needed to turn my temporary license into a permanent credential. That meant grad school. I started taking the courses I needed but hated them. Everything that they taught felt irrelevant to my students' reality. Professors expected me to turn in homework, write papers, and make all sorts of commitments that interfered with my life outside of school. I wasn't willing to pursue a degree just to move up the career ladder, much less to simply tread water.

So when my temporary teaching certificate expired at the end of my second year of teaching, I knew it was a signal. As much as I loved being back in the Bronx, I started looking for an exit.

Just as I was looking for a way out, a buddy phoned me one day with what sounded like a fairy tale—except it was real. A distant relative of his had died and had left my friend a big house in rural Arizona. He was the sole heir. He was heading out west to settle the estate.

"It's three hundred acres and a ranch house. Plenty of room," he told me.

This image of a house in the desert fired up my imagination. Maybe it could be an oasis. In the Bronx, I could feel trouble creeping up on me. Some of my friends were changing, getting caught up in drugs and petty crime. Some got into much deeper trouble. More than one had been diagnosed with AIDS. I was terrified of this plague. There were no medications yet, and it was an awful death sentence.

"So what are you saying?" I asked my friend.

"I'm saying you can come with me. Get a fresh start. Figure out where your head's at and what your next move's gonna be. Who knows? Maybe you'll be back here and maybe you won't."

That's how I found myself in Prescott, Arizona. In this unfamiliar landscape of cactus, sand, and an abundance of white people, I didn't find easy answers. But I did have an epiphany: Wherever you go, there you are. And you bring yourself with you.

It didn't take me long to settle in. Right away, I got hired as a playground supervisor at a school with a large population of Native American students. I didn't know anything about their history or culture, but I was eager to learn. I saw so much in common with my former students. These children were living in abject poverty, just like the students I had taught in the Bronx. In a wild way, the lonely and isolated reservations seemed like horizontal versions of the housing projects I knew in the South Bronx. Substance abuse was rampant here, too. Instead of crack, glue and alcohol were ruining families.

Crack makes life go at hyperspeed. It comes on like a barreling train. Anybody who gets caught up in crack can't get enough stimulation fast enough. Emotions come flooding in, shifting moods in an instant. Glue and alcohol do the opposite. They slow everything down. On my way to work in the morning, I'd see guys sitting at the side of the highway looking as stationary as cactus. At night, they'd still be in the same spot, baking in the desert sun. When the wind blew sand in their faces, they didn't even flinch. Their reflexes were deadened.

I learned to recognize the look and affect of children born with fetal alcohol syndrome. Their expressions were blank, devoid of emotion. I made it my mission to make a connection and get them to smile. I dressed up as Clifford the Big Red Dog and volunteered to teach reading on the reservation. I threw myself into it with all of the energy I brought to the basketball court, and children responded. I wasn't just a playground supervisor—I was the Prime Minister of Play! On a good day, I'd get three hundred of my fellow children involved in capture the flag and other playground games. I'd be right in the middle, having a ball. It was like conducting an entire orchestra, great fun, but I started wondering what else I could do to really improve the odds and outcomes for these children.

After six months of playground duty, I got serious about teaching. Semiserious was more like it. I knew I was a long shot for graduate school at Arizona State University but figured I should visit the campus and plead my case. Sheer luck and destiny connected me with Professor Stan Zucker. Dressed in shorts and an awful Hawaiian shirt, he seemed far more approachable than the head of the department. In fact, he listened to me intently. An expert in special education, Stan—as he preferred to be called—agreed to give me a chance.

Like me, he was a transplanted New Yorker. If I came across as outspoken or a little too loud to others on campus, Zucker recognized the voice of a fellow Bronx native. He could give me a look that made me check myself without thinking. He could see through my bullshit and knew, without my telling him, that I was carrying baggage, and lots of it. Like me, he was a night owl. His evening class schedule appealed to me. I figured I could fit grad school into my life without giving up my part-time job at a sandwich shop or curtailing my active social life. He signed on as my graduate adviser. I quit the playground job and moved into on-campus housing in Tempe so I could be close to classes.

Zucker looked like he had wandered away from a Grateful Dead concert. On first impression, he reminded me of the white guys who came to the South Bronx to cop-and-go, make a quick deal and get out. He had the beard, ponytail, and serene smile you'd expect of a middle-aged hippie. I knew this type all too well, or so I thought. You'd never guess from his affable, laid-back demeanor how smart he was. Or how demanding. I found out the hard way.

"Missed you tonight, Steve." That was a greeting I grew to dread. If I skipped class, Zucker would hunt me down. He knew I worked at the sandwich shop near campus, so he'd show up there at closing time.

"Had to work late, man," I'd say, and see his head shaking before I could finish my excuses. Some nights he found me on the basketball court, sweaty from a pickup game that went on longer than I realized. "Whoa! Guess I lost track of time," I'd start in, and see the head shake coming my way.

"What are you doing here, Stephen?" he would challenge me. "You don't need to take up a useful spot in my program. You've got to cut this shit out." In a classroom full of graduate students, I was a standout for all the wrong reasons. By skipping class and missing assignments, I got Zucker's full attention. The easy thing would have been to let me fail or drop out. But he wasn't about to let me take that route.

What was hardest for me was coming clean about how little I knew. I had bargained and charmed my way through undergraduate school without learning essential skills. My academic gaps were enormous. How do you do research? How do you write an academic paper? How do you cite sources? I excelled at making excuses, but those stopped working when I got to grad school. I was ashamed to admit what I didn't know.

What did Zucker see in me? When I was at my worst as a student, I reminded him of the youth with behavioral challenges that he taught earlier in his career. He saw me as a big kid in sagging shorts who needed to turn around behavior that wasn't serving his own best interests. When I did come to class and railed against the injustices of public education, he caught a glimpse of himself at a younger age. He knew I was right, even if my message was too blunt. He wanted to help me harness that raw passion for the sake of children who need a forceful advocate. He saw that I could connect with people when I wasn't pissing them off. With the right training and maturity, I could be part of a meaningful solution.

"I wouldn't have gotten to where I am," he later confided, "except that I kept falling into opportunities that people gave me. I knew there was hope if you were willing to take advantage of opportunities yourself."

Hope appealed to me, especially after I had a health scare. School was arduous, and as classes progressed, the stress added up. My hectic schedule and self-indulgent lifestyle didn't help. I went from having a cold to some sort of chest infection that would not go away. The breaking point was waking up one morning with half the hair from my head on my pillow. I knew something was way, way wrong! Weeks earlier Magic Johnson had shocked the world by revealing he was HIV positive. Information and more misinformation were running rampant, and my symptoms and my own risky behaviors had me scared. The day I tested positive for HIV, I saw it as a death sentence. I went to the bank and withdrew my life savings—a few hundred dollars—in small bills. I bought dozens of ninety-nine-cent hamburgers and gave them away on a street corner in the worst part of town. When I ran out of burgers, I started handing out dollar bills to strangers. I ultimately passed out on the street and was left there penniless, shoeless, and without ID. I woke up in a Dumpster and walked seven miles back to campus—barefoot, in tattered socks, in one-hundred-degree heat. Determined to move forward, I finally got up the nerve to get retested. That's when I learned that the first result had been a false positive. I didn't bother to tell my adviser about that wake-up call. Even I understood that I was dancing way too close to danger.

Zucker was so demanding precisely because he knew that his graduates would go on to work with special-needs students. If he didn't adequately prepare us as teachers, we would let down the children who deserve better.

"We have a special thing in special education," he would tell me. "We can't let future teachers get away with not doing the work. I won't just dock your grade for an incomplete. If you don't do the assignments, you're not going to develop the skills you will need as a teacher."

Grades didn't motivate me, but his faith in me flipped a switch. It was the ultimate collision, connection, and co-learning. He took my success personally. In a special education program, I became his special project.

It took a while, but our heart-to-heart talks got through to me. In hindsight, I can see that Zucker was giving me a private tutorial in educational theory that applies to all students, not only those labeled special ed. One lesson in particular has stayed with me to this day. It guides my overall approach to teaching and learning.

"There are only two reasons why kids can't do something," he would go on to explain. "They're either noncompliant, which means they don't want to do it, or they're incompetent, which means they don't know how to do it. Our answer, in either case, is always to teach. You don't give up on the kid. You, however, are *both* noncompliant and incompetent. I'm a teacher, so I'm not giving up on you."

Once I understood that lesson, I knew it would stick with me for life.

Bit by bit, I started to grow into the opportunity that he was offering me. If I owned up to not knowing something, Zucker was ready to help me fill in the gaps in a way I could understand. As I got more invested in my studies, I began meeting the academic goals that Zucker helped me set for myself. I was ready to pour my energy into becoming the impact player that he envisioned. Took me a while, but I graduated the program with honors.

During my student teaching, I asked for the assignments that nobody wanted. Schools with the worst poverty, the most marginalized populations—sign me up. I was determined to teach harder, teach smarter, and apply the insights I was learning in graduate school. Both theory and practice convinced me that it is insane to assume all children learn the same way. Working with special-needs students, I focused on finding their strengths. What were they good at? What were they passionate about?

Passion, purpose, and hope have always been the cornerstones of my work, but you have to infuse them with the right support. Passion is the thing that will get children to come to school. Purpose is what keeps them coming back. Hope is what drives them to keep trying, even when it's hard and against all odds. I've seen students get so stuck that they start to believe they aren't able to learn. My job was to convince them otherwise and provide the support they needed to succeed. I'm a fast talker by nature, but now I needed to be a fast observer. I had to figure out in a heartbeat whether students were attentive and understanding the lesson or drifting in a state of confusion.

Long before accountability became a term favored by pundits and policy makers, it was a reality in my classroom. I told my students, "I'll hold you accountable. You hold me accountable right back." We kept that promise every day and built a culture of mutual trust.

Our bargain included these agreements:

ON MY SIDE

I will provide you with a daily agenda, entry activity, and exit ticket.

I will take time to answer every question that any student asks.

I will provide whatever tools you need to help you succeed.

I will treat you with dignity and respect.

I will come early, I will stay late, and I will always be here to help you.

ON THEIR SIDE

We will always make our thinking visible.

We will respect and love everybody, even when it hurts.

We will make sure that everybody knows the homework assignment.

We won't give up just because something is hard.

We'll ask questions when we don't understand.

We will never yuck at somebody's yum.

Now school wasn't something done to them; we were all in this together. Students who had seen themselves on the margins of education became stakeholders in their own success.

The approach began to get results. As my underachievers turned into superachievers, I ran into the same resentment I had experienced in the Bronx. To be fair, many of my colleagues in Arizona were well-meaning people. I would challenge them by asking, "Would you send your own children to school here? Is this how you would want your child treated?" People didn't want to hear it, especially not from a young upstart from New York.

By the time I finished my student teaching, I had adopted a theory of education that has stayed with me ever since. My views are not complicated: We have to stop placing the blame on poverty. Poor children can rise to high expectations, but first you have to have those expectations. No child rises to low expectations! For me, it starts with love. We've got to love children until they learn to love themselves. I learned that power when Stan Zucker gave me a chance and encouraged me to show my students the same respect. Meeting, learning, and working with Stan was a true opportunity that I was and remain determined to forever pay forward. Through him, I learned that teachers have the power to change lives.

As soon as I completed my master's degree in special education, I was recruited by a wealthy suburban school. This predominantly white school served a small and needy subset population of children from the reservation, who were only there because of zoning. The school wanted a babysitter for the "rez-kidz" and other special education students who were isolated from the rest of the "high-achieving" and well-to-do student body. I wanted results.

Reservation students ("rez-kidz") had even less reason to trust a white guy than my Latino and black students back in the Bronx. We found common ground on the basketball court. When my team of Native American students beat the school's varsity team, I caught flak from administration. The varsity kids, predominantly white, wanted to win championships for the status. If they got college scholarship offers, even better. For the Native children, scholarships could be life changing. If some of my students earned those coveted spots on the varsity team, we would upset the natural order of things. My students earned those spots. But sadly, they never got what they deserved.

The same thing happened in academics. Thirteen of my special education students qualified for the state writing championship that year. Their successes earned me the title of Arizona Teacher of the Year, in my rookie year. That caused more grumbling among my colleagues. At the end of the year, I was called to the principal's office and asked not to come back for a second year.

"Why don't you apply at an inner-city school?" the principal suggested. He gave me a great recommendation but made it clear that I wasn't wanted in his community.

One afternoon, a beat-up envelope that looked like it had traveled a hundred thousand miles landed in my mailbox. It had followed me from one forwarding address to another, to another, to another, starting from my parents' home in Rockland County. I tore open the envelope and broke out in a big smile when I saw the name at the bottom of the note: Vanessa. A photograph of her in cap and gown fluttered into my lap.

Two years after I left the Bronx, she had done it—buckled down, stayed clean, and gotten her high school diploma with honors. Now she was heading on to college and thinking about a career in counseling. Paying it forward. I grinned, remembering that little powder keg who taunted me in my first teaching job. If this was how it felt to make an impact, I was all in.

What was remarkable was how much her note affected me. Her timing could not have been better. Here she was thanking me for inspiring her, when she had given me that same gift right back. Even though I hadn't been perfect, I had been enough. If I had been able to change a young person's life even when I was still prone to screwing up myself, imagine what good I could do if I went back and kept myself more focused and grounded. Show up to grow up. Bring your body and your brain will follow.

Everybody needs second chances, I thought. Even me.

CHAPTER 4

PUTTING DOWN NEW ROOTS

Fall 1994—After several years in Arizona, I was itching to go home and give myself that second chance. The illness that earlier had been mistakenly diagnosed as HIV was actually an airborne allergy known as valley fever that was indigenous to Phoenix. It was acting up again. In Arizona, I struggled to find the job that was the right fit. I had done a lot of growing up. By then, I was a father myself. I planned to raise my daughter, Michaela, with my college girlfriend/future wife, Lizette. We had managed to keep our relationship going long-distance during my time in Arizona. Now we were ready to start our life together back in the Bronx.

The daughter of Dominican parents, Lizette was a first-generation American full of ambition. Growing up in a household where no one spoke English, and the oldest of three children, she taught herself the language so she could keep up in elementary school. That made her the family translator. Like a lot of children who shared her background—and like a lot of my students—she had to grow up fast.

When we met, I was a college senior in no hurry to slow down. She was a seventeen-year-old freshman, at least a year younger than most of her classmates. Our first date was April Fool's Day, 1984, the day Marvin Gaye was killed. After a night of slow dancing to "What's Going On?," she went home and told her mother she had met the man she was going to marry.

She turned out to be right, although we didn't tie the knot until years later. At our wedding, we danced to Marvin Gaye.

When I came back to the Bronx from Arizona, I didn't get back into teaching immediately, at least not in the traditional sense. Initially, Lizette and I saw an opportunity to start a small restaurant in a former crack house that we bought for $600. The interior was stripped down to nothing, thanks to rumors that drugs might still be hidden away somewhere in the walls. Or maybe the pipes. The neighborhood—two train stops from South Bronx High School—was rougher than ever. But our location was within walking distance of schools and small businesses. That meant plenty of foot traffic. Plus, we delivered.

The place was profitable from day one. Lizette compared the experience to earning an MBA. For me, running a small business offered daily lessons about the power of feedback. In graduate school, I had learned that prompt, specific, actionable feedback is one of the most powerful tools for learning. In the restaurant, I lived that lesson by noticing our customers' likes and dislikes and then making adjustments accordingly. We learned about assets and liabilities every day by keeping a close eye on the bottom line.

We sold the best soup in the South Bronx and offered $1.99 specials out of a tiny place with a roll-up door and twenty seats—eight stools and three tables of four. Every day, we delivered on the promise of fast, fresh, clean, and polite with our secret sauce of passion, purpose, and hope. This was the most dangerous block in the South Bronx, but our little restaurant was a safe haven. To Lizette, it felt like a more diverse version of the café on *Friends*. People would come in for a cup of coffee or bowl of soup and stick around to tell us about their lives. Our customers looked out for us, walking us to and from our car. We never experienced a single incident of violence personally, although we did have the windshield stolen right out of our car.

Our best customers were students who wanted homework help and teachers who needed to unload about their daily challenges. Along with rice and beans, I served up algebra lessons and gave feedback on five-paragraph essays. No extra charge for homework help and a free meal for an "A" paper. I hired special-needs students for delivery routes and paid extra if they picked up cans and bottles to recycle. We sponsored dances and donated food to proms and graduations. Hearing all these children's stories and questions made me eager to return to the classroom, where I could apply everything I had been learning.

Somehow, our little restaurant had become the interactive asset-based community development classroom I had envisioned years ago, and only blocks away from South Bronx High School. Yes it was profitable, but we loved the human dividend and what we were building more than the income we were deriving. Remarkably, even here, it all tied to local children and local schools. Every day offered a chance to tackle incompetence and noncompliance and build a culture and community where all benefited and thrived. In our little community, food was a nonnegotiable. Here, all were served with dignity and respect while celebrating and supporting achievement and accomplishment.

"I don't think you've ever left the classroom," Lizette told me. "You're just teaching from behind the counter."

We soon sold the restaurant for a profit and bought an apartment in the Bronx. Lizette started what would become a successful career in Manhattan's financial sector. I returned to teaching and never looked back.

"Hey, guys, please clear out! Can't you see there are children here?"

At recess and lunch, I made polite and respectful sidewalk sweeps to keep addicts and dealers out of sight of our middle-school students. This quickly became part of my daily routine as a new teacher in the South Bronx Creston Avenue/University Avenue corridor on 184th Street. Rudy Giuliani had just won the mayor's race on a law-and-order campaign, but his cleanup efforts in Manhattan were only pushing more drugs, crime, and homelessness into the Bronx. Some days, there would be a line of fifty people waiting to buy on the sidewalk and more customers at the curb in double-parked traffic.

Some of our students—still way too young to drive—were already using intravenous drugs themselves. Many suffered the consequences of their parents' drug use; this was the first generation of children born addicted to crack. Crack babies of the 1980s had become dysfunctional students of the '90s, and no one knew how to deal with them. They had problems with impulse control, aggression, and concentration. They behaved as if they had faulty wiring, on constant short circuit. These were issues I had noticed in some of my young restaurant customers, too. Some of the faculty had their own demons and addictions as well.

In this whirlwind, I was lucky to work under school leaders who inspired greatness. Principal Pamela McCarthy was an African American woman from the neighborhood who expected teachers to work hard because she believed that children deserved no less. Another administrator named Nancy Berlin—white, Jewish, and inspired by Eleanor Roosevelt's example—treated students the way she wanted her own children to be treated and her staff like family.

On a particularly cold winter day, Nancy came to observe my classroom after lunch. Right away, I started making excuses. She had recently coached me on better ways to use the chalkboard to focus students' attention, but that day's lesson didn't reflect any of her good strategies. "It was so cold at recess. My hands got too numb to hold the chalk," I told her. The following day, Nancy presented me with a pair of black leather gloves. That gift reminded me to have no excuses, ever. Our students deserved the best from us, each and every day. Warm and stylish, those gloves made me a better teacher. Every time I put them on, I felt loved and valued. I relished them at recess. I wanted to pass that good feeling on to my students. (Twenty years later, I still wear those gloves.)

Assistant Principal Karen Armstrong, whose mother was an army sergeant, was the school's chief disciplinarian. The first day we met, she followed the sound of my big, booming voice right into my classroom. "My office is just down the hall," she told me, with a no-nonsense look. "I'm in charge of math, science, and special education." And me.

In a school system that felt like it was coming apart at the seams, these leaders were fair and honest. They gave me room to innovate in my class-room as long as my sometimes nutty-sounding approaches helped students learn. Mindful that the system was not receptive to disruption, I knew I couldn't change entire schools but longed for and clung to leaders who at least allowed me flexibility and freedom within my four walls. That's why I followed them from one school to the next as our education system played musical chairs. During the six years I taught under their leadership, our school name changed three times but we never left the building. Each time, the district simply slapped a new sign on the exterior. Inside, it was the same old story.

Imagine if the school system itself could foster devotion, dedication, and loyalty to facilitate change the way Pam, Nancy, and Karen had me hooked to them. We all collectively worked and prayed to create more and more spaces like mine, sacred and accessible. One classroom at a time, if only my classroom, we kept our dreams alive.

Miguel was a street-smart seventh grader when he was assigned to my special education class. He'd spent the year prior spying on our class and plotting to get into it. On his early-morning walk to school, he side-stepped crack pipes and hypodermic needles. He pretended not to notice when drug runners sidled up to parked cars to hide their packages on top of tires. It was better not to know anything. Police routinely stopped chil-dren his age to shake loose information about neighborhood dealers or accuse them of being lookouts. By thirteen, Miguel had learned not to act afraid even if he was quaking inside. Looking soft or scared would make him a target.

Like many of my students, Miguel didn't really belong in special educa-tion. The son of immigrants from Honduras, he was significantly behind grade level in reading because he was still learning English. He didn't do well with teachers who handed him a book, pointed to a seat, and told him to get busy.

"They think I'm slow," he told me, "but really, I'm just not that good at English." I thought about my father and his early challenges with reading.

When Miguel got tired of pretending to read, he would take a nap on his desk or stir things up with his classmates. In an instant, he could orchestrate chaos. That got him labeled as trouble.

My goal was to create a place where children like Miguel wanted to spend time. Miguel wound up with me via default. I kept wondering, what if by design we had classrooms and teachers that children actively wanted to be a part of, to work toward and with? What if I could channel all that creativity and energy to good use? What would it take to make my classroom into an oasis where all students could find success? How could I build a culture that built on the strengths of students like Miguel instead of making them feel like losers? I was determined to find out. I wanted this reality for every student, every teacher, and every classroom. What if every student had a teacher they wanted to be with, a classroom they wanted to call home and loved to spend time in? What if every teacher and every classroom had a big screaming WELCOME sign on the door that spoke a unique language? How awesome school would be then!

"Yo, Mr. Ritz! What's the plan today?" Miguel would ask when he bounded into class.

To a visitor, my teaching style might have looked spontaneous. In fact, I spent most evenings fine-tuning lesson plans, anticipating where students might struggle and how to help them. Miguel liked knowing that I always had a plan. When children know what's expected of them, they can do so much more. One day I was teaching a lesson on long division and told the class, "Here's one way to solve the problem, but there might be a thousand other ways to solve it. If you can come up with a better solution, tell us."

Miguel's eyes lit up when he realized he had worked out a shortcut. "Mr. Ritz, your solution takes three steps. I can solve it in two!" I handed him the chalk and invited him to teach us his shortcut.

That happened to be one of the days when I brought my young daughter to school with me. By this time, Michaela was a kindergartner. There sat this skinny, bright-eyed kid, surrounded by all the middle schoolers. She wasn't scared by their size or tough looks. She did the same lessons and loved reading with my students. She saw herself as one of the gang, just a little smaller. "It's mellower when she's here," Miguel observed. Twelve years later, she would go on to write her college application essay about her nonbiological brothers and sisters from her dad's classroom who became her extended family.

Again and again, I watched students who had been labeled "special needs" or "low performing" respond to the invitation to learn about their world. I experimented like crazy to design experiences that would open their eyes and engage their curiosity. We never had to travel far to find adventures.

To understand the principles of force and motion, we built our own bicycles out of junked parts and took a forty-two-mile bike tour that touched all five boroughs. When fourteen of us rode through Greenpoint, Brooklyn, and saw business signs in Polish, my students asked, "Are we in another country?" Every outing reminded me that their understanding of the world stopped as soon as we left their immediate neighborhood. A deep-sea fishing adventure, intended as a reward for good behavior, quickly turned into a ship full of seasick students. One of the most eye-opening and heartbreaking moments for me happened on the way back to shore, when one of my students pointed to Staten Island and innocently asked, "Is that Africa?" Nobody laughed at his poor understanding of geography. In our classroom, there were no dumb questions. I was reminded of the vast differences in life experiences that students bring to school. Experience, or lack thereof, can unfairly dictate outcomes.

One afternoon, my own curiosity pulled me into a pet store a few blocks from school. I was fascinated by a display of aquariums. I bought a small fish tank for our class and watched my students gather around it to catch a glimpse of neon tetras and goldfish. Every day, I would stay after school to take care of the tanks. "What are you doing there, Mr. Ritz?" Miguel wanted to know. "Can I help?"

I had no idea what I was starting. As an educator, I understood the importance of setting a "hook" to grab students' attention and get them interested. But I never could have predicted what a monster hook this would become; I think I landed a whale. Having some sort of living thing that was dependent on the children—for its food at the very least—made a huge difference in students' lives. It tapped into a sense of empathy and compassion that I realized was at the heart of my own value system. What was special about a fish tank was that it was self-contained and, if maintained properly, gave off no odor, had no poop to scoop, and didn't attract vermin or pests. Watching the fish swim had a calming effect on students. That made it ideally suited to the classroom.

The children loved having fish in the classroom so much that I quickly graduated to a fifty-five-gallon aquarium. The lessons came fast and furious.

"What kind of shape is this fish tank?" I asked.

"Rectangle!" someone called out.

"It would be if it were flat. But this tank has three dimensions, so it's a . . . ?"

"Rectangular prism!"

"You got it. And if I want to know how much water to put inside this tank, I need to know a certain measurement. What's that measurement called?"

"Volume?"

"And volume is measured in what kind of units?"

"Cubic?"

"Right! So who wants to help me figure out the volume of this fish tank?"

There was no shortage of volunteers for any job that required standing by the fish. Students would pull out rulers to measure length, width, and height. How many cups, pints, quarters, half gallons, or gallon jugs would it take to fill an empty tank? Estimations and trials helped them visualize what ten gallons looked like and then what fifty-five gallons looked like.

Then we learned other stuff.

We learned together about how to create the right habitat for fish—the right temperature, the right filter, how often to change the water. Big fish ate some of the little fish, which was the story of these children's lives. I wanted my little fish to constantly outswim the big ones. It wasn't all about your size or even your speed, either: Schools of fish were protective. Those fish families had your back. By sticking together, they could ward off predators or take down an enemy. That was just like the way a good peer group could help my students fend off bullies.

Miguel was quick to volunteer for fish duty. He was a natural when it came to testing the water chemistry, cleaning tanks, and keeping the equipment humming. Watching his immigrant parents work two jobs each had instilled a strong work ethic in him. One morning before school, he confided, "Mr. Ritz, I never knew I was good at stuff like this." He astonished me when he went on to reflect, "You're showing us how little things are connected to way bigger things and how all of this connects to school." Years later he would tell me, "School used to feel like a storage locker or a time-out for children. You turned our class into a diving board and the world into our swimming pool." I was witnessing this miracle daily, and the children kept showing up ready to dive in and do it again and again and again.

Maybe the most important lesson of all was nurturing. Teach children how to care for a living thing and you've given them something no textbook can provide. When we teach children about nature, we teach them to nurture. And when we teach children to nurture, we as a society collectively embrace our better nature. The day one of our guppies gave birth, we all watched in awe. We marked the important date on the calendar, then I went out at lunch and bought a Fudgie the Whale ice cream cake from Carvel. We all sang "Happy Birthday" to our school of baby guppies.

When I saw how eager my students were to learn about living things, I rebranded our special ed classroom as a biodiversity center. No student wants to be placed in a "special education classroom," but everyone wanted to visit our "Biodiversity Center"! It went from being the room filled with the lost, lonely, and misguided to being the coolest place in the school. It took children who were often the victim of circumstance and consequence and made them the children of privilege. They became the veritable ringmasters of a living, breathing circus, and their new status came complete with important responsibilities. It was interactive and, most importantly, it was alive!

On 184th Street, in the heart of the hood, on a block without a single tree, bush, plant, or blade of grass, we had a natural wonderland. A pair of housebroken iguanas, four feet long from snout to tail, calmly sat on the desks of students who were reading quietly. We fed them bananas and kale. When a giant tortoise smuggled from the Galápagos Islands was confiscated at Kennedy Airport, we volunteered to take care of it. We fed her strawberries and mustard greens. And we eventually had twenty-five hundred gallons of freshwater and saltwater fish swimming in the classroom . . . including a school of piranhas. One tank alone held three hundred gallons. I bought display racks from a local retailer and filled an entire wall with what I called our "imaginarium," a place of wonder, inquiry, and aspiration. Every new creature we introduced generated the need for information and research, and suddenly my students were delighted to do it.

Did I ask permission for all of this? No. Asking for permission is begging for denial. If I asked permission for just about any of the things I did with my students, I would still be waiting for some rubber stamp somewhere. I just showed up at work hauling boxes with air holes punched out. After all, I was keeping all this stuff contained behind my own classroom doors.

Karen Armstrong, our no-nonsense assistant principal, did her best to keep an eye on my classroom menagerie and me. She ran interference when other teachers questioned what I was up to.

"Have you seen the resources he's bringing to this school?" she would tell them. "Have you seen how the students respond?" It wasn't just the children. When I took a busload of students to a reptile show, we had siblings, parents, and grandparents join us.

Although Karen was a stickler for following the rules, she saw the value of being flexible. "Steve," she told me after joining us for one of our adventures out of the city to see how maple syrup is made, "you're giving these children experiences they never would have had in life."

Running across the street to break up a fight after school one day, I was hit by a van. I still remember leaving the ground and hearing my students exclaim, "Look at Mr. Ritz fly!" I was rushed to the nearest hospital emergency room. That afternoon, at Lincoln Hospital, I was the only patient who was not handcuffed to a gurney.

While I was out nursing a surgically repaired ankle, I worried about who would take care of the animals. Miguel stepped right up. With the key from the custodian, he took over all the duties without being asked—and then some. He got a little too good at animal husbandry. Unknown to me, he trained our giant monitor lizard to jump for food. When I came back to school, I opened the cage one afternoon only to have this three-foot-long reptile pounce on me. It attached itself to my arm with what looked like the jaws of death. As I was trying to pry the thing off me, Miguel walked in, saw my distress, and doubled over laughing.

"Yo, Mr. Ritz, I forgot to tell you—I trained it!"

The big lizard was sent away to a new home.

Twenty years later, Miguel and I continue to share this story with each other and our families.

Despite the occasional mishap, this lively environment was great for motivating students. I believe every child deserves a safe, nurturing, aspirational environment, a place where children can work, dream, and aspire to a better, brighter future. They all deserve a place where they have a sense of daily purpose and responsibility. A classroom that students cannot wait to enter each and every day is a place that drives competence and compliance.

A student who had perfect attendance for a month earned the right to feed our twenty-one-foot-long blind albino reticulated python, Blackie.

Blackie terrified our assistant principal but was good for encouraging student attendance, especially on feeding days. We announced these feeding days weeks in advance. Eventually, during the hottest summer on record, Blackie got us into trouble. In a prank gone way bad, the night custodian let Blackie out of its cage. Unknown to me, the custodian used to enjoy letting the snake out to wander the empty hallways, then would lock it back up again. This time he forgot to close the cage properly. I learned of this when the phone rang at our house in the wee hours.

"This is Irma. May I speak to Stephen?"

"It's two thirty in the morning. My husband knows no Irma."

Lizette hung up on her.

The phone rang again.

"This is Irma Zardoya, the superintendent."

By four a.m., I was walking the building with Michaela and a SWAT team looking for the runaway snake. A helicopter hovered overhead with a spotlight trained on the building. We headed to the basement, hoping to find Blackie in the abandoned swimming pool. All we found were rats— bigger than the baby rabbit we had brought along as snake bait.

My school had to close down for a week and a half. Summer school students were moved to a different building. In the evenings, the snake kept appearing in windows—snapping and lunging at pigeons—and then ducking back inside, scaring the pants off passersby with its beady red eyes. When rumors spread that a crazy white guy was unleashing snakes on the community, the mayor's office called the school to investigate. It was like an urban legend—*We've heard that this snake can swallow a child whole!* Finally, after eight days of setting traps and pounding our knuckles on cement walls to try to coax Blackie out of hiding, my daughter and I found him hidden inside the janitor's closet. During the hottest week of the decade, on the hottest day on record, Blackie was chilling in a water trap we had set there, anxious for a sip of water.

Michaela thought it was all a great adventure—"just another day with Dad."

After a brief period of offers from people who wanted to adopt the snake or skin it for accessories, we found it the right home and donated it to a facility in the wealthy suburbs of Westchester. He was like the reptilian Fresh Prince of Bel-Air. The custodian got a transfer, too, but not to the suburbs. Karen Armstrong was thrilled to see them both go!

Two years later, I taught a self-contained class of twelve students—all boys—who were labeled emotionally handicapped, with disabilities ranging from Tourette's syndrome to autism. Some had been my students for multiple years thanks to a practice called looping that lets teachers build long-term relationships with students. The adventure movie *The League of Extraordinary Gentlemen* had just come out. Inspired but not wanting to plagiarize, we called ourselves the League of Distinguished Gentlemen. "The boys," as they were known throughout the school, had never been referred to as gentlemen before. For a writing project, we planned to write memoirs and publish them as a book. Each boy would have his own "gentleman name" and chapter.

I told my gentlemen to use all their senses to describe the world around them and the things they liked and didn't like. We talked about how writers will immerse themselves in something to learn how to describe it well, like a writer who goes to the jungle to study an animal that she wants to write about.

This led "Gil" to break a window.

He wanted to describe the sound of a window breaking, so . . . he broke it. That's how I found myself on the receiving end of a call from his mom: "Mr. Ritz, did you assign my son to throw a rock through a window so he could be a better writer?"

"That . . . wasn't *exactly* what I said."

He did describe it really well, though.

When we were done editing, I had the book published. And by "published," I mean that my wife took the manuscripts to work and had them make a ton of photocopies and use fancy spiral binding and glossy presentation covers. Then we had a book signing where we invited parents, guardians, and school staff to receive their copies of our publication, logically titled *The League of Distinguished Gentlemen*.

This called for a celebration, so naturally that meant food. I bought a thousand chicken wings to give away. The Chinese restaurant manager donated free fried rice. Student authors signed copies of their book for their family, favorite teacher, and principal. In front of everyone, I gifted each student with a fountain pen, a highlighter, and a journal to keep the momentum going. They were so proud!

Their stories were not prettied up or sanitized. Although special education exists for noble reasons, it can be a cruel place to find yourself as an adolescent when peers are looking for any reason to mock and bully. By and large, that's what the stories told in ways that were both insightful and upsetting.

One student, a little person named TJ, wrote a story called "The Glue Trap" (see the Appendix). It was all about how being in special ed had made him feel like a rat stuck on a glue trap—how the stigma "sticks to everything" until he just wanted to gnaw off his own leg to escape. He named names about teachers who made him feel bad and described the injustices he saw in the program. Another student wrote about the teacher who had written IDIOT on his forehead with a black Sharpie and made him walk to school that way. Miguel, my star animal trainer, helped to orchestrate that teacher's firing. Sure, I could have censored these stories, and that might have made the staff feel more comfortable and kept me out of hot water, but I wasn't about to invalidate these boys' truths. Ironically, the very school we were part of had forged them. They were my extraordinary gentlemen, and they deserved to be heard.

I realized then and there that if we were going to address the root problems that challenge children, we need to let children self-identify the problems they perceive as the impediments to their success. No parent brings a sick child to the doctor and asks him to tell the doctor what feels good;

rather, we encourage children to describe what hurts, where and why, so the expert can address and assuage the problem. As educators, we cannot fear hearing that our behaviors and actions are causing harm or pain. We need to hear it, acknowledge it, unpack and deconstruct it, and then get children to a better place. We all love to hear and share the good, but we also need to acknowledge the painful and our roles collateral to it.

Some of the stories were about more lighthearted things, like a boy who described his mother's lasagna in such terrific detail that your mouth watered by the end and you really hoped you'd get invited to dinner at his house one day. I asked if I could buy some from her to take home to my family, and Heriberto was right—she made the best lasagna. For the rest of the year, I bought lasagna from her every Friday.

One boy described how much he loved playing capture the flag. Another described my "Look of Death" in the classroom and how he tried to avoid being on the receiving end. Overall, the book was critically acclaimed and controversial. The book went viral, and everyone wanted a copy. The first printing of 750 copies disappeared in three days! We even had requests for additional copies. People wanted signed editions. I loved and cherished every page!

The people at Lizette's workplace loved it, too. It gave them a window into a world they knew nothing about, and their hearts went out to my children. That's how we got our first corporate sponsors. They donated used computers to the class to help make a difference for the students. It did. That year, we placed five special education students in a summer program at Fordham University for gifted and talented youth. No surprise to me, my students took first, second, and third place at Fordham's summer science fair. No surprise, either, that Miguel was number one!

The computers enabled me to turn my students loose to learn about programming. A quiet boy named Alberto who had Asperger's syndrome and mild dyslexia was a particularly quick study. One day, federal law enforcement agents came to my classroom to find out who was tinkering with NASA satellites. They caught him in the act.

"What the fuck, man!" he said. "I was right in the middle of something and they tried to handcuff me!"

"Not cool, Alberto!" I told him, while silently marveling at his abilities.

After that, you'd hear his name called over the loudspeaker every so often. At first I worried that something was wrong, but it turned out that the front office was calling him in whenever they had a computer problem they couldn't figure out. Schools were going digital at this time, and the board of education had outsourced the implementation to a private technical team. The professionals had a big contract but were way behind schedule. It took Alberto, a special ed kid, to hardwire the whole building. When AT&T donated one hundred used computers, it was Alberto who got the equipment to work. He set up a computer for every teacher, made the library digital, and sent excess equipment home to students' families.

"Man, I should get paid for this," he'd muse.

"No joke. You will someday," I told him.

He went on to a successful IT career and still keeps in touch.

Teachers are forever bringing their work and their students home. It is not as if you place the day in a cubby, on a shelf, or in a locker and punch out and go home. That's especially true if you are committed, and make no doubt, I was committed. Teaching was much more than what I did; it was who I was. I brought my whole self to work daily and I also brought it home daily. Giving yourself over to this profession can be overwhelming and overbearing but so incredibly rewarding. I wanted to bring that experience home to Lizette and share it with her personally; I wanted her to catch the fever. After all, she couldn't come to work with me daily. So we decided to expand our family.

Lizette and I had been trying to have a baby for two years, and in summer 2003 we finally got the amazing news that we were going to have twins.

Michaela would get to be a big sister—twice! We barely had time to celebrate, though, before we found out that one of the twins didn't make it through the first trimester. That was devastating.

The rest of Lizette's pregnancy was difficult. On New Year's Eve, twenty-two weeks in, her water broke, way prematurely, and she was hospitalized for nearly two months. I would go to school and then sleep at the hospital each night. In February 2004, under emergency circumstances, our son, Max, was finally born . . . but he passed away the next day.

Lizette was inconsolable. I was so angry with the world. Why was it that people who didn't care about children at all, or who would abuse or neglect their own, could have children easily and we couldn't? Why would this child, so loved and so wanted, never get a chance at life? I wore the black gloves Nancy Berlin gave me on the day we buried my son, and I tried to make sense of anything at all.

We became top fund-raisers for the March of Dimes. Because we wanted our son's legacy to exceed his short time on earth, we started the Max Foundation. The staff and students at my school were wonderful to us during this painful time. They cared, they asked how they could help, and I knew their hearts were broken with us. When I broke down sobbing after school one day, Karen Armstrong folded me in her arms. "I'm going to hold you in my heart," she promised. "We're a family here."

Then came another blow, just a few months later. One of my favorite students, a big kid named Victor, was a gifted athlete. I spotted his raw talent one day in the schoolyard when I saw him throw a football and knock a seagull out of the sky. Another day, Victor got into a fight at recess and had another boy in a chokehold. I told him to let go and he did, but the other boy fell back and cracked his skull. Victor was suspended.

Every day during his lengthy suspension, he came and sat on the hood of my car. I could see him from my classroom window. I started leaving him homework assignments, books to read, and lunch. I left my car open so he would have a place to stay in the subzero weather. When the suspension ended, I helped him get a football scholarship to attend a private prep school

PUTTING DOWN NEW ROOTS

in North Carolina, far away from the Bronx. Two weeks after he got there, he passed out on the football field. Within seventy-two hours, he was diagnosed with leukemia. At the same time my wife was hospitalized during her pregnancy, so was Victor. I visited him every day, shuttling across town from one hospital to the other. Throughout those weeks, I never missed a day of work.

Victor never left the hospital. After a five-month battle, Victor passed away. Three months after burying my son, I had to bury Victor, too. I wore Nancy's black gloves to that funeral as well.

How do you go back to school after that? I could barely walk into the building. There were no good days at that time. Before this tragedy, our assistant principal used to call me a ray of sunshine. Now there were only tough days and tougher days. When you bring your whole self to work, that means you also bring your pain.

I spent the summer with my wife and daughter, who needed me near, and promised to find a job closer to home. Every moment mattered. If I could escape my painful memories, cut twenty minutes off my commute each way, and also be able to walk my daughter to and from her school, that meant the world to me.

That's what led me to Walton High School the following September. It was so close to home that I could check on Lizette during my breaks. It was such a relief to walk away from the pain of seeing the locker that used to be Victor's, and the seat in the classroom that once was his, that I didn't even research what I was getting myself into. Walton was one of the lowest-ranking high schools in the entire state.

As I walked through the metal detectors on the first day, all I could think was: Let the heartbreak end. Let my life get a little better. Let me do right by these children and my family.

CHAPTER 5

HOW DAFFODILS BROKE UP A FIGHT AND STARTED A LEARNING REVOLUTION

Fall 2004—When I arrived at my new school, I discovered that Walton High School was a four-story holding pen with almost four thousand teenagers packed into a building meant for eighteen hundred. The graduation rate was 17 percent. In fact, it was slated to be closed—a fact I never knew until I arrived there. I was oblivious. Mayor Michael Bloomberg had taken control of the city's schools two years earlier and increased the number of school safety officers to crack down on discipline. He wanted to bring structure and innovation into an archaic system and break up massive schools into smaller ones. I didn't disagree with the fundamental need to disrupt a system that had failed so many students. But what Bloomberg and his reformers didn't anticipate is how long it takes for new school culture to take root and thrive.

From the moment you arrived on the Walton campus, you sensed chaos. In fact, you felt it even before you entered. Graffiti and neglect screamed anything but welcome. People parked randomly and often argued for parking spots. Hordes of students loitered outside, and there were massive lines to enter the building. Brazen sexual activity occurred everywhere and openly. The campus appeared to be cloaked in marijuana smoke. Inside, it was crowded, loud, and frantic. All the adults carried walkie-talkies, and each on a different channel. Radios and announcements blared endlessly. Faded paint on the drab walls seemed caked on in inches, not coats. There was always something urgent happening or about to happen. Everything in the building was geared to try to capture and create control. But the reality was, there was none of it. There was no sense of order to anything; it was sheer, unadulterated chaos.

We had eighteen armed police officers stationed at the school, thirty-eight safety officers (which were basically unarmed police officers), and seventeen deans of discipline. I was one of them. In fact, I had been promoted higher up in the chain of deans within just a few weeks of joining the staff. The reason wasn't that I was tall or able-bodied. It was that I knew many of these students from my years of work at middle schools serving the same community. Those children—now young adults—respected me and knew I cared about them.

My extra job title may have emphasized discipline, but my personal strategy was all about relationships. My goal was to differentiate between noncompliance and incompetence—and then to teach to both accordingly. In some ways, that attitude made me an instant outlier to those who wanted instantaneous law and order. The problems here were huge, and there was no immediate fix. This would take time. I thought of my days at South Bronx High School and my Arizona State University mentor, Stan Zucker.

A police van was permanently parked out in front of the school to haul kids off to the police station in groups each day. It was so bad, students were routinely maced in the hallways. There were more than two hundred felonies committed at Walton that school year. But even when students were caught doing egregious things, they saw me as their ally. They would ask the police to stop while they were being hauled out in handcuffs because they spotted me down the hall. "Hey, Mr. Ritz!" they would shout. "How's your wife? How's Michaela?"

Even those bonds with students were no guarantee of peace in my classroom. At any moment in this overcrowded building, tempers could flare. The wrong look or an angry word from one student to another would be enough to set off a skirmish.

I had no idea what ignited the tension between two of my students on an otherwise ordinary October day. There was no time to find out. When I saw a big guy and an even bigger girl push back their chairs and spring to their feet, I knew from the body language that they were ready to fight. I was pretty sure the girl would do the ass-kicking. I made a beeline for the two of them, trying to keep the other students out of their reach. I was about to try to call for help (the phone system was pretty spotty) when I saw the boy, a kid named Gonzalo, reach under the radiator. That's when everything seemed to go into slow motion.

He yanked something loose and out spilled . . . flowers. Dozens of bright yellow flowers on long green stems. In Gonzalo's hands, those blooms shone like miniature suns.

The class gasped as if he had pulled a rabbit from a magician's hat. The flowers were just as unexpected and incongruous under the fluorescent lights. Fists instantly stopped flying. *What the . . .*, I thought to myself. The boys now clamored to give flowers to the girls. The girls wanted a stem or two to take home to their mothers. And the science teacher in me had to figure out what the hell had just happened.

I didn't even know that the flowers were daffodils. Weeks earlier, I had stashed a box of flower bulbs that someone had donated to the school behind a radiator because I didn't know what I was supposed to do with them. I had no idea how steam from the hissing radiator had forced the bulbs to bloom and the box to deteriorate. My students were just as clueless. Youth who lived in neighborhoods of concrete and barbed wire had just experienced what we educators call a teachable moment. This wasn't magic—it was nature. And it was amazing! Now we had a mystery to solve, a real experience with scientific inquiry. Turns out that was a teachable moment for all of us.

I could have let that moment pass and gone right back to the lesson plan for the day. But there was something so poignant in my students' response to those yellow flowers that I was moved myself. For the first time in weeks, I felt the stirrings of something that felt an awful lot like hope. No way was I going to let this good feeling end with the bell.

When class ended, I took time to really look through that big box that held the donated flower bulbs. I found a letter inside. Turns out the package was from BK Bulbs out of Holland, which was donating the daffodils and inviting us to a New Yorkers for Parks event at Poe Park that was coming up in just a week. The idea was that students and community members would show up for a Saturday of volunteer work to plant bulbs and beautify the park.

"You guys want to go to the park?" I asked the same class of students the next day.

"Hell, yeah!" was the unanimous consensus.

Those bulbs were not supposed to bloom in October. They were still supposed to be just bulbs, and we were supposed to plant them so they'd come up the following spring. But because I screwed up and stashed them under a steaming radiator, we got to deliver a special treat to the park. Our flowers would stay in bloom right through Thanksgiving until first frost of winter. Call it beginners' luck. Clearly, we were all beginners when it came to gardening.

Poe Park, just three blocks from our school, is listed on the National Register of Historic Places because of the absolutely unremarkable little cottage where Edgar Allan Poe lived when he wrote "Annabel Lee." Most of my students didn't know anything about Edgar Allan Poe, but we all loved Poe Park. For the community, the park was significant for a variety of reasons. Poe Park has always been a place for people to convene—some for good purposes, some not so good. For the LGBT community, it's known as a safe place to gather. Gangs and drug dealers have used this public space, too, but not usually for fighting. At night, it's often a camp for the home-less. By day, families come here for picnics and playground visits. Many of my kids had been here to smoke weed and make out with their dates. Twenty years earlier, I used to meet Lizette at Poe Park for our dates. In our microversion of New York City, this was our Washington Square Park.

Eleven of my seventeen homeroom students showed up the morning of the event. When we got to the park, we found city workers and a big group of older volunteers with lots of gloves, garbage bags, shovels, mounds of soil, and thousands and thousands of bulbs. My students were the only young people who had come to work. Everyone had to sign in, and the vol-unteers welcomed each young person enthusiastically.

"This enters you into a raffle, too!" one of the volunteers said as she collected signatures on her clipboard.

The first objective was to clean out debris in the park, and I was impressed by how well the students got right to work. No one stood around; they were all actively helping, giving and taking orders, working as a team.

When it came to planting, they were even more amazing. They took direction and outworked everyone else around us. They didn't want to stop for breaks, and they wanted to see the job to completion, no matter how long it took. We kept getting complimented on what great workers they were, which wasn't my doing—they were just really into it.

Even the drug dealers stopped by to give my students a quick smile.

The longer we were there, the more attention we drew. The more we worked, the better the place looked. The results were so obvious, it became contagious. It's not the norm to see eleven inner-city teenagers come together to garden in the park, and people loved it. Newspaper photographers snapped their pictures. Elderly people stopped to talk about how much they loved to garden when they were young. For once, my students were getting positive feedback from their community rather than distrustful stares.

At the end, two of my students won raffle prizes, too. One won a pair of sneakers, and another won front-row concert tickets to Lincoln Center to see a salsa band that turned out to be his grandmother's favorite. He was thrilled. The prize included not only the pair of tickets but also a chauffeured car to transport his grandmother and him there and back! This was an experience they never would have had otherwise, and it affected him deeply. This tough guy came back from that concert a changed man. He had been able to do something wonderful for the woman who raised him, and all because of something that started at school.

"YO RITZ! LOOK! WE'RE IN THE PAPER!" Peter declared. Sure enough, on Monday morning there was a big article about the daffodil planting in the local Bronx news, along with the kids' pictures and names. This was the coolest thing ever for them. Their parents and guardians had something to tack on the fridge, and other students around school were impressed.

The six students in my homeroom who hadn't shown up were now pretty pissed they had missed it. The others were getting a whole lot of attention, and now I had something to motivate the ones who had stayed away. I made sure to leverage that.

"Hmm, I didn't see you there on Saturday," I told those who missed out. "We might be doing more stuff like this, but are you sure you want to be part of it?"

This was not a normal event for the students in that homeroom, which was filled with the young adults nobody wanted. Some didn't have the literacy skills to read a Dr. Seuss book after a decade or more of public education. Their whole lives had been defined by what they couldn't do. Some coped by zoning out. Others had short fuses, ready to go off with no notice.

Many of these children had suffered life experiences that far exceeded their developmental capacity to handle. One girl's mother sold her clothes and feminine hygiene products for quick cash. Another came home from school to find her apartment in ashes after a crack pipe was left to smolder on a mattress. Some already understood that their parents or grandparents kept them in school just to work the welfare system or get SSI benefits, which required children to show up to school at least part of the time. Despite their tough, street-smart exteriors, these were adult-size children.

Even kids who carried guns and had criminal records responded like kindergartners when I read them stories. They soaked up love and positive attention like a dry sponge tossed into a wet sink.

I wanted to build on the momentum we had going from the park event. And there was no shortage of ways to do that. New Yorkers for Parks had handed us flyers listing similar events all over the borough. We had enough work to last us sometime into the next century.

But first, I thought, we should make our team official.

"Graffiti and gang tags get painted over almost before they dry. I'm giving you an invitation to make a lasting imprint on your community, and for good reasons," I announced on Monday. "On your desk, you will find an application. We're going to start making 'green graffiti.' We're going to make our community more beautiful by finding ugly spots, cleaning them up, and planting flowers. If you want to join the Green Teens, you need to fill it out and type up a résumé."

"Are you serious?"

"Of course I am. We're going to put a lot of effort into this team, and I need serious people. I want you here, but only if you're responsible and ready for it. So I'm only going to pick the best ones."

Calvin greeted my proposal with suspicion. "You think we want to get our hands dirty? I'm not into that," he said. He was a muscular kid with no body fat. If anybody looked like he could handle physical work, it was Calvin. He had missed the first Saturday workday and was well aware of the sneakers that somebody else had won in the drawing.

"Don't worry, Calvin. Dirt washes off. You guys are going to have a chance to do something great for your neighborhood. That's permanent."

Calvin muttered to himself, "This guy's got some balls."

I told them that I would be accepting applications until Thursday. When I had to cover an honors class the next day, I saw my homeroom students peeking in, thinking that those students were filling out applications, too. I played along.

The application asked questions meant to highlight grit and determination, not academic qualifications. I prompted students to tell me:

- Why do you deserve to be part of this team?
- What challenges do you face that you will work on while you're on the team?
- How can this team help you?
- Are there any places you hope we can work on?
- What do we need to know about you?
- How are you special?

These questions allowed students to self-diagnose and give me insights into their talents. Whatever made them special was exactly what I wanted to celebrate. It turned out they all identified that they wanted to fix their own, immediate neighborhood. That was an eye-opener for me. And it seemed completely doable.

Every one of my homeroom students turned in an application—including Calvin. "I decided to take a chance on you, Mr. Ritz," he told me. "You're a pretty wild guy, but I think you're gonna come up with something cool."

That Thursday morning began a little bit of theatrics. I knew if I had just announced at homeroom that they'd all gotten in, it would be anticlimactic and they'd realize I'd made them fill out those applications for no good reason. So I worked it differently.

"I got a couple hundred applications for the program, so it's going to take us another day or two to go through them all," I explained. "We even had some kids from the Bronx High School of Science apply, too. I asked two master gardeners to help me decide who's going to make the cut, because they're going to help teach us."

Some of my students were visibly deflated. I put them up against the *elite* high school students from up the street? What was I, a traitor? Now they'd never stand a chance.

The two mentors I mentioned were real people I had contacted through the New Yorkers for Parks group. I'm a guy who isn't afraid to ask for help with my crazy projects, and I knew I was going to need help with this one. What did I know about starting a gardening program? I hadn't even recognized a daffodil.

The guys arrived at school to help me deliver the news. I had the secretary page the first student, José, to come to the main office. When he arrived, expecting to be in trouble for something or other, the secretary instead told him that some people wanted to meet him.

There I stood, ready to make introductions.

"José, this is Darrell Penn and Paul Sawyer. They read your application and résumé, and they wanted to come meet you in person."

José's eyes widened. He had no idea what to say.

These weren't some middle-aged white guys in garden gloves. They were young, hip, handsome, well-educated African Americans. They brought instant credibility to the Green Teens—and to me.

"Hey, José. I really liked what you had to say in your application," Darrell started in. "I noticed that you said you have an interest in learning a new skill, and I think that's a great goal. Learning how to garden and build landscapes is a good move that can be a real asset to you as you consider your career options." Hearing this message from a cool, smart guy who looked like José and his classmates—that was riveting.

"You sound very dedicated and willing to work hard. We think you would be an asset to the Green Teens program," Paul added. "Congratulations! Welcome to the team. We're looking forward to working with you." Paul knew the neighborhood well enough to rattle off local legends. He instantly clicked with the students.

It was like José had just won a prize, awarded by the best possible judges.

We continued on like that all day and the whole following day, breaking it up so that students were told during all different periods and compared notes with each other.

"Did you get in?"

"Nah, man, I didn't get called. You think they're still calling people?"

"I don't know. Good luck, man."

Finally, we had announced the names of the students who were annointed to get into the Green Teens. Whaddya know? All seventeen applicants from that homeroom made the list. The air was electric.

"Can you believe it, Mr. Ritz?" José asked. "We all got in!"

"That's really amazing," I said. "There must be something special in every one of you that makes you stand out." I saw students exchanging looks and nods around the room, giving props. I piled on. "Think about it. People who didn't even know you saw something in your applications that made them say, 'Wow, these are the best of the best.'"

To get through the school doors each morning, students had to pass through a metal detector and undergo the scrutiny of armed security guards. Boys in one line, girls in another. Backpacks and shoes off to make sure nobody was hiding a weapon. Boys had to remove their belts. Girls often had to remove their earrings. With four thousand teenagers needing to be screened at a school designed for eighteen hundred students, the process could take forty-five minutes. No mercy if you were at the back of the line when the bell rang, even if you had hauled yourself out of bed early enough to get to school on time. While they waited outdoors, hungry and irritated, students had nothing welcoming or even interesting to look at. Out of boredom, they'd often rearrange the white plastic letters on an ancient announcement board to spell out "fuck you." That summed up how most of them would describe the school culture.

Calvin was one of the first Green Teens to start paying closer attention to that environment. "This place is just dirt," he announced one morning when he arrived at homeroom. "There's no grass, no flowers. Even the trees look mangled. It's sad."

Calvin lived within walking distance of Walton but still struggled to get to class on time. Some days, he didn't even try. I found out where he lived and occasionally showed up on his doorstep bright and early. Being on the Green Teens was a privilege that required good attendance.

"Man, I can't hide from you, Ritz," he said.

"I don't want to lose you, Calvin," I told him, and watched the corners of his mouth turn up. When he smiled, the grin went ear to ear. I caught a reflection of myself grinning sheepishly at my old mentor, Stan Zucker, when he had held me accountable.

We started digging up that hard-packed dirt at the school entrance and preparing the ground for flower beds and rosebushes. Every new task offered another metaphor and more opportunities to spark curiosity.

"Why do we need to dig in compost?" asked Krystal.

"Yeah, where does this stuff come from, anyway?" Porsche chimed in.

"And why does it smell different from dirt?" Precious wondered.

By hefting shovels and pushing wheelbarrows, my students came to see that everything is salvageable. Kitchen scraps, leaves, and grass clippings could be recycled into rich loam. Nothing is beyond redemption, not even dirt. Imagine their reaction when they found out that the best soil in the world—brown gold—was elephant shit. I got it from a guy I knew at the Bronx Zoo and didn't tell the students until they were knee-deep in it. By then it was too late.

Getting to use simple hand tools and shovels made these students feel special. For the first time, they had access to stuff that most of their classmates didn't. Even better, they had access to Darrell's and Paul's tutelage. While we worked, the mentors talked to them. They were a perfect tag team. Darrell was a Princeton graduate who loved talking about the value of education. He gave the students not only the gift of gardening training but also the gift of a relatable role model. Paul worked two miles from our school. He had a great job—with benefits—managing local parks. He knew these students' backyards better than they did, and with that came incredible credibility. Here was a chance to put young people of color and power in front of young people of color with *no* power.

The more my students got their hands dirty, the more they started noticing the natural world all around them.

"Yo, Mr. Ritz, how can a plant grow out of a crack in the sidewalk?" Luis wanted to know.

"I saw a plant on top of the train track. How'd it get up there?" wondered Franklin.

Their questions opened the way for conversations about seeds, life cycles, and habitats. We talked about science, naturally, but also about the toughness of organisms that could survive and even thrive under harsh conditions. They all got the parallels between plants and people.

Once we had spruced up the school entrance, we tackled the courtyard behind the cafeteria. We chipped out the cracked cement, spread soil, and then planted it with ornamentals. Students from other classes started coming to the courtyard to eat lunch or hang out, and that brought my Green Teens some long overdue respect. I brought my classes out there during the day, too, for special projects.

One morning, I led my homeroom students to the courtyard, where they discovered a pile of materials. There were plastic straws, pencils, pens that had run out of ink, and other junk. "How can we use this stuff to tell time?" I asked. They didn't understand my question. "I've got the time right here," said Franklin, pointing to his digital watch.

"Or you can listen for the bell," added Krystal.

They knew I was up to something when I drew a circle in the dirt and stuck a straw in the center. "Notice anything?" Now they were curious, moving closer to get a look at the shadow cast by the sun. That was our introduction to sundials. Learning to trace the trajectory of the sun this way was like learning a secret code. I'd see my students out in the courtyard before school, checking the "real" time, making sure the sun was still working. Their questions opened up more lessons about the solar system, ancient civilizations, and art. Using junkyard scraps, we made some amazing outdoor timepieces, as beautiful as they were functional.

Once we had things looking pretty good at ground level at Walton, we set our sights on new opportunities during and after school. Those mangled trees outside the school entrance that Calvin complained about became our training ground to learn about pruning. More metaphors. A good arborist can look at a tree full of deadwood and broken limbs and imagine it leafed out and healthy. When students heard that they could earn $45,000 a year as certified tree pruners for the city, I had trainees lined up in work gloves, eager to learn.

"What do you say we get you guys certified?" I asked.

"Like . . . right here at school?"

"I know a guy," I said.

It really was the story of my life.

If I didn't know a guy, I knew a woman who knew a guy, or an aunt's best friend's brother-in-law who knew a guy. Every meaningful connection in life is one phone call, one handshake, or one secret door knock away.

There were always instructors willing to come to my school to help teach my students. Mostly they were working contractors who needed to hire good crews. It was in their best interest to train these young people early and put them to work rather than having to hire out-of-towners or provide paid training to new recruits. So we got all the students certificates showing that they had passed the tree-pruning course. They appreciated earning certificates that, unlike report cards, reflected what they could do, not how many hours they sat in class. We planted more trees around campus just to create more pruning work for ourselves. Our plan was to keep ourselves very, very busy.

Our timing could not have been better. Mayor Bloomberg had just challenged New Yorkers to plant a million trees across the five boroughs. This was his vision for a greener, greater New York, creating a sustainable city for the twenty-first century. Contributing to a healthier planet was important, but what I cared most about was getting my hands on some of the city's free nursery stock. We had the student power to plant it and nurture it. Local organizations like Trees New York were eager to connect with my students and me. All it took was a phone call to make the connection. This opportunity made dollars and sense to all of us.

Within the semester, the school property looked so much neater and gave us the satisfaction of finishing a job. But students would have to wait for spring for their efforts to pay off in full—we didn't have any more radiator bulbs left for instant gratification. That was all part of my plan. Now my students had a reason to come back after winter break and remain until spring to see everything bloom.

Even though they liked working around the school, what was far more exciting to my Green Teens was the chance to get *away* from school and not be penalized for it but instead rewarded. We started signing up for anything and everything—wherever there was an opportunity to volunteer to take part in a beautification project around the Bronx, we were in.

My daughter, Michaela, was a regular visitor at Walton, just as she had been at my previous schools. She welcomed any chance to hang out with Dad, even if I was working. She started joining us after school when she was near the end of elementary school and looked up to the big, burly Green Teens like they were her older brothers and sisters. Everyone was protective of her, making sure nobody messed with Mr. Ritz's daughter. In a class where hostility and hormones were the norm—boys hating certain boys, girls getting into drama with other girls, and boys and girls always on the edge of something—everyone had a smile for this skinny, nerdy kid with the big backpack. She smiled right back.

Our Green Teens projects were good equalizers. Everybody got their hands dirty. Michaela dug in like everyone else, happy to be included with the big kids. Watching this little kid tackle the work with vigor spurred my students to work harder. They didn't want to disappoint her. And each time they finished a project, they took time to appreciate a job well done. They all learned something about grit and getting it done right. We were a family.

Michaela didn't seem to notice the piercings, tattoos, and tough attitudes that intimidated many adults. To her credit, she never looked down on high school students who couldn't read as well as a sixth grader. By then, Michaela was also on a first-name basis with the staff at our neighborhood library branch on Sedgwick Avenue. She inhaled books the way my students gobbled up junk food, pop culture, and whatever the media would market to them.

Even as a youngster, Michaela understood that my students faced challenges she didn't. One particularly tough-looking kid with a big red streak in his hair and a belligerent attitude to match let everyone know that he had no respect for authority. He seemed surprised when I addressed him with words like *please* and *thank you*. My daughter was the first to notice the change in him. "He softened up," she told me. "I think he figured out that you really do care." I watched her team up with another boy who struggled to keep up in class. He always needed more time than everyone else. But working outdoors, he could take all the time he needed. "You are the very best seed planter!" she told him. He beamed.

To show my eager students where their advanced landscaping skills could take them, I planned outings to spectacular sites like Woodlawn Cemetery, the historic Bronx burial place of New York's rich and famous. Maintaining this sprawling, tree-studded green space requires the attention of a well-trained, well-paid grounds crew. Students were amazed to discover the graves of Miles Davis, Herman Melville, Duke Ellington, and survivors of the *Titanic*. A lesson in landscaping turned into a stroll through history.

It was also an introduction to living-wage employment. Wandering past the magnificent mausoleums built by wealthy families, my students came to their own conclusions about class and social justice.

"Man, rich people get better places to live even when they're dead!" Franklin said, drawing nods of agreement from his peers. All these experiences led to greater awareness and curiosity about the world.

The rewards of our Green Teen efforts started to become more tangible. Even the least likely students turned into believers. Students who had never experienced good results in class could now see the payoff for their effort. They were getting their first taste of what the experts call intrinsic motivation. They weren't working for grades or gold stars or a pat on the head from me. They were setting their own goals for what they wanted to accomplish.

"Mr. Ritz told us we could do something great for our community," I overheard Calvin say to a classmate. "That's no lie. Whatever he's up to next, I want to be part of it."

Hard work makes you hungry. I kept myself fueled with regular visits to the fast-food outlets and bodegas that line the retail strip under the train tracks on Jerome Avenue, bordering the Walton campus. I kept an open tab at the bulletproof Chinese joint where I'd often buy plates of noodles for students who were short on lunch money. Same at the local Spanish restaurant that doubled as a nightclub. I didn't realize why students perpetually kidded me about going there so often until they eventually told me that it was a prostitution hot spot at night. The twenty-four-hour laundry/fast-food joint on the corner was my go-to spot for morning break. I could get two slices of pizza and an extra-large soda for three bucks. A street vendor sold paper cups of frozen *coco helado* that came in coconut, banana, cherry, mango, and all the other flavors and beautiful colors that I just couldn't resist. Fried chicken from every state in the Union was available within three blocks of the school; I was on my own edible Manifest Destiny mission, determined to try each one.

My weight ballooned. At 240 pounds, my XL T-shirts were getting tight across the gut. One pound at a time, I didn't notice. But it adds up fast. My blood pressure skyrocketed with my weight. Instead of recommending changes in diet or exercise, my doctor prescribed medication. I was taking so many pills that one morning I got them confused. The last thing I remember was arriving at the Walton campus before school with Michaela. I woke up in an ambulance, clutching my cell phone. I did not know how I got there. My daughter had called 911 on another teacher's phone. Clearly, I was no longer the wiry basketball player I had been. Most days I was too busy to care. Even an ambulance ride didn't convince me to pay attention to my own health.

In the midst of all this, the school still faced more than its share of behavior challenges. The halls were so crowded that students bumped into each other all day long just moving from one class to the next. The building was at 194 percent capacity; it was a warehouse, not a school. I could hear students making their way to my classroom. When they were calm, they would say, "'Scuse me. 'Scuse me. 'Scuse me," all the way up to the second and third floors. But tempers were perpetually short, and it didn't take more than a stray elbow for a "'scuse me" to turn into a "fuck you."

What was wild was how quickly we were seeing progress. In my class alone, the daily attendance rate shot up from 40 percent to more than 90 percent. The only school-wide assembly held that year was an event orchestrated by the Bronx borough president's office to celebrate the successes of my Green Teens. Each student was presented with an award in front of the entire student body.

Little by little, one plant at a time, we were creating a more inviting habitat. Even with the noise generated by passing trains, diesel trucks, and the foot traffic of four thousand teenagers, you could stand on the front steps of the school and hear birdsong above the din. As our green efforts took hold, the whole campus felt like it was coming out of a long winter's sleep.

And then we got to meet Rumpelstiltskin himself!

Bronx Parks Speak Up is a local tradition that goes back more than two decades. Sponsored by the Bronx borough president's office, this annual one-day event brings together community activists, politicians, environmentalists, and others who care about adding more green spaces to the county. An invitation to attend brought me and my Green Teens to Lehman College, which happens to be located right next to Walton High School. My students were the only youth participating. Nobody had considered inviting youth before, even though parks are designed with the young in mind. None of us had set foot on the Lehman College campus before that weekend. There might as well have been an invisible wall between our two institutions, and they were only seven hundred feet apart.

Russ LeCount, a third-generation Bronx resident, wondered what brought all the teenagers in Green the Ghetto T-shirts to a parks conference. He listened closely as my students and I described the beautification work we had been doing at Poe Park, on our own campus, and at other locations across the borough. At the break he walked up, offered me his hand, and said, "I'm going to make you a hero."

For perhaps the first time in my life, I was speechless. What could an old, bald, white guy in red suspenders, black army boots, a flannel shirt, and high-water pants possibly have to offer me and my students? This gentleman wasn't just white; he was fluorescent! Literally glowing! I shook his hand but was ready to turn and run. This was a collision I was eager to avoid.

It turned out that LeCount had been attempting some green graffiti work of his own to stem the crime, drug use, and illegal dumping that was threatening to destroy his neighborhood. He wanted to turn a decommissioned street into a community garden. He had started hundreds of seedlings and needed to get them in the ground. "I've got the trees, the shrubs, and the shovels. You've got the kids. How about we team up?" he asked.

The connection made good sense. How could I refuse?

Once I got to know him better, I respected LeCount for his technical expertise. The guy knew his plants. He had put serious time into learning about propagation and cultivation techniques and was willing to share what he knew. Not only that, he had tools for us to borrow.

By then, my students knew enough about landscaping basics to tackle a bigger project. We faced a daunting challenge in LeCount's Wakefield neighborhood. This is the part of the North Bronx where the No. 2 and 5 train lines end. Two decades earlier, during the era of the Subway Vigilante, I had ridden these same trains with my South Bronx High School students. Back then, we all feared for our safety. Now I was coming back to rebuild the community with a new crop of students.

In the 1970s and '80s, these trains sported some of the most fabulous graffiti in the city. People would risk arrest to hop the fence of the train yard and tag the cars with crazy designs. By the time my Green Teens arrived, the neighborhood had earned a reputation for a different kind of danger. It was lined with cheap liquor stores and seedy motels that rented rooms by the hour. The nightly shift change at the train yard meant that eight hundred men were off work and eager for entertainment. Blocks near the tracks were notorious for off-track betting, crack dealing, and prostitution. One house in the neighborhood was like a retail mall for illegal activity: crack on floor one, heroin on floor two, prostitution on floor three.

Geography exacerbated the problems. A few blocks north of the train yard is the dividing line between the Bronx and more affluent Westchester County. In Westchester, any amount of drugs in your possession is a felony. Get caught with lesser quantities in the Bronx, though, and you just get slapped with a desk appearance. That created a price differential. A five-dollar bag in the Bronx would cost twenty-five dollars in Westchester. A steady stream of customers made the short trip from Westchester to the Bronx and often lingered in our borough to use. Meanwhile, dealers and pimps used the transportation corridor to flood the market with their goods and services of all sorts.

LeCount, a tough-talking war veteran with a pale, bald head and beer belly, was tired of watching his neighborhood turn to shit. He didn't hesitate to blame others for everything that was wrong. When my students first met him at Bronx Parks Speak Up, one of them whispered to me, "Mr. Ritz, where did he come from? Are you sure he's from the Bronx?" He looked as out of place as a Viking—or Rumpelstiltskin. To his credit, LeCount looked past the labels that others had put on my students. He appreciated their willingness to work. He showed them abundant patience. When my students agreed to dig in, he picked up a shovel, too. As they worked side by side, he told stories about the old neighborhood. Turns out his father, an ironworker, helped build Walton High School; it was sublime!

Our ambitious plan was to turn five blocks of decommissioned Bissel Avenue into a community garden. An elevated train track borders the sprawling rectangular space on one side. Along the other side are modest single-family homes that had seen better days. Before we could plant anything, we had to take out the trash.

"Time to put on the work gloves, put on the kneepads, get down, and get dirty," Calvin told his peers.

What began as a school project quickly turned into our shared obsession. We kept at it after school, on weekends, and eventually during the summer. The first phase took about a year of effort by the Green Teens. Within eighteen months, the project had expanded to include students from other schools along with adult volunteers, many of them Vietnam veterans from the neighborhood. By summer 2007, I had secured funding through the city to pay for sixty youth jobs.

We started with the biggest items: junked cars that people had been using for shelter or prostitution or both. Most had been stripped on-site, the pieces sold off to pay for drugs and tricks. We sold the scrap metal from the remains of forty or more junkers and invested the profits in materials for building fences and hothouses.

Just removing the garbage made the place look better. "People would come by and say, 'Wow, you guys are doing a great job,'" Calvin remembers proudly. "To think that kids would spend their time to do this—that made people think better of teenagers like us."

Each phase of garden construction offered more hands-on lessons. We could see the progress when we compared the two hothouses we built, side by side. We applied all the lessons we learned on the first one to make the second one better. The first had a dirt floor; the second was finished inside with pavers. Eager learners practiced their basic carpentry skills on picnic benches before building an elegant wooden gazebo. As soon as we finished it, neighborhood families started using the gazebo for weddings and *quinceañera* celebrations. For a water source, we rigged up a decommissioned fire hydrant with spigot and hose, turning it into a gangster sprinkler. We got supplies from anyone who had stuff to share. Excess construction materials? Bring it on. Home remodeling leftovers? Love to have 'em. We said yes to everything.

Eventually, we shifted from thinking piecemeal—what should we build next?—to thinking systemically. What was the bigger vision for this five-block space?

When we spread wood chips to create a meandering pathway connecting the blocks, local residents started coming there to stroll and admire our progress. We had an unlimited supply of free wood chips, thanks to city programs like Christmas tree recycling. All that mulch had to go somewhere. Drivers were only too happy to dump it at the end of the residential streets bordering Bissel Gardens. Big mulch piles created temporary barriers so people couldn't drive cars into the garden area. Once we created pathways, they provided more permanent barriers to shift public behavior. Before long, people from the neighborhood started signing up to tend their own small garden plots. Calvin, reflecting on that long-term effort, summed it up in a sentence: "We took a place that was just garbage and made somewhere to sit in the sun, have a picnic, and hang out."

That's how a neighborhood liability became a community asset. Highly visible projects like Bissel Gardens caused my students to get noticed and appreciated for their skills and smarts. Receiving praise was a new experience, and they liked it. Students who had legal troubles were able to work off court-ordered community service hours on these projects and some got paid to keep working during the summer. They liked that, too. Clearly, we were onto something.

Word quickly got around that there was a group of students at Walton High School who were fixing up the Bronx. We were in the newspapers several times, and News 12 had taped a segment featuring them. That was more exciting than the papers—everyone got News 12, even if you couldn't afford premium channels. And what played in every waiting room across the city, from doctors' offices to government buildings? News 12. Some of my students were awaiting probation hearings when they saw their own faces flash across the television. That must have been a heck of a reference to use when trying to convince the authorities that they were improving their lives.

They didn't realize that the news on Channel 12 repeats throughout the day. They thought they were a lot more important than they were when they saw their segment keep coming up. They called their friends, they called their families. They were TOTALLY FAMOUS!

We showed up wherever we were invited, which included businesses, nonprofits, and public areas. They provided supplies; we provided free labor. Big projects like Bissel Gardens took months, but many of the changes we were making were noticeable almost immediately. My students thrived on that fast feedback.

Within a short time, we got word that the New York City Council wanted to honor us.

"I want to see all of you men in ties," I said.

"I don't have a tie!" Luis said.

"You can borrow one of mine."

"Can I, too?" asked Ramon.

"Okay, how many people don't have ties? Raise your hands."

Hmm. I was going to need more ties.

We showed up at an expensive restaurant on Union Square, where my students carried themselves with such dignity. I'd never seen all of them dressed up before. It was an awesome sight.

The city council presented us with a Golden Daffodil Award, which thrilled the students to no end. The council assumed that they were the honors students—the brightest the Bronx had to offer. I wasn't about to correct them. For once, my students had a chance to be seen without labels. The fact that these council members had redefined my students in their minds allowed these young adults to redefine themselves, too. They were an *award-winning team.*

Success is addictive. It was a whole new world for this group of teens— and we were just getting started.

CHAPTER 6

DRUNK ON TOMATOES

Spring 2005—A year after our cleanup efforts at Bissel Gardens, our friend Russ LeCount and one of our Green Teens suggested we try growing vegetables there. Everyone endorsed the idea. My students know how it feels to be hungry. Their families and neighbors are all too familiar with what the US Department of Agriculture calls "food insecurity," meaning limited or uncertain access to adequate nourishment. My students don't need a fancy term for having empty cupboards and growling stomachs. If it's not their own stomach, it's a friend's or sibling's empty belly. I was moved to hear them talk about how they wanted to help somebody else. I knew they would learn by doing for others. Life has taught me again and again that you get by giving.

When we first started talking about growing food, my students reminded me just how hard life is for them. I used to think that soup kitchens were purely for hard-core alcoholics and homeless men. I didn't think about mothers and children relying on shelters for hot meals. My students taught me that a community resource called POTS—Part of the Solution—was a lifesaver for Walton families, offering meals, a food pantry, showers, and a range of social services to those in need.

When I suggested that we find a way to help Part of the Solution, my students were immediately on board. "We can be part of the solution ourselves? That's cool," they agreed. They had plenty of empathy. But when I started to lay out ideas for an urban vegetable farm at Bissel Gardens to raise produce for the shelter, they looked at me as if I had suggested a trip to Mars. Farming was so far removed from their experience that it seemed crazy to them, like a fantasy.

To be honest, many of my students equated farming with slavery. They were surprised when I told them that a century ago, the Bronx was known for its farms and greengrocers. Later, during World War II, the borough was dotted with small victory gardens tended by patriotic families. Students from immigrant families spoke up about relatives back home who tended vegetable plots.

"My grandmother keeps an avocado pit in the middle of the table. That's her idea of farming," piped up Luis.

In a sense, we were all returning to our roots when we set out to plant our first vegetable farm next to the train tracks.

Spring was the time to plant so we could have a summer harvest. That made sense from a gardening calendar, but it also made sense to me as a teacher. I wanted to motivate my students not to drop out, to come back to school for the next term, and to keep working with me over the summer when I could line them up with paying jobs. The chance to see their efforts come to fruition—to be there for the harvest—proved tantalizing.

Deciding what to plant was a group decision. This was my stealth strategy to make sure students felt ownership of their garden. I wanted them to learn through inquiry and curiosity, not just by following my directions. Frankly, when it came to vegetable varieties, my Green Teens and I were equally clueless. What we all knew best were what my students call "hood vegetables." That's the grimy, brown-at-the-edges lettuce you might find in a bodega cooler if you're lucky. If you happened upon a street vendor, maybe you'd come across an eggplant or tomato. Nothing fancy, nothing organic, certainly nothing that demands a premium price. Those are hood veggies.

To get us thinking about what else we might want to grow, I arranged an afternoon field trip to Whole Foods Market, which had opened its first Manhattan store a few years earlier. About a dozen of us took the train from Walton High School to the Upper West Side.

As usual, as soon as we spilled out of the subway exit in Manhattan, the sidewalk around us cleared out. Well-dressed pedestrians took one look at this crew in their hoodies and baggy jeans and crossed the street. From a safe distance, a few took a second look at our ragtag crew with the tall white guy leading the way. On any day we stood out, but especially when we ventured outside our home neighborhood. And make no mistake—we were worlds away from home, even though it only took us thirty minutes by subway to get there. To bystanders, we probably looked like Mr. Kotter meets *The Wire*. My students were used to sidewalk clearings and second looks. They knew the sound of car door locks clicking when they approached. Unfazed, they followed me toward our destination.

As soon as the grocery doors slid open to welcome us, my students realized they had entered an unfamiliar environment. No bulletproof glass here. No cashier in a cage. No fluorescent lights glaring overhead. The nonchalance my students wear on the street—part of their invisible protective armor—gave way to full alert as they started to size up this place. Heads whipped around. Necks craned. Eyes grew wide. This was interesting!

Two steps inside the door, we all came to a sudden halt in front of the bounty that spread out before us. Red, yellow, and green apples nestled in perfect pyramids. Lemons, oranges, and limes threatened to overflow their bins. Even potatoes came in colors we had never seen before. Purple potatoes? You must be kidding. And the peppers! There must have been thirty varieties of peppers—big and small; orange, yellow, green, red, purple. In our neighborhood, you wouldn't find such a display of brilliant color outside of a gumball machine or inside of a liquor store.

Not only was the place spotless, but it smelled so damn good. Bodegas in the Bronx have their own special smells. Some burn incense to cover the stink of weed or other chemicals wafting from a back room. Some smell like roach spray. This place, however, smelled like an orchard on a summer day, something my students had never experienced. It was intoxicating for all of us.

Whole Foods is an environment that's been artfully designed to make you fall in love with everything you see. We fell hard. It was love at first sight of Fuji apples, Anjou pears, and Japanese eggplant. My students had never had such a quality retail experience before, and certainly not around food. If they got their hands on a few extra bucks, they would buy inexpensive bling like belt buckles that spelled out their names or clothing to elevate their status. They shopped from street vendors and dollar stores, not retail emporiums with high-tech lighting and clerks who looked like they spent their off time in a yoga studio. Everything here was so *nice*. They were even giving away free samples. I could have told my students we were in a food museum instead of a grocery store and they would have said, "Cool, Ritz. Cool."

That initial sensory stimulation lasted only a minute or two but seemed like an hour. Time stopped while we took it all in. It felt like we had stepped into a 3-D still life or a hologram. Even I needed a moment to return to my senses. When I did, I noticed a security guard studying us with a quizzical look. You could almost see the thought bubble over his well-groomed head: "What the hell are *they* doing *here*?"

Usually my students know when they're being watched, which is most of the time. Sadly, they've come to accept that treatment, especially if they're outside their neighborhood. They were so enthralled by their first Whole Foods experience that they forgot they were being eyed. For a heartbeat, they got to be drunk on a perfectly ripe tomato. They got to feel intoxicated by a cornucopia of fruits and vegetables. They got to let down their guard and remember how it feels to be innocent. But just for a moment.

When they noticed the security guard standing by, they wiped the childish delight off their faces. They resumed the slouch and impenetrable expression that they use to put a buffer between themselves and strangers.

I held my breath, hoping nobody would say or do anything to cause an incident. A store like this tempts you to graze. Nothing's hidden behind glass or stashed away in vending machines. I didn't want a stray hand to reach into the bulk bins of dried fruits, nuts, and single-origin chocolates. I didn't want one of my children to get antsy and knock over a display.

As it turns out, I didn't have to worry. My students introduced themselves to the security guard and explained that they were urban farmers from the Bronx, here for research. The guard looked surprised but was only too happy to join our entourage. Truth be told, a skinny security guard working in a fancy Upper West Side store doesn't pose much of a threat to my kids. Produce may be bigger and better in Manhattan, but our security guys are beefier in the Bronx. My girls could have taken this guy single-handedly. Once my students sized up the situation, they started firing off comments and questions.

"Yo! This is big business, yo!" said a student named Urckle, pointing to the price of collard greens.

"Check it out—eight dollars a pound for basil," Keisha followed up. "Damn! White people got money." We came from a neighborhood where people shopped with food stamps and WIC coupons, not credit or debit, much less platinum and gold cards.

It didn't take long for my students to start thinking like entrepreneurs. "Ritz, why aren't we growing stuff like this? The food we can buy in the Bronx looks like shit," said Toya. "This is good stuff. How do we do this?"

"Point taken, Toya," I responded. "Can you please use more appropriate language?"

"Yeah," added LeQuann, making a connection to lessons he had learned on his own time. "These prices are like the difference between street weed and hydro. Why grow the cheap shit when we can grow the good stuff?" His instincts were dead-on, even if his retail experience came from the street. He understood value differentiation as well as any business student.

After half an hour of exploring the aisles, I was the one getting antsy. I knew we had another train ride ahead of us to get back by the end of the school day. The bell schedule wasn't my only concern. This had been such a glorious afternoon, I wanted to wrap it up before anything spoiled the mood. It felt like a perfect first date.

Little did I know, but this was the start of a beautiful relationship. A year later, my farmers would return to Whole Foods and sell some of their own fancy homegrown produce, right in these aisles. They'd come back eventually to install a high-tech garden installation. Instead of being eyed as potential shoplifters, they would be treated with kindness and respect for their accomplishments. At their side would be the vice president of the United Federation of Teachers Career and Technical Education division, Sterling Roberson. Years later, I would be invited to speak to the Whole Foods Tribal Gathering of corporate bigwigs who make buying decisions and weigh the merits of social initiatives. My students would grow enough produce to donate thousands of pounds of fresh vegetables and fruits to Part of the Solution. That's a tradition we carry on to this day.

Little did I know that two years later, I would deliver a speech at Columbia University called "From Crack to Cucumbers," highlighting what happens when you give children who are apart from success a chance to be a part of it.

Those adventures were all on the far horizon, beyond our wildest dreams. For now, we had work to do. Time to roll up our sleeves and turn an urban lot into our glorious vegetable plot. Get down and get dirty. Gourmet peppers, heirloom tomatoes, and sorrel lettuces, here we come!

CHAPTER 7

OUR GARDEN IN THE SKY

Fall 2005—"Di-a-a-a-blo!" screamed Luis, cupping his hands around his mouth to amplify his shout. The first time my Green Teens stepped onto the flat roof of the Bank Note Building, soaring five stories above Lafayette Avenue in Hunts Point, they unleashed some creative exclamations and a few expletives too colorful to repeat.

Our sky-high perch put us at the most strategic vantage point in all of the Bronx. Under the midday sun, there were no shadows to dull the colors. We could see down the whole length of Manhattan Island and as far out as Long Island Sound. The city skyline appeared in front of us as suddenly as if we had turned a page on a pop-up book. Central Park looked like an emerald forest. At that moment, for the first time in our lives, we were eagles over America.

Watching passenger jets rising from the tarmac of LaGuardia, Ramon said, "I timed it. There's a plane taking off every thirty seconds. Where they all going?"

Most of these young people rarely ventured beyond the Bronx. Our 360-degree view showed more of the world than most of them had seen in their lifetime.

"It's like we're in a James Bond movie," said Janette. Tall and covered with ink, Janette was the kind of girl who took no nonsense and intimidated most of the boys. She waved Calvin closer to the edge to get a better view.

"I'm not crazy about heights," he confided, inching forward nonetheless.

"Yo, check it." Ramon pointed to an island sparkling in the cerulean water of the East River. His peers craned their necks to take a look. Upon closer inspection, we could see how the sunlight glancing off razor wire on the chain-link fence made it glitter like jewels. Seagulls by the thousands circled high above as if taunting the inhabitants below. We were looking at the largest penal colony in the world.

"Rikers," Luis said with a nod of recognition. Statistically, four in ten of his peers would do time there before age twenty-one. Several of my students had already done short stints inside, but they were awed by the sheer size of the place—a huge floating island in the middle of a beautiful bay. To think this massive hunk of land was devoted to a prison; it was mind numbing.

As they looked back toward the Bronx, the sights were more familiar. "Look at that crack house," said Emanuel, pointing to a building where buyers scurried in and out like ants at a picnic. We could see the street corner where prostitutes were going about their business in broad daylight.

My students matter-of-factly picked out landmarks from their own life stories: "There's where my friend was shot." "There's the spot where my brother got busted." "That empty lot is where we used to live before our building burned to the ground."

Then the students started counting the garbage trucks that roll into the Bronx by the thousands every day, dumping 40 percent of New York City's trash on our doorstep and driving up asthma rates with diesel fumes. The familiar stink of exhaust and garbage didn't float this high, though, and these high flyers instinctively faced into the breeze to get a lungful of clean air.

It was a good metaphor for our day—today, we were rising above the garbage down below, both literally and figuratively. I couldn't imagine a better place than the Bank Note to inspire audacious thinking. The American

Bank Note Company Printing Plant building, built in 1911, was originally used for printing money. Like my students, the freestanding landmark had been neglected for years. Built like a brick fortress, its imposing structure sits on a hill in Hunts Point on a parcel of real estate big enough for a college campus. The building is five stories tall with a footprint of 425,000 square feet. The roof alone could hold two football fields.

By helping to create a green roof up here, we would keep thousands of gallons of wastewater runoff out of the city sewage system and remove pollutants from the air. More than that, by converting hundreds of square feet of roofing into a suitable growing space, we would transform a tired Bronx landmark into a symbol of the future.

When we arrived at the Bank Note Building on that fall day, I couldn't help but laugh.

"What's so funny, Mr. Ritz?" asked José.

"I tried to rob this place once," I said.

Everyone started laughing with me. "No way," they said.

When I was a kid, my buddies and I, after watching way too many *The Little Rascals* episodes, hatched a plan to rob the Penny Factory. That's what we called the building because of all the money that used to be made inside. We spent hours fine-tuning our plan in the backyard of one of my buddies' grandmothers. She lived around the corner and downhill from the Bank Note in a house tucked between commercial warehouses.

Our plan had all the elements of a classic caper. We would split into two squads, sneaking up on the building from different directions. One kid was assigned to cause a distraction by getting stuck on the fence while the rest of us rolled a red Flexible Flyer wagon down the hill to haul away the loot. In case a chase ensued, we would stymie our pursuers by throwing marbles onto the roadway. We didn't care about the paper money, even though five million pieces of currency and stock certificates came off those presses in a day back then. We just wanted coins to buy candy and ice cream. We lost our nerve when we realized the building had a real guard up on the roof, holding a real rifle.

Now here I was returning with my handpicked crew, many with criminal records. What an irony. I was the one who had planned a heist. Now I was holding the keys to the place, thanks to a bunch of youth that society had labeled as troublemakers.

Until now, Green Teens had been doing urban landscaping and gardening on abandoned properties at street level. Every one of these students had more than proved his or her worth by hefting shovels and pushing wheelbarrows, but now we were entering the big leagues. We had been recommended for a large-scale sustainable building demonstration project that involved a big budget, private investors, nonprofit partners, and plenty of public scrutiny. We couldn't afford to screw up. This was no Little Rascals caper from my youth. We would have to marshal our talents, strengths, and ingenuity as well as work with skilled union workers who might resent a bunch of rookie schoolkids underfoot.

I was determined to prove these capable young people were up to the challenge, but something else motivated me, too. I had heard my borough derided my whole life as one of the ugliest communities in the country. In my lifetime, presidents Jimmy Carter, Gerald Ford, and Ronald Reagan had all stopped at Charlotte Street to get their picture taken and make a big speech about how they were going to improve the Bronx. In the end, they did nothing.

Showing up for one day didn't mean anything. What did mean something were people like my mom, committed to the daily challenge of actually making change happen. She worked six blocks away from Charlotte Street as a special education teacher at Morris High School. In thirty-one years, she never missed a day of work.

Now here we were, part of something bigger than ourselves.

It's true that the Bronx is the poorest congressional district in the nation, but where an outsider might see a dearth of opportunities, I see abundant energy. The underutilized talent in low-status and marginalized communities is the greatest untapped resource in the world.

I wasn't the only one who could see the raw beauty and hidden assets in this industrial center. Majora Carter was an emerging local champion and founder of an organization called Sustainable South Bronx, which had its offices in the Bank Note. She was the brains (and beauty) behind the green roof project and had welcomed us because, of course, I knew a guy.

Majora had been telling a local plumbing supply owner—our mutual friend, a guy named Bob Bieder—that she couldn't seem to find good workers for this big project. He asked her, "Have you heard about Stephen Ritz and his kids at Walton?" We'd never done a roof project before, but we had done ornamental plantings, we had lots of certifications, we won awards, and heck . . . we were on TV! What better reference was there? Plus, we would contribute our labor as volunteers for the chance to learn new skills.

The first day we met, Majora watched from her back office as I walked in with my Green Teens. She hung back a few minutes, checking us out. My shorts and T-shirt didn't look like typical teacher attire. My students looked older than she expected. But something about us must have made a good first impression. "I've never seen a teacher interact with his students in quite the way you do," she told me in an aside. "When you talk to your students, I can feel the respect. It's a partnership. You all look like you're here to be part of something. Cool."

Stepping out to the lobby to shake hands, Majora wasn't exactly who my students expected either. With dreadlocks, Green the Ghetto T-shirt, hip-hop belt with her name on it, and a dazzling smile, she looked unlike any construction boss they had ever imagined. There was no cigarette, no beer belly, no tattoos, and no scowl. She was all warm and bubbly, no rough edges. She was a woman. And she was black.

"She's in charge?" I overheard one of my guys saying under his breath. They'd never heard of a social entrepreneur before, let alone a black woman giving orders on a big project. For girls on our team like Janette, Precious, and Cassie, she turned out to be more than a figurehead; she was calmly, completely, and lovingly in charge.

They later learned that Majora had been awarded a MacArthur "genius" fellowship for leading urban revitalization efforts. She was raised right here in Hunts Point, the youngest of ten children, and came back after college to launch her career. She was determined to show that communities like this one could be national leaders in sustainability. She welcomed community use of projects like the Bank Note and literally gave me the keys to the building so we could contribute our efforts to the green roof. She didn't know it, but to my students, she was a fairy tale in the flesh. They weren't about to let her down. Neither was I.

Although our heads were in the clouds, my team soon started to appreciate the challenge of transforming this unfriendly surface atop the Bank Note into a fertile ecosystem where seedlings could take root.

"Why's it so freakin' hot up here?" asked El Bori as he lifted his sneaker off the sticky tar roofing. We had two Josés on our team. We called the bigger of the two Big José. The smaller one, who called himself El Bori (a term for Puerto Ricans born in the United States), had a mop of curly hair and was always the first to ask a question.

The heat snapped us out of our reverie. Tons of asphalt and a century's worth of black tar roofing made the Bank Note Building a heat sink. If it's 90 degrees in Manhattan, I guarantee it's 105 in Hunts Point. Looking down at the street, we could see the faded yellow lines shimmy in the heat. Up here, without a stick of shade, we were sponges for the sun's energy.

"Yo Ritz, why the hell are we putting a garden up in the sky where nobody will see it?" El Bori asked, setting off a round of laughs. It was a crazy idea, I agreed, and might not even work. But what if it did? We would be making our own mark on the Bronx in a bold way.

Green roofs were good for the environment, soaking up storm water that would normally overflow the sewers and create flooding on city streets. They were good for air quality and for keeping buildings cooler in summer and warmer in winter; this led to cost savings and extended roof life for owners. They were also good for tax incentives—getting a building green certified meant a tax credit year after year. On top of that, they were just attractive. Most green roofs were ornamental, but this project had the added bonus of being an edible garden. It was more accessible than most green roofs, with an easy-access door from inside and a parapet around the perimeter to keep visitors safe. When we were finished, people would be able to come right up to the roof and pick their lunch.

It wasn't going to be easy, though; just getting to the job site required a Herculean effort. Although we could get from Walton High School to Hunts Point in fifteen minutes by car, school rules required us to use public transportation. That meant jumping through endless bureaucratic hoops to secure seventeen Metro cards, even though they cost the district nothing. With Metro cards finally in hand, our train trip took an hour and fifteen minutes each way and cranked my anxiety into overdrive. The circuitous route—the No. 4 train to 125th in the heart of Harlem, then transfer back uptown on the 6 local to Hunts Point—took us through every stop in the Bronx. Each time the train doors opened, I braced myself for drama. What if an old boyfriend, old girlfriend, or rival gang—all three equally bad—boarded our car and wanted to start something?

I could handle the hassles of permits and insurance and releases. I wasn't even nervous about my students working on a rooftop. But a train ride across town? Oy! My blood pressure and heartbeat skyrocketed!

Walking from the subway stop to the Bank Note Building took us through a rough neighborhood, even by my students' standards. Public urination and drug dealing happened in plain sight. You couldn't help but notice that the century-old monastery across the street from the Bank Note had erected a twenty-five-foot cinder-block wall to keep out prostitutes and drug dealers and their customers. Walls send messages. My students and I were on the wrong side of it, exposed to elements over which I had no control.

Once we stepped into the Bank Note elevator, I felt the tension start to leave me as we left behind the ugliness at ground level. We had somewhere better to go.

"You're going to have to trust people you don't know," I cautioned my students, "and they're going to have to trust you to get the work done right."

Once we began our rooftop garden project in earnest, we shared responsibilities with a union crew. The union guys were mostly white, clean-cut, and highly skilled. My students were everything but, and their body ink and fashion choices only exaggerated the differences.

Around these grown-ups, my muscle-bound students at first tried to come off as cocky and cool. Behind the swagger, though, they were as excited and curious as little kids. Thank God for El Bori, who had a knack for breaking the ice with his incessant questions. "Can plants breathe up here?" he asked. "I mean, will they get enough oxygen?"

Luis gave him a scornful look and said, "Plants need carbon dioxide, dickhead. We're the ones who need oxygen." Even the union guys laughed.

Before long, my students were peppering their new acquaintances with questions: "How'd you get hired for this job? Did you have to know somebody?" "How much do you make an hour?" "How'd you learn to work that crane?" The adults didn't mind answering as long as they were on the clock. My students quickly learned to leave them alone when it was time for lunch or break.

All chitchat stopped when the real work started. First order of business: Move thousands of pounds of building materials from the street to the roof. For that task, we had cranes that could reach five stories high. The crane operators' task was to maneuver pallets that weighed a ton apiece. These six-foot cubes couldn't just be hoisted up and dropped at random. Operators had to swing the crane arm out at precisely the right angle to avoid hitting the building parapet and then set the pallet down in a spot where it could be unloaded. My students were their eyes on the roof, giving directions over two-way radios.

Lesson number one: Don't screw up.

Over the radio, I overheard an impatient male voice squawk: "How far to the left do you want it?"

"A little bit," said Ramon.

"Whaddya mean? *A little bit* doesn't mean shit, you dumbass. How many feet over?"

All the lessons my students had bitched and moaned about in the classroom were critical here. Precise measurement mattered, down to the inch. In math class, being off on calculations by a few feet seemed like no big deal. On a job site, a simple rounding error could mean that two thousand pounds of materials get deposited in the wrong spot. And now you and your buddies have to pick them up and move them where they belong.

Clear communication was essential. Being too proud to ask for directions or clarification was going to bite you in the ass. I watched attitudes change in a heartbeat from "Who gives a shit?" to "This shit matters."

Once the pallets were in position, students set about unpacking the cubes. As they unrolled hundreds of feet of edging made of recycled plastic, they were amazed that so much could fit inside a six-foot cube. Here was a math lesson in volume that I didn't have to teach them. They started remembering formulas for perimeter and area, testing textbook lessons against reality.

To frame the garden beds, we used plastic modules that fit together in a grid like giant Legos. My students learned why it makes sense to measure twice, cut once. They got the hang of using a T square to make sure corners met in precise right angles. The project manager had no tolerance for sloppy work. Understanding the X/Y axis and formulas for calculating area suddenly mattered. Now algorithms not only made sense but could translate into real dollars. It turns out that math skills could be extrapolated to job skills. Who knew?

Big José, a burly teenager with a thick beard who could easily pass for forty, was a quick study when it came to envisioning how the parts needed to come together. Even better, he was quick to recognize which of his peers were good at what. He noticed who was meticulous when it came to measuring and cutting, who could follow a schematic, who should concentrate on carrying heavy stuff. The leadership skills he had picked up on the street took on new importance on the rooftop. His peers responded to his example, realizing we would never get this job done if we didn't pull together.

What was funny about it was that he was withdrawn in class. I had never seen this take-charge side of him before. Outside workers assumed he was a supervisor, so he was an effective buffer for the other students.

Each time we came back on the train for another workday, we could see progress. Assembling that first section of framing took us more than two hours; the next, just ninety minutes. After we lined the perimeter of the roof with perfect rows of rectangular beds came the painstaking job of fitting each bed with material designed to retain rainwater. Accuracy was critical. You couldn't leave gaps or water would leak through and damage the roofing underneath. When the water retention layer was in place, we were ready to add the planting medium. It came rolled up like sod, which required more measuring, cutting, checking, and double-checking.

Once the beds were in place, the union guys packed up. It had been a month since we started work. Now it was up to us to do the tender work of planting and nurturing.

A rooftop is not the most hospitable environment for plants. The ones that survive have to withstand intense heat and cold, high winds, and drought conditions while growing in a thin layer of soil because a roof can't support much weight. To get our rooftop garden off to a fast start, we began with sedum and succulents that come ready for planting in big mats. These tough little plants can withstand desert conditions. They're lightweight, but they can store tremendous volumes of water to get them through droughts. Working with engineers, my aspiring technicians calculated how much load the roof could bear down to the square foot.

My students had experience with vegetable gardening at ground level from our earlier work at Bissel Gardens. Now they had to figure out how to grow food on the roof. We decided to start with ever-bearing strawberries. Not only were they hardy, but their shoots would help hold the growing medium in place. This meant nothing would blow away, ensuring the longevity of the project. Bit by bit, we were emulating the natural world. My students learned there was a vocabulary word worthy of the SAT to describe their efforts: *biomimicry*.

"How long before we get to eat strawberries?" Janette asked as she tucked a row of young plants into the soil. It was going to take months of waiting, weeding, and watching before we'd harvest our first berries.

"Betcha we have salad next week," said Melvin, pointing to the leafy lettuce plants that were practically growing before our eyes.

As a teacher, I understood the power of students seeing the fruits of their labor. We came back to that rooftop week after week. You can't turn your back on a garden and expect it to thrive. Persistence and patience weren't the only lessons. They also experienced the joy of watching a living thing grow and knowing "I did that." Succulents that were no bigger than our thumbs at planting became bright green groundcover. Blueberry bushes and tomato plants that looked fragile in early spring shot up and got heavy with fruit as the weather warmed.

One day, something orange and black flew by and El Bori asked, "How the hell did a butterfly find its way up here?" Observing butterflies as they sampled nectar on our rooftop delighted even my toughest-looking team members. Students who thought the only birds of New York were garbage-eating pigeons looked with wonder on the winged creatures that came to visit our rooftop. These were no rats with wings. They came in amazing colors like red, orange, white, and blue. None of us knew the names of the birds we were seeing, but it didn't make a difference. To us, they were all magnificent.

Not every green thing was welcome. Local and invasive species were carried to the rooftop by wind and winged creatures. By spring, we had to weed out the invaders. Creating a thriving culture was an ongoing effort, requiring constant tending. I didn't have to explain that metaphor for my students. They lived it.

As my Green Teens transformed this industrial eyesore with their patience, resilience, grit, and nurturing touch, I could see a profound transformation happening in them. When they stepped onto that rooftop back on day one, they were unsure and untested. Nobody had attempted a green roof of this scale in the Bronx, and certainly nobody before had entrusted a major urban construction project to a bunch of ragtag kids. My Green Teens got the chance to prove themselves, and they took it.

During lunch, on the hot rooftop overlooking the world, I would read from classics to them, including words from Walt Whitman: "This is what you shall do: Love the earth and sun and the animals, despise riches, give alms to everyone that asks, stand up for the stupid and crazy, devote your income and labor to others, hate tyrants, argue not concerning God, have patience and indulgence toward the people, take off your hat to nothing known or unknown." They smiled and nodded as I read, and asked for more. When we finished that project, it was such a huge success that we were soon in demand to create many more.

Every single one of those students graduated from high school. One hundred percent got their high school diploma in a school where the normal graduation rate was 17 percent. Young people who had been on track to be dropouts or inmates—the least likely to succeed by all the experts' predictions—started finding their way to college and apprenticeships. As soon as he graduated, Big José signed up for an environmental stewardship program for young adults with Majora Carter and Sustainable South Bronx. He was in her first cohort of graduates. The South Bronx training program earned him certification to work in the new green economy where a world of opportunities awaited. It became his ticket out: He began working as a contractor to rebuild New Orleans after Hurricane Katrina and has worked steadily ever since.

Meanwhile, I continued crossing paths with Majora Carter. Seeing me at one community event after another in the South Bronx, often with students along, she would remark, "Steve! You just keep showing up!" Instead of seeing me as a goofy teacher in shorts and T-shirt, she came to recognize me as a fellow fighter for social justice.

"We both know you have to be in it to win it," she would say. Like me, she was also running into headwinds from critics who didn't understand her approach or who envied her successes. She challenged both of us to keep thinking bigger, saying, "How can we support our community and the people who are so left out, left behind, let down?"

Her words spurred me to action. Inspired by Majora and our blossoming borough, I had a renewed and permanent call to action: People should not have to leave their neighborhood to live, learn, and earn in a better one! It has become my battle cry ever since.

CHAPTER 8

THE RUBBER ROOM BOUNCE

Fall 2006—Our well-publicized successes at Walton High School generated some unsolicited job offers for me. Small schools were springing up across New York City in response to Mayor Bloomberg's call for school reform. Overcrowded and failing high schools were getting carved up to house smaller academies and charter schools. Many focused on high-interest themes like the arts, social justice, and environmental science. These schools were intended to be the breeding ground for innovation, with less top-down control and more autonomy.

On the surface, this approach made a lot of sense. Small clearly seemed better than massive schools that were overcrowded, underperforming, and impersonal. And in fact, some of these new schools became success stories. But I was about to learn the hard way that many new schools failed to deliver on their promises—to students or to teachers. If a small school had a poor leader at the helm and no oversight, it could quickly turn into a fiefdom. When these schools went wrong, they went really wrong.

My first stop on the school reform merry-go-round was at a small high school academy. I was recruited away from Walton by the offer to build an academic program focusing on a green, interdisciplinary curriculum plus job training. It seemed like an opportunity to turn what I had learned from the Green Teens into a more sustainable, school-wide program to engage a broader swatch of students. No such luck. Instead of giving me room to innovate, the principal handed me a teaching script that I was expected to follow to the letter. He was an acclaimed school leader, even revered in certain circles. As I got to know him better, I realized that his leadership style favored fear and intimidation. He didn't want to be held accountable or inspire innovation; he wanted allegiance. In public, he spoke eloquently about social justice but told another story behind closed doors.

"We're going to improve attendance so that all students can learn," he promised the community. "If kids aren't at school, we'll bang on doors and call parents until we get them there."

So I did just that. When I went out of my way to encourage one special education student with poor attendance to come back to school, the principal went on the attack. "That kid's an animal!" he roared at me. "I don't want to see him in this building ever again."

Determined to do better for our students, I kept questioning his decisions. I exposed teachers who were saying one thing and doing another, or willfully violating policies. His do-as-I-say attitude did not correspond to his actions or our intended outcomes. Clearly, I was getting on the principal's nerves. He stopped me one morning in the hallway and said, "Ritz, you don't seem to like my answers. Why don't you take your questions right to the top? The chancellor is coming to the Bronx next week. Why don't you use your professional development time to go see him?"

He might have been joking, but I loved that idea. Instead of sitting through another waste-of-time staff meeting, I could go listen to Joel Klein, chancellor of New York City schools. I was starved for inspiration. Maybe he would deliver it.

The event took place near Hunts Point, just a mile from the Bank Note. This turned out to be the day when Klein spoke out against the "bitter irony" of black students trapped in squalid public schools half a century after *Brown v. Board of Education* had overturned school desegregation. Klein drew headlines for his remarks. Just showing up in the South Bronx would have been newsworthy. The room was filled with VIPs. Others arrived en masse to have their photos taken with the chancellor. I wasn't there for the photo op. I did not even know what Chancellor Klein looked like, but I was a believer who wanted to see and bring change.

Klein was impressive, but it was Deputy Chancellor Eric Nadelstern, a Bronx native, who lit a fire under me. He spoke of the need for new leadership. In that crowded auditorium at Fanny Lou Hamer Freedom High School, I felt like he was talking directly in my ear. How capable was I to lead others toward lasting change?

That day, Nadelstern helped me appreciate the difference between diversity and inclusion. In a system that continues to fail so many children, simply acknowledging our differences isn't enough. Inclusion is the game changer. If diversity means playing multicultural music at a school event, then inclusion is getting everyone out on the same dance floor together. It had to start with new and improved leadership. By the end of his remarks, I was revved up and ready to boogie.

Two days later, I ran into Nadelstern again. His mother lived up the street from our apartment, and he was coming to take her to breakfast. I spotted him on my way to work. He had stopped at the local bank to use the ATM. Excitedly and groupie-like, I screeched my car to a halt and jumped out. Slowly, I approached him, not wanting to be perceived as a thief—a reality my students lived daily—and I politely and cautiously stopped him on the sidewalk at six in the morning to tell him how much I had appreciated his speech. Amazingly, he remembered my face in the crowd—the tall guy nodding along with such enthusiasm. Our sidewalk encounter got me revved up all over again. In that moment, I went from excited to committed.

Within a month, I was enrolled in a principal leadership program and asking questions to provoke my classmates. In a session on budgeting, they wanted to focus on funding summer remediation programs. I was incensed. I knew this was geared to adding to their incomes and not to student outcomes. "Why are you predicting in October that students will be behind grade level by summer? How dare you predict their failure? Why don't you redirect money and resources to help them succeed?"

When I compared the schools I knew best to other schools across the district, I brought up more hard questions. "Why are metal detectors only used in certain schools? Why should predominantly poor children get treated as if they are little convicts? What are we doing to disrupt the school-to-prison pipeline?"

I know that I offended some of my colleagues when I insisted, "No child rises to low expectations." My goal was never to offend but to inspire. I wanted these future leaders to realize that everything we do in the classroom, starting with the attitude we project, has a major impact on a child's life. If a child doesn't succeed in school, we should never blame the child. We should teach differently, we should look at the environment and examine what we are doing to facilitate success for that child. When a plant fails to grow in an environment, we don't blame the plant, we look at the environment and the plant to determine cause and effect; certainly my students were worthy of the same respect we afforded plants!

I was impatient not only for answers but for real change to fix a broken system. Most of my fellow principal candidates were career oriented and income focused. They didn't want to shake up the system. They didn't even want to improve the system. They wanted to rise within it, gaming the system to their own advantage. I might not have all the answers, but I was determined to work to find them. I vowed to become the kind of leader who, while not always right, is committed to getting it correct.

While I contemplated my next move, I struggled under school leaders who had no business being anywhere near children. As the department of education continued its school reform chess game, schools were opened and closed seemingly at random.

In one two-year period, I was transferred or reassigned to three differ-ent schools, all on the same campus. The school where I started was quickly closed by the department of education for poor results. That principal, forced to retire, was sued for anti-Semitism by his staff. I wasn't a direct victim but was named as a witness. I transferred to another academy where the principal was downright illiterate—in both English and Spanish. She made me write her principal reports for her. Another school leader threat-ened to call immigration authorities if undocumented parents didn't go along with her outrageous demands. It was appalling, watching people build careers on the backs of those they were supposed to serve.

One of my placements started well, although unfortunately it didn't end that way. The principal recognized my ability to reach out to commu-nity partners and made me coordinator of student activities. With a flexi-ble schedule, I was able to start a school garden and arrange many special events, including a performance by Bad Boy Records recording artists. I was able to leverage my out-of-school relationships to inspire students and faculty alike. We were connecting dot after dot. I agreed to put in extra duty with a group of special-needs students, all of whom had previously failed the Regents Exams. My job was to make sure they passed the test so they would graduate on time. And they all did. While I was I thrilled and proud to help students pass, this really drove school data, which was at the heart of her agenda. The reality was, many of these students would have benefited from an extra year of instruction instead of being pushed out the door in their prescribed time period with a passing test grade under their belt. The inequities were obvious and everywhere. It was never about students first.

Occasionally, I also had to cover for absent colleagues.

"Good morning. I'm Mr. Ritz. I'm filling in today," I said to get the attention of a noisy science classroom. "Let's talk about the earth."

A girl wearing neon high-top shoes and the coolest hat I'd ever seen perked up at my words. She had opinions galore about the sorry state of our planet and how we humans needed to be better stewards. When I asked her to tell me a little about herself, she said, "I'm Chardyna and I'm an artist." That funky hat with the painted brim and crushed velvet details was one of her creations.

Talking with her after class, I learned that Chardyna had enrolled in this academy because it claimed to have an arts focus. "I live for art," she told me. "My grandmother taught me to draw the funnies when I was a little kid. So why aren't there any art supplies at this school?" she wanted to know. Good question.

Chardyna became a regular at the popular after-school programs that I coordinated. I made sure she had access to art supplies and enriching opportunities offered by partner organizations. Her talents blossomed on anything that involved drawing, textiles, or design. For one project called Redesign Your Hood—sponsored by Cooper Hewitt, Smithsonian Design Museum—she helped to design a homeless shelter.

Chardyna faced homelessness herself due to a chaotic home life. As a teen, she endured crisis after crisis. Her mother was seriously ill. Their home burned to the ground, which meant she had to move into a shelter. Not surprisingly, Chardyna fell behind in coursework.

Rather than surround her with the support she so dearly needed, the principal sought to push her out. If a troubled kid moved away or chose to transfer out, that would be considered a clean discharge. The school could scrub her from its records and no longer be accountable for that student's academic progress, in turn impacting the school's performance ratings. The tragedy was, students would get transferred all around the system but never catch up academically. The principal, known as a school turnaround expert, was skilled at gaming the system. In a system that screams for transparency, she manipulated students' lives behind closed doors.

Chardyna pushed back. "This is my *life*," she argued. "I'm not just a number on your spreadsheet." She knew she was missing credits, but no way did she want to quit or start over at ninth grade. Her success on out-of-school projects and in the real world showed that she was talented and capable.

I did my best to intervene, but that only turned the principal against me. Even though my file was filled with letters the principal had written citing my positive work at the school, our relationship fell apart fast after this. When Chardyna refused to go along with an outright lie—an accusation that I didn't have permission to take her on a field trip when I actually did—things escalated. She was assigned to a room by herself with a security guard at the door. "All these rules," she told me with a weary sigh. "They don't seem like they're for the best interests of the students."

As life at that school became more and more difficult, I learned how important it is to have values and to stick to them, particularly in times of difficulty, stress, and opposition. If you don't stick to your values when they and you are being tested, they're not values; they're simply best wishes and a part-time hobby.

In the midst of a system that was manipulating truths, telling half-truths, and hardly seemed fair or honest, my students and I became obsessed with truth and justice. To all of us, it was abundantly obvious that the school we were a part of was not about students. Rather, it was about status quo and the principal's legacy. Through my own professional development, I learned about an amazing author and artist named Robert Shetterly, the creator of a portrait series and Web site called Americans Who Tell the Truth. I admired his skills, honesty, tenacity, and ability to capture the essence of a person via a great portrait and short, eloquent quote. Students loved his artwork, and his short quotes were excellent, elegant prompts for DO NOW activities related to content area instruction. Shetterly's work was the most inclusive and diverse collection of heroes I had ever seen assembled. It was perfect for my students.

In early 2007, Barack Obama announced his candidacy for president of the United States. How awesome was that? I was so excited and inspired. When I saw a T-shirt picturing him saying "*Sí se puede*," I realized it was that beautiful and that simple. "YES WE CAN!" I also loved the inclusivity of an African American being quoted in Spanish language. Overnight, my simple and direct response to any challenge and any opportunity became

"*Sí se puede!*" I loved saying it, children loved hearing it and screaming it, and it was easy and straightforward to understand. Best of all, we could never be misquoted or misunderstood. All it took was three simple words: SÍ SE PUEDE! When I came to understand that these words originated with Cesar Chavez, founder of the United Farm Workers union and a human-rights activist, it was even better!

In that spirit, I decided to reach out to Robert Shetterly directly and invite him to our school. SÍ SE PUEDE, he willingly agreed. He came and captivated my students in a way no other adult had done. An older, reserved, very eloquent gentleman, he looked into our eyes and asked us about our truths. How could we build a better life for ourselves? He told us the best way to predict our future was to own it, plan for it, and to prepare for it; to not accept lies and half-truths. His presentation, simple and eloquent, was one of the most meaningful and impactful my students and I had ever experienced. It left us all in tears and determined to act, as if we could be the next series of heroes portrayed in his portraits and books. He encouraged us to question authority and closed with a quote from the nineteenth-century reformer Elizabeth Cady Stanton: "The moment we begin to fear the opinion of others and hesitate to tell the truth that is in us, and from motives of policy that are silent when we should speak, the divine floods of life and light no longer flow into our souls." Then and there, the next generation of Americans Who Tell the Truth were born. We took to school and advocacy in a way we had never imagined. SÍ SE PUEDE was our battle cry!

A huge takeaway was how empowering Shetterly had been by simply listening to my students. The strength of his presentation beyond his skills, talents, and passion was his ability to listen to and hear my students. He valued their voices and issues, which in turn gave them additional ownership of their own ideas. From that day on, I promised to incorporate student voice and student accountability into every aspect of my pedagogy. I always knew this was important, but Shetterly—a random visitor—reinforced in a brief visit what I had been doing for years. It was thrilling. By letting children make their thinking visible and actionable, and supporting them in the process, I could help them to become truth-sayers. Their voices, dreams, and lives mattered. They could take ownership of their destiny. A culture of truth, honesty, rigor, and accountability holds the ingredients for any successful organization. We were surely the right people. We were simply in the wrong environment. That school and that principal were just not ready for us or our emboldened SÍ SE PUEDE attitude.

The last straw was watching the principal try to scrub standardized tests to boost our school performance. Tests that showed failing grades would get scrutinized by a team that would somehow "find" missing points. When I refused to go along with any of this, the vice principal called me to the office for a meeting. It was a Wednesday morning.

"Congratulations," he said with a smile. "You've been transferred. You're out of here." He told me the address of my new school—a math and science magnet in Washington Heights—and said I needed to check in at eleven a.m. that day. I started to get suspicious when I looked up the school Web site. It didn't match the address the vice principal had given me.

When I arrived, I didn't see a school name in front of the building. Instead, there was a sign that said "Academic Center." Hmm.

When I walked inside, I realized the trick: I had been sent to the city's notorious Rubber Room for insubordination, and nobody had the decency to tell me the truth. The Rubber Room is where the New York City Department of Education sends teachers to await disciplinary rulings. The place serves as a time-out for teachers.

After I signed in that first morning, security guards pointed me toward a big open room where I found a sea of adults crowded around a jumble of desks and tables. Others were camped out on the floor, snacks and coffee cups spilling around them. I started to sit down in an empty chair and a woman called me out, saying, "Hey, that's my seat! I've got seniority. I've been here three years." Later that afternoon, I won the daily Rubber Room Scrabble tournament that had been going for years.

In this holding pen where there was barely enough air to go around, I saw the best and worst of education. I met brilliant teachers whom I would love to have teaching my own daughter. Some taught lessons to each other just to keep their classroom skills sharp while they waited for their disciplinary cases to be resolved. Others, their breath stinking of booze at ten in the morning, didn't deserve to be anywhere near children. One guy landed here after throwing a bagel at his principal. Another told me he had smacked a kid, "but only one, and he deserved it."

Some wanted to stay here as long as possible, drawing their regular teaching paycheck and earning a second income by day-trading on their laptops. I wanted to get back to teaching as fast as possible.

The principal who sent me to the Rubber Room apparently didn't realize that the hiatus from my classroom duties and her daily fabricated witch hunts would give me time to search for a new job. Frankly, it was the stupidest thing she could have done. Cell phones are permitted in the Rubber Room, and I used mine to good advantage.

I called my old friend Majora Carter to fill her in on my latest dilemma.

"Majora, you'll never guess where I am."

"What now, Steve?"

"The Rubber Room!"

She was initially horrified and then shocked by how upbeat I sounded.

"I've already found a new job," I explained. It turned out that the Walton campus was being reconstituted as home to several new, small high schools. By working the phones, I had just been hired at one of them called Discovery High School. I couldn't wait to start. In fact, I saw it as a homecoming.

After three days in the Rubber Room, the trumped-up charges against me vanished. The principal who was so determined to outsmart me had never even filled out the proper paperwork to start disciplinary proceedings, and now with a new job secured within the system, it was too late for her to backtrack. What's more, I had it in writing that she had offered to sell me a "Satisfactory" performance rating as long as I never spoke publicly about her school policies. With a signed letter of intent for a new job, I was on to my next teaching adventure.

Meanwhile, as I started my new job, Majora and I continued to bemoan what was becoming a familiar pattern. Educational "saviors" would sweep into the Bronx with big ideas to fix education. They didn't know the neighborhoods or the people. When their ideas failed to stick, they left in a hurry.

"I'm thinking about proposing a new school," Majora told me one day. The board of education was continuing to solicit ideas for new and innovative small schools, especially in the Bronx. Although Majora was gaining national visibility for her efforts to develop green jobs for adults in the South Bronx, she was seeing daily evidence of how schools were failing young people. Adults were showing up for new jobs unprepared. "We're catching people after they've been failed by systems," she told me. "I look at what you accomplish with students and think, *Wow!*" What if workforce development programs for adults didn't have to start with remediation of basic skills? What if schools produced more young people like Big José, ready and motivated to tackle his next career move? Majora wanted me on board as an adviser, and I eagerly accepted.

Our first big idea was to propose a public school dedicated to sustainability and career pathways, emphasizing and partnering with local employers and community resources. It would be 100 percent local, an ecosystem within and for the community. We knew there was no shortage of employers in the South Bronx looking for qualified young people to hire. We wanted to build these employers and other neighborhood assets right into the school design, creating a true school-to-career pathway; literally a "one-stop shop." We didn't realize that we were ahead of our time. The model we envisioned then would later be called a community school.

Designing our own high school to fill all the gaps we saw in the current system "may be a crazy idea," Majora cautioned, "but crazy ideas have to be tested in the real world. If we don't try, we'll never know."

We spent more than a year fine-tuning our proposal for Sustainable

South Bronx High School. Everybody we talked with wanted their picture taken with Majora Carter. The board of education liked our school concept but wanted to put it in Brooklyn; that was diametrically opposed to who we were and what we were about. We had nothing against the children or communities blossoming in Brooklyn, but we were focused on our beloved Bronx. In our immediate neighborhood, Bronx schools were failing Bronx children. The notion of at-risk children getting on a subway for a ninety-minute ride each way made no sense to us despite our grand plans. We said no thanks and went back to the drawing board.

We poured our best thinking into our next proposal for the Majora Carter Achievement Academy. We practically finished each other's sentences as we planned the experiential model that would have students learning by doing, using the South Bronx as our real-life classroom. We expected to see a host of benefits—academic, social, economic, environmental.

In our conversations, the two of us discovered that we brought different styles to leadership. Majora is a deep thinker but considers herself naturally introverted. In contrast, she told me, "You're like a ball of energy that's best when it's rolling around, gathering mass." By this point, my waistline had expanded so much that I even looked like a ball. Majora was too tactful to mention that my extended belly was shaped like a watermelon, but she did coach me to tone down my energy a little so that others could appreciate my ideas "without feeling like they're drinking from a fire hose." We had deep discussions about situational leadership.

For our second proposal, she asked me to come on as principal. Her advice and our collaboration paid off. Letters of support arrived from a range of organizations and power brokers, including former president Bill Clinton and Van Jones, who headed sustainability efforts for President Obama before becoming a television commentator. The Smithsonian Institution, Cornell University, and the United Nations Food and Agriculture Organization's director of education all championed our plan. By then, the program director at the United Nations had seen my students in action at demonstration sites and joint projects across the city. We had partnered at several schools, and he had seen me conduct professional development for teachers about designing a green curriculum. He appreciated the logical connections to his work.

Our proposal, one of a hundred new school ideas submitted for that round of competition, was turned down without even getting a hearing from the department of education. Politics and egos no doubt played a part. We heard through the grapevine that those in charge weren't willing to name a school after a woman who was a lightning rod for disruption. I'm sure my proposed leadership role, with my reputation for being outspoken, unapologetic, and unabashed, didn't help either. In our shared disappointment, we both vowed to keep up the good fight. "We have plenty to do," Majora reminded me, "but boy, that would have been the most amazing school."

We even tried a third time. We figured that maybe the selection committee didn't want to take a risk on me as a new principal, even though I had completed the leadership training program and met all the qualifications. To sweeten our chances, we asked the department of education to suggest its own champion principal for our proposed Bronx Vocational Academy. Bronx Borough President Ruben Diaz Jr. wrote a phenomenal letter of support, citing our prior work and demonstrated histories of accomplishment and committed partners in the Bronx. We even got letters from students testifying to our success and submitted them as part of our application. (See an example in the Appendix.) Together, we spent a year working with this vetted school leader, only to get turned down again. Nobody told us why thirty other proposals moved ahead but ours did not.

Short of starting a public school from scratch, how else could I harness a green curriculum to engage more students and benefit more communities? I had plenty of proof that the benefits were profound and measurable. Local jobs and new industries were emerging before our eyes to absorb the talents of people in our community. My students were poised, ready, willing, and able to apply those talents.

I wasn't the only one who saw opportunities. Revitalization was happening across the South Bronx by 2006. Ruben Diaz Jr. was constantly talking up the New Bronx. The place was no longer burnt or burning. It was ready to blossom. I didn't want to see opportunities kicked down the road—I wanted to seize them now!

What I needed was a breakthrough to make my approach easier for others to adopt. While continuing to experiment in my own classroom and on community gardening projects, I was still looking for a model that could be scalable and replicable. That's how we could grow beyond my one green classroom, one Herculean teacher who was willing to move heaven and earth. I didn't know it yet, but a series of fortuitous accidents were about to show us the way forward.

No lobbyist can bribe nature. In the end all politicians and everyone else must accept nature's mandates and the consequences of violating them. In that is my optimism.

—PERRY MANN

PART II

PLANTING THE SEEDS

CHAPTER 9

HITTING THE GREEN WALL

Fall 2009—Back when I was a rookie teacher at South Bronx High School, my goal was to stay one day ahead of my students. Over the years, I've become a better-prepared, more knowledgeable educator. But I've never had a grand plan. My strategy in life—not just in school—has always been to pay attention to my three favorite Cs: collisions, connections, and co-learnings.

A major collision happened during my second day in the Rubber Room for that trumped-up charge of insubordination. Ironically, it was the same day my students and I were going to be featured on *Good Morning America*. We had spent months helping to build a beautiful community garden in Harlem. This was the day of the grand opening. The film crew needed us in Harlem at six a.m. I didn't have to check in at the Rubber Room in Washington Heights until eight. Plenty of time to meet both obligations with a smile.

The garden was an ambitious collaboration between two groups that didn't usually mix: my students from the Bronx and youth from a community-based organization in Harlem. As tough as the Bronx can seem to an outsider, it was familiar turf to my students. My students were predominantly Latino and Afro-Caribbean. They didn't know what to expect across the river in historically African American Harlem. The bulk of what they knew about Harlem came from innuendo, rumor, and MTV. But from the first day they arrived on 143rd Street in their work clothes, ready to get down and get dirty, they were welcomed with open arms.

It didn't hurt that a few of my students happened to be very attractive young ladies. The boys from Harlem were eager to get to know these pretty Bronx girls. The girls weren't so interested in flirting. They were some of my hardest workers, and that worked to our advantage.

"Don't stand here talking to me. You got work to do," Michelle told one of the guys.

"Yo, start moving that compost," Tameika ordered, pointing to a mountain of mulch to make sure the boys understood her directions. The guys rolled their eyes but put in twice the effort to earn the respect of these demanding girls.

There was plenty of hard work for everyone. It took us months of weekly return trips by subway to build that garden in a brickyard. That's what we call it when an apartment in the hood gets flattened, leaving behind nothing but broken bricks and other debris. Coming back to that lot every week or so, we could see the transformation from bricks to bounty. Not only was the place looking great, but more and more people from the neighborhood were pitching in. That was a good indicator they would keep the garden thriving when our initial construction work was done, just like at Bissel Gardens. For many reasons, it was time to celebrate.

As the camera crew prepped us for our interview with Chris Cuomo, the *Good Morning America* correspondent, I took in the scene. The garden looked especially lush in the morning light. Just after dawn on this gritty Harlem street, with sunlight hitting the brick pathways and dew clinging to the leafy greens, we had chanced upon the time of day that photographers love. When the sun kisses the earth good morning, that's the magic hour. My students were deservedly proud and excited about their media debut. Just like the plants, they were shining in the sun and beamed out on television across the country.

Looking over my shoulder, I spotted something else green and gorgeous. Positioned behind us was a freestanding wall that was practically exploding with luscious, flowering tomato plants. There were hundreds of them. This living structure was a surprise gift for the new garden. I'd never seen anything like it but could tell at a glance that one eight-by-eight wall would produce more food than our entire garden.

What a collision! As soon as the crew took off my microphone, I stepped up for a closer look. I had a million questions about how this wall was designed and what was required to maintain it. Who could tell me more?

I got the name of the vendor. Once I started my new job at Discovery High School, I invited him to come visit my school. Discovery was one of the new smaller high schools housed on the same Walton campus where I had launched the Green Teens several years earlier.

"Do you have any idea what you could do with this thing in a classroom?" I asked him once he found his way to my room on the third floor. He didn't. Up to that time, most of the green wall installations had been in commercial or industrial settings. It didn't take long for him to appreciate the opportunities in education.

"Put one of these things in my classroom," I explained, "and I won't have to transport students an hour by subway to get them to garden sites. We could integrate plants into our lessons every day." I suspected that our big classroom windows would bring in enough light to keep plants alive.

What's more, if my students learned to install and maintain green walls, they would find all kinds of avenues for learning about technology, biology, data collection, engineering, and more. Plus, this thing just looked so damn cool! I saw it as a way to bring our green graffiti indoors.

When I paused to catch my breath, the vendor offered to donate some surplus materials from trade shows and let us experiment. Game on. With a green wall in my classroom and a manufacturer interested in my feedback, now it was time for some serious co-learning. Our driving question: How could we improve this product, and maybe improve education, by combining forces? How could we make one plus one add up to something greater than two? I couldn't wait to find out.

My students and I had our first installation set up and ready to plant within a day. Almost as quickly, that first green wall changed the learning environment in all the ways I had anticipated, and then some.

"This place feels *so alive*," said Vianey, stepping back to gaze at our wall full of seedlings. What a contrast from all the other classroom walls that were chipped, gouged, and covered with layers of paint to hide years of graffiti and other abuse. Our green wall reached almost to the ceiling. We positioned it close to the third-story windows so that our seedlings could soak up sunlight.

People came from all over just to see it. First it was my students' friends from other classes, who had heard reports about our latest crazy project. Then more visitors started dropping by—curious colleagues, teachers from other schools on the Walton campus, neighbors who caught wind of something interesting happening up on the third floor. When we added red, purple, and blue LED lights to extend the growing time, reporters came to investigate rumors of school windows glowing at night. What the heck was going on up there?

"These lights are so bright, I bet planes and helicopters can see them from the sky!" Edgar speculated. He was one of my most precise planters and was eager for the lights to shine on the seedlings he called his "babies."

Having an indoor living wall allowed us to create the first edible classroom in New York City and in the nation, born and grown right here in the Bronx. Just as I had hoped, my students got curious about healthier eating by growing their own juicy tomatoes, fragrant herbs, sweet strawberries, and practically anything else they could imagine. Best of all, this bounty wasn't available only during certain seasons or grown in a location far from campus. It was right in our classroom all year long.

"Mr. Ritz, my grandmother asked if we could grow jalapeños for salsa on our wall," Lupe told me one day. That question led right into lessons about propagating and pollinating peppers. I showed students how to pollinate using feathers and toothbrushes. One curious learner brought in an electric toothbrush to see if that would work. Everyone considered that a more high-tech approach to pollination, even though they discovered that low-tech methods were just as effective.

It was a surreal sight to see fifteen teenagers going from plant to plant with feathers and toothbrushes, doing the work that bees do outdoors. The principal walked in one day and asked what was going on. Imagine his surprise when the students told him, "We're having sex with the plants!" Then they explained the process of pollination in more technical terms, showing off their expanding academic vocabulary and their readiness for the science portion of the Regents Exams. I could have lectured them about sexual versus asexual fertilization for weeks and they wouldn't have remembered a word of it. Now they could demonstrate their understanding with accuracy. We called our session "plant parenthood." They owned this knowledge.

It was all highly engaging, bell-to-bell learning, with no time lost to transportation or other logistics. Plants grew quickly, generating enough produce to send bags of fresh food home. Parents and grandmothers got so excited, they started stopping by class to pick up their fresh vegetables in person. Some parents even brought us seeds from their favorite plants and herbs to grow on the green wall. It was a joy to see families coming to school for a positive reason, not to hear about their children's academic or behavioral problems. This was exactly the sort of game-changing, scalable green experience I was looking for.

Green walls grow fast, but they don't grow themselves. You plant them with scores of seedlings, each rooted in its own little cell filled with growing medium. You can swap out these plants quickly if you want to grow something new. When my students discovered we could also use the walls to make living art, they wanted to experiment with plant colors and textures.

We spent a month creating a living mural that spelled out DHS—for Discovery High School—in red and green plants. This project helped students learn about graphing, scale, and proportion along with botany. They designed their mural on paper first, then went from sketches to graph paper, then figured out how to scale it on an X/Y axis. We prototyped with colored paper and fine-tuned the design before planting the wall with red sedum and leafy greens. The final step was like paint by numbers, only with colors that were alive.

That was all great for inquiry learning and self-expression, but all the experimentation meant that students were going through plant stock quickly. Where could we get enough seedlings to keep growing these hands-on learning experiences?

In our green classroom, the care and tending of seedlings became the responsibility of some of my most developmentally delayed students. They were geniuses when it came to getting little plants to grow. They were patient, and they loved the process. They took the time to do it right. Other students relied on them, which fostered inclusiveness in our classroom. We had important jobs for everybody.

State Senator Gustavo Rivera lived near the Walton complex and stopped by one day to visit our edible classroom. I didn't have a clue who he was or even how the political system worked. I gave him the same treatment as any other visitor: full immersion in a deliberately noisy, active classroom where ten different things were likely to be happening at once.

That day was especially busy. In our classroom, we were busy hosting our first farmers' market for the community, selling produce we had grown indoors along with student artwork. We had invited a local chef to give a cooking demonstration. A crew of kindergartners were about to arrive from the elementary school next door to hear a story about vegetables. First graders were coming to visit and were going to become bees, with costumes and toothbrushes, and be taught by my students. We even had visitors from an exclusive and famed private school on the Upper West Side, Calhoun School, where another teacher was experimenting with a green curriculum to engage his students. So many people had arrived, the crowd was overflowing our big classroom and spilling down the hall. Demand for our produce was so high, students filled a shoebox with more than $2,000 in cash.

Even though my students had been marketing the event around the neighborhood with flyers that they made, nobody expected such a big crowd. A team of students who were in charge of budgeting had projected sales of $300. Frankly, I thought that was optimistic. I was hoping we would break even. The senator walked into the midst of this chaotic celebration.

"Welcome, Senator! So glad you're here. Follow me," I called out over my shoulder.

Distracted by all the activity, he raced to keep up. Rivera was a big guy with broad shoulders like a football player. He was impeccably dressed and crisply pressed. He had a shiny shaved head and a baby face. Not quite sure what to make of him yet, I escorted him to another classroom where adults stood in the back wearing expectant looks.

"Wait here," I told him, then ducked out again.

A few minutes later I reemerged, leading a gaggle of kindergartners holding hands. They wore name tags shaped like veggies, had bee wings pinned to the back of their shirts and antennae affixed to their heads, and immediately began waving to their parents standing at the back of the room.

"Hey, kids! I have someone special here for you today," I said, glancing over to see Rivera's face take on a look of alarm. "Meet the senator!"

With that, I left the politician to entertain a room of five-year-olds. This was not his typical audience. Fortunately, his aides were with him to feed him softball questions for the young children, like "What's your favorite vegetable?" When I returned a few minutes later, Rivera was shaking hands with all the parents in the room and confessing his lack of experience dealing with youngsters. "Is it obvious that I don't have children?" he asked, drawing sympathetic laughs.

I rescued the senator and gave him a fast-paced tour of our program, trying to explain all the benefits of an edible classroom and how this idea could transform public education if we could just expand to more schools.

I had barely launched into my pitch when he grabbed my arm and said, "Stephen, chill! I can tell you have a million ideas, but I'm only getting maybe half of what you're saying." I was reminded of Majora's advice: Don't blast people with a fire hose of information.

So I took a breath and started over. This time I tried to be more deliberate about the connections between growing plants and growing healthier communities. That he understood. Representing the district with the worst health statistics in all of New York State, Rivera was eager for solutions. He encouraged me to keep at it and promised me that our paths would cross again.

Before he left that day, Rivera took time to work the room filled with my high school students. And he worked it hard. I watched him walk up to every single one of my students, make eye contact, offer a handshake, and say, "Hi, I'm your state senator. I work for you." My students were astonished. They had never met a public servant who was there to serve *them*. This guy could shift from English to Spanish in a heartbeat and spoke to teenagers without being patronizing. With insightful questions or comments about music, fashion, or neighborhood concerns, he quickly found common ground with everybody.

"Remember, Stephen," he advised me on his way out the door, "what we need are affordable, replicable programs."

Much as I welcomed the many opportunities afforded by our green classroom, I still wasn't satisfied with the setup. The green wall wasn't quite perfect for classroom use. In fact, my students and I started tinkering and modifying our first wall almost as soon as we had it assembled.

"Ladies and gentlemen, we have a problem," I announced at the start of class. "The custodians are mad at us."

Every teacher knows that you want to stay on the good side of your janitorial staff. I never wanted our hands-on learning to leave behind a mess that they had to clean up. But that's exactly what was happening. The first time we watered our green wall, some of the growing medium washed out onto the floor. When the night custodial crew arrived, there was a muddy mess to mop up. I asked them to leave it for my farmers to clean.

Students were furious. One day earlier, they felt like they had invented the wheel by assembling and planting that green wall. Now they had to do grunt work. As I handed out sponges, I challenged students to think while they mopped. "Look, we don't want to have to clean the floor every time we water, right? And we can't stop watering or the plants will die. So what do you think is causing this mess?"

"Gravity!" one kid blurted out, getting right to the root of the problem. Because we had set up that first wall at a ninety-degree angle to the floor, any water we poured on top made a rapid descent to the bottom, washing out soil along the way.

"Man, how can we ever fight gravity?" I challenged him.

That got everyone analyzing the wall instead of grumbling about the mess.

We designed experiments. How much could we tilt the wall without tipping the whole thing over? Students who had never understood slope in algebra class now got it. We sketched and prototyped our way to solutions. But there were always more variables to consider.

"Let's put this thing on wheels," Jonathan suggested another day.

"Why wheels?" I wanted to know.

"With wheels, we could bring it everywhere!" he exclaimed. "This wall is so cool, everyone will want to see it. We can show them what we're learning."

Another student chimed in: "Yeah, Mr. Ritz. You want us to make our thinking visible, don't you?"

"You got it." I smiled to hear her repeating my favorite classroom request. *Wow. These students are so right*, I thought to myself, *and poised to transform education and influence the entire green tech industry.*

Figuring out the right wheels created more problems for us to solve. We had to make sure the wheels didn't mark up the floors. We needed the wall to be easy to turn to get around corners but stable enough while we moved it so that it wouldn't tip over. Should the wheels lock or rotate? What about in reverse? We had variables galore to test and analyze.

Finally, we were ready to push this thing out of our classroom and use it as the perfect prop for our twenty-first-century version of show-and-tell. The first day we managed to wheel our fully planted wall into the elevator, down three stories, and into the cafeteria, we felt like we had run a marathon. But the big finish was still ahead.

A cafeteria packed with six hundred noisy teenagers came to a full stop when we rolled in. What in the world was this? When other kids spotted *my* students pushing the wall, they made all kinds of faulty assumptions.

"Yo, what is that, a weed wall?" somebody shouted out. It was no secret that some of my students had been known to partake of marijuana.

"No way!" Bianca shouted back. "Growing weed is for amateurs. This is so much cooler. It's food—and we built it and grew it ourselves!"

Instead of being on the margins, my students were now in the spotlight, educating their peers about the benefits of vegetables and healthy eating. Young people they never mixed with in classes crowded around, asking questions. My students had become the experts.

When I saw how all students responded to the green wall, I knew that this technology could have wide appeal in classrooms across the country, and not only with special education students. But not without more modifications. I kept thinking of Senator Rivera's advice: "Make sure it's affordable and replicable." We weren't there yet on either requirement.

The industrial green wall model that I started with came shipped flat. I didn't mind that it required assembly. I was motivated and eager enough to recruit some student muscle to move that unwieldy package up three stories, and then figure out how the pieces all fit together. The assembly work was a phenomenal opportunity for my students to read for a purpose, follow directions, and enjoy the satisfaction of putting together something cool with their own hands. But I also knew that most teachers would sooner forget it than have to haul the pieces and oversee the assembly.

What's more, this thing was expensive. I was lucky to be working with donated materials. How many schools—especially public schools like ours, serving high-poverty communities—could afford the $5,000 price tag, let alone for something to do with plants?

I was certain that a smaller model would appeal to a bigger education market. How big was just right? We needed data, so I sent my students—now called research assistants—out to measure doors, hallways, stairwells, and elevator openings all over campus.

"Hmm, you sure these measurements are right?" I asked them when I saw their calculations. "You all have the same numbers."

They went back out and measured the doorways again and again and again, until finally they said, "You don't get it. The numbers are supposed to be the same, Mr. Ritz. These doors are all the same size!" What a great lesson in standard units of measurement, and they figured it out all by themselves.

We shared our feedback about measurements with the green wall vendor, who sent us new, smaller models and modifications to test. We were all learning together.

As my students/research assistants got more sophisticated about problem solving, they hatched the cool idea of adding a spongelike material to the growing medium so that it would expand when it got wet. They knew all about the properties of sponges from mopping up our classroom messes. "We think it will work, Mr. Ritz," they told me, "but we don't know what stuff to use to soak up the water."

"Well, now you're getting into materials science," I told them, adding some academic vocabulary to the lesson. "Sounds like you want to find something that's highly absorbent but not toxic for plants. Those are your technical requirements, right?"

Right.

"Hmm, I'm no expert in materials science," I admitted. "Who do you think could help us figure it out?"

Without a moment's hesitation, Alejandro blurted out, "Ask Michaela! She knows all those geeks and nerds. There's bound to be somebody at her school who knows the answer."

By then, my daughter was a student at the highly esteemed Bronx High School of Science. Her school was just a four-block walk from ours but it might as well have been in another universe. This legendary academic powerhouse attracts students from all five boroughs. It's a selective school, which means students have to test their way in. Michaela and her classmates had access to state-of-the-art science labs, computers, and an observatory for learning about the stars.

Students from the two campuses typically avoided each other, getting on and off the No. 4 train at different stops. They didn't need advanced degrees in sociology to figure out who belonged where. They could size each other up with a glance, passing judgment on the spot about each other—and themselves. Michaela was a solitary pollinator, flitting from campus to campus, at home in both worlds. That made her a conduit of information, giving students on both campuses a window into the mysterious other school down the block.

Michaela convinced her brainy classmates to work on a solution to our messy problem in their fancy science lab. They came back with several mad scientist ideas, including one suggestion to use a gelatinous, transparent growing medium instead of a solid so that you could see the plant roots. My students tested and evaluated various proposals like an R&D team. They were getting better and better at problem solving.

In fact, some of my students got so good at working on green walls that they were hired for special projects by private industry and individuals. Several of them even installed a green wall at Rockefeller Center in Manhattan. They were no longer just greening the hood; this was prime real estate! They installed another one twenty-one stories up in a skyscraper in Boston and put a green wall in a Whole Foods Market in Manhattan. Just as I had anticipated, our classroom experiment was opening up career opportunities and attracting allies in the emerging green economy.

It was no secret that I wanted to keep the learning going after the final bell. I was always there after school, eager to work with any students who stayed around to help. I routinely opened and closed the building. I knew every custodian by name—day crew as well as night shift—and often sent janitors home with fresh produce from our classroom. When a foster care agency called to see if I would start an after-school job training program for their most difficult youth, I invited them to just show up. We could always use more participants willing to learn by doing.

A social worker arrived in my classroom a few days later, accompanied by a young man named Nadje. He was an immigrant from the Ivory Coast of Africa who had already lived through a lifetime of tragedies. His mother died when he was twelve and his father sent him to the United States to live with an uncle. Family conflicts escalated into physical abuse. An anonymous complaint had landed him in the foster care system at age fourteen. Now almost eighteen, he was about to age out of foster care and needed to figure out how to support himself. He was desperate for job skills and still needed to pass science exams to graduate from high school.

"You'll learn plenty of science here," I promised him. It didn't take long for me to appreciate Nadje's sharp mind and his facility with doing things by hand, like pollinating delicate plants with a feather. I made a point to emphasize the academic vocabulary he would need to pass high school biology. But I got concerned when I overheard him say to another student, "Why are we working for this white guy for free?" I explained that volunteering would help him develop skills that could lead to a paying job, eventually.

"You're starting as an unpaid intern," I told him, "but you'll work your way up." To make him feel better, I told him that I was also a volunteer, putting in my own time after school to expand our program. He was dumbfounded.

"Then why are you so happy and smiling all the time?" he wondered. My only answer was another smile.

Our visible projects earned us a reputation that sometimes led to special projects. This enabled me to facilitate hiring students for paid jobs. When I had a chance to place a few students for a paid summer position installing a green roof on a private home, I naturally thought of Nadje. I showed up at his foster home and told him to pack a bag. "And bring a swimsuit. We're going to the Hamptons, Nadje!"

"You gotta be kidding me," he said, wide-eyed. He had no idea where the Hamptons were but liked the sound of getting out of the city for a few days.

Not only did Nadje receive a nice paycheck for that job, but the gig included a plush place to stay with a stocked refrigerator, and it covered all transportation costs. He did such good work, he was recommended for other projects. I watched this kid from such a difficult background make friends everywhere he went. From the Hamptons to the hood, he attracted buddies that he called "my brother from another mother."

When we came back from the Hamptons, I made sure every student opened a bank account. Nadje used his to save for his first apartment. I didn't find out until later that he was sending money back home to the Ivory Coast as well.

"Mr. Ritz," Nadje told me with a smile, "you touch my heart." He touched mine right back.

True to his word, my new friend Senator Gustavo Rivera stepped up as an advocate for healthier communities. He literally stepped up. During a summer health fair in 2011 to kick off a new initiative called Bronx CAN (Change Attitudes Now), he stepped onto the scales at a community center. TV cameras zoomed in to show the result: just over three hundred pounds.

Boy, was I amazed. Not only was he as heavy as I was—almost to the pound—but I had never seen a politician hold himself so publicly transparent. There was no arguing with the scales, even though he didn't look that heavy. Here was a guy telling a hard truth about himself—in public. He was leading by example, being honest; just like a Robert Shetterly portrait. We needed more of that attitude in everything.

Rivera pledged to drop twenty pounds that summer and promised to share his progress at health fairs scheduled for the coming months. And he planned to do it without going away to a fancy spa or hiring a personal chef. Nope, this Bronxite was going to get slimmer and trimmer while eating in the same hood as everybody else. Our county may have come in dead last in a health outcomes comparison of New York State, but Rivera was convinced that his community had all the assets it needed to do better: our own health care experts, local food providers, and physical spaces to get exercise.

Game on. "If Rivera's going to drop twenty pounds, I'll lose forty," I promised everyone who would listen, including my family and my students. His pledge was all it took to fire up my hypercompetitive spirit.

I followed the senator's example and started practicing moderation. No more chips and soda. One slice of pizza instead of three. Small, healthy snacks like nuts and apples to keep me energized throughout the day. Lo and behold, those first twenty pounds practically flew off! I felt better. My clothes weren't so tight. And people noticed. Their feedback motivated me to keep going. Just like the senator, I was holding myself accountable. If I was going to teach my students to lead healthier lives, shouldn't I do the same?

Meanwhile, I had fresh problems to solve. Students from other classes wanted to get involved on our green projects. That caused friction within the school. The principal was delighted to see my special ed students engaged and successful. Their academic results were so strong, they boosted the entire school's performance. But my class was an anomaly.

He wanted his mainstream students to stay focused on college prep, not get sidetracked into vocational education. That was his vision for the school and for their future. I was a disrupter, and this principal abhorred disruption. Clearly, he was on a mission, a noble one at that. It was just a different mission from mine, and to me, mine was equally important. The stakes were so high on so many levels.

We probably didn't earn any bonus points with the administration when we adopted a new name—Green Bronx Machine. Years earlier, I had nicknamed the students in my Walton homeroom the Green Teens. That program had ended when I changed jobs. Now we were onto something bigger and more powerful than just an isolated class project. A beloved colleague who used to give guest lectures to my students suggested our new name. Green Bronx Machine captured our ambition to be an engine for community change. We wanted to use our green projects to lift up the lives of everyone, not just children and teens. One of my students designed a logo with green gears. It was a cool brand, but it said nothing about Discovery High School. We were thinking bigger.

Through the rumor grapevine, I heard the principal call Green Bronx Machine a distraction. Other teachers grumbled in the faculty room about my students showing up with dirty hands and messy clothes from tending the green wall. Nobody shared their concerns with me directly. I heard it all secondhand.

I knew the bloom was off when I came back from summer vacation. I had been reassigned to a small, windowless classroom in the basement. Formerly the book supply room, it had a ceiling so low I had to duck to get in. No room for a green wall there. Our edible classroom had to be dismantled.

Once again, the tall poppy was getting cut down. As I packed up my gardening supplies, it dawned on me that one green classroom had not changed the culture of the school. But it had changed outcomes for a critical subset of students. Students considered to be the least likely to succeed were thriving. With my first cohort of students at Discovery, attendance shot up from 40 percent to 93 percent. They had become community legends.

"We felt like rock stars," one student told me. "Man, we went to Rockefeller Center. We were on TV. We went to the Hamptons. We met an astronaut!" And all because of the power of a plant. Talk about SÍ SE PUEDE!

Like the bittersweet feeling you get when the seasons change, I could sense my years on the Walton campus drawing to a close. The eternal optimist in me wasn't about to give up. I was determined to see this as a set-back, not a failure. By paying attention to the three Cs—collisions, connections, and co-learnings—I had managed to bring the multifaceted benefits of gardening, green technology, and healthy eating right inside my classroom. The idea was too good to give up, even if this administrator didn't share my vision. "The opposite of courage is not cowardice, it is conformity. Even a dead fish can go with the flow," wrote activist Jim Hightower. I was no dead fish, and I simply knew I had to swim upstream and spawn. Everything I had learned here could be transplanted and expanded to reach even more children.

Clearly, the Green Bronx Machine work went far deeper than any-thing we had done previously with the Green Teens. What's more, it was 100 percent school centered. The projects and work we were focusing upon could be readily absorbed and integrated into any and every school, across all content and subject areas as well. Having an overarching, tax-exempt organizational status meant the work could have an oversight body and not be dependent upon one teacher in one school. We now had the internal framework and infrastructure to ensure that our reach would and could forever exceed our grasp!

If I could get others interested in greening their schools, maybe we could create a bigger disruption and change public education for the better. It was time to share my hard-earned insights with a more receptive audi-ence. SÍ SE PUEDE! Little did I know, but the ideal audience was queuing up and eager to listen.

CHAPTER 10

WHO THE HELL IS TED?

Winter 2011—On a cold winter evening just before the holiday break, I lumbered down to the Lower East Side of Manhattan to meet with a woman named Diane Hatz. We had only exchanged e-mails and had one brief phone call. I had no idea yet who she was or what she did as curator of the TEDxManhattan event. I didn't have a clue what TED was. I figured it must have something to do with a guy named Ted, not an organization that disseminates "ideas worth spreading" in short talks before big audiences. In retrospect, I guess I should have done a Google search.

Nor did I know what it meant to trend on Twitter. I didn't even know what Twitter was. I had no idea how links went viral on YouTube. I was a social media newbie. All I knew was that a mutual acquaintance had introduced us via e-mail (using my trusty AOL account). My TEDx tryout in her apartment was our first collision. I was about to get a crash course in how far and how fast information travels.

Sitting in Diane's living room, I launched into my story about Green Bronx Machine. Or at least I tried to. Diane reminded me of an adult version of my students. She was so curious, smart, and eager to learn that every couple sentences, she would interrupt me with a new question. Her tiny apartment could barely contain her intellectual energy and her endless questions. "Do you have any data to back up these stories about kids improving their attendance, academic results, and behavior once they get involved with Green Bronx Machine?" she wanted to know.

"Of course I have data," I told her. "I just haven't gotten a chance to tell you about it yet." Then she saw how many photographs I planned to include in my talk. My students had taken most of them. Her introductory e-mail to me had recommended fifteen to twenty slides. When I showed up with hundreds of images, that was just the teacher in me being overprepared.

"Four hundred and fifty photos? Are you kidding me? No," she said point-blank, leaving no room for negotiation.

By the time we were done talking, she had booked me for a TEDx Manhattan event in early 2012 on the theme "Changing the Way We Eat." She didn't tell me until much later that after hearing my story, she changed the event lineup to create a spot for me.

From our first conversation, Diane understood the significance of what we had been doing under the radar in the South Bronx. As the founder of a network called Change Food, she was on her own mission to create a more fair, sustainable food system that makes healthy, nutritious food accessible in every ZIP code. She knew just the people who would be keen to hear more about our disruptive work in one of the poorest communities in the country. Hundreds would pack the TimesCenter for the event, and thousands more would tune in via viewing parties around the world to watch the live stream.

I didn't know about any of these things. Viewing parties? Never heard of them. Live stream? No clue. When I tried to imagine a "good food movement," I drew a blank. I was so focused on my own green classroom, I had no idea what was happening more broadly. I pictured backyard vegetable gardeners and tree huggers. What would we possibly have in common? Clearly, I needed to be educated.

But I knew enough to recognize a good opportunity. This was going to be my first big presentation about Green Bronx Machine, and my students and I were thrilled to share our story. To be honest, though, my debut on that big stage could not have come at a worse time. I was still teaching at Discovery High School on the Walton campus. Conflicts with the principal and my own health issues were making my life a daily hell. Each seemed to exacerbate the other. Not only had the principal relocated me to a basement room with no windows, but he then assigned me five different classes to teach each day. That meant I was all over the building, carting materials up and down stairs, teaching a hodgepodge of courses. A year earlier, I was teaching in the first edible classroom in the country. Now I had no green wall. No living classroom. No designated space for Green Bronx Machine activities. Not even any daylight. I received his message loud and clear.

To make matters worse, I needed outpatient surgery to treat a hernia. I had put it off as long as possible and planned to schedule the procedure during winter vacation so I wouldn't miss any school days.

When you wake up after an operation surrounded by doctors, you know it's not good news. Still groggy, I counted way too many white coats hovering around my bed.

"Complications," one of them told me.

Instead of sending me home from ambulatory care same day as I expected, they were scheduling another surgery for the very next day. Only later did I learn that my heart had set off alarms while I was under anesthesia. During surgery, I started bleeding internally. My condition escalated postsurgery to the danger zone. It didn't help that I was still overweight even after losing forty pounds. I was out of shape, prediabetic, with sky-high cholesterol. My liver wasn't in great shape either. My years of out-of-control consumption had turned me into a poster boy for chronic disease. Lizette spent the next week sleeping on the floor of my hospital room. This was not the holiday break that either of us had imagined.

When it was showtime for TEDxManhattan, I was still recovering from surgery with two drainage bags taped under my clothes. I was running a fever of 102 from postsurgical complications. I was determined not to cancel. This was a chance to showcase my students' accomplishments and share some good news from the South Bronx. Day after day before the holidays, my students had stayed after school to help craft our story. They analyzed what we had accomplished like historians, deciding which events were significant and which photos best captured our experiences. During winter break, while I was stuck in the hospital, they had been planting and tending a beautiful green wall to display on the TEDx stage.

This was *our* moment—their story as much as mine. There was no way I would let them down. We couldn't afford tickets for my students to attend the event. Even if we could, the event had sold out months in advance. I had no idea it would be standing-room only. Yet I could feel my students' presence as I got ready. Earlier that morning, Lizette and a handful of Green Bronx Machine volunteers transported the green wall to the stage at TimesCenter. I was too weak to help.

Diane took one look at me and said, "You really shouldn't be here, Stephen." She didn't want me to take the stage. "There will be other opportunities," she said. "Canceling one talk is no big deal."

It was to me. I was there to speak for my students and everything they had accomplished. That day, I was a voice for the voiceless. I came to sing my students' song.

Watching from backstage, I could see hundreds of people pack into the venue. I was mystified. Who were all these smartly dressed people? Why were they willing to spend their Saturday listening to people like me talk about food? While I waited my turn to take the stage, I met the most amazing individuals who were also there to spread good ideas. Being in their company literally took me to a better place. I was riveted to their stories and started feeding off their energy.

A former Vietnam medic named Howard Hinterthuer described how he and fellow vets have found peace and better health through organic gardening. "There's nothing more optimistic than planting a garden," he said, "because you're making a bet that you're going to be there at harvest time." Wow. He was talking about veterans suffering from posttraumatic stress and depression, but he could have been describing so many of my students. I was reminded of the Vietnam vets who helped us build Bissel Gardens.

They worked side by side with my students to help heal the whole community. I knew personally how much veterans loved to garden. Betting on the harvest was what my work was all about!

Michelle Hughes, director of GrowNYC's New Farmer Development Project, shared stories of immigrants using microloans and entrepreneurship training to establish small family farms outside New York City, closing the distance from farm to urban table. I knew I had found a kindred spirit when she told the audience, "We help people see inside themselves that they have the skills they need." How often had I seen my students recognize their own potential through our Green Bronx Machine projects? Many of our South Bronx students were immigrants themselves, from families that understood the multiplier benefits of growing food to nourish communities.

After years of feeling isolated in education—the crazy teacher with the gardening projects, the gangster-educator working with youth on the margins—I found my community. In a room filled with tree huggers, vegetable lovers, foodies, and assorted mixed nuts, I was no longer an outlier. We were all equity warriors! I couldn't wait to make connections. Each person who spoke taught me something new and inspiring about food and equity. Their messages filled me with hope and gave me fresh ideas. They were just as interested to learn from my experiences. I felt like Popeye getting his spinach, only these vitamins were going straight to my brain. I remember thinking, right before I went onstage, "I am in the perfect place at the perfect time."

That epiphany gave me enough of a boost to get back on my feet, even though I looked like I needed a stretcher. I practically ran onto that stage.

I behaved the same way I do in the classroom to grab the attention of antsy adolescents. It wasn't an act. This was genuine excitement and a sense of urgency about changing lives with the power of a plant. The audience responded to my energy and emotion the same way my students do. They sat up, leaned forward, tuned in. They even smiled and clapped at my one-liners. ("When I need to get my students to listen, I say, 'Quiet. The plants are having sex.'")

A few minutes in, I was on a roll. I was also nervous about the strict time limit for TED talks. When the audience interrupted me midspeech with a standing ovation, I begged them to sit back down. The clock was counting down—I only had six minutes left! I didn't learn until later that it was the first standing ovation in the history of TEDxManhattan.

Diane was perched backstage in her black dress and black leather boots, watching me work up a frenzy. She knew I was on a mission, but my health had her worried sick. She had insisted I use a stool onstage to conserve my energy, but I was roaming around far too much to sit down. What she didn't know was that I was literally gasping for air. When I flailed my arms like I was working a bellows to pump air into my lungs, she thought I was just excited. She was also worried that I'd never get to what she considered the good stuff.

"Don't forget to give them some data," she had coached me countless times, including right before I went onstage. "That's what will help people understand how many positive things happen to kids because of growing plants. It seems simple, but the impact is enormous."

When I finally got to the numbers at the end of my talk, the audience erupted again—standing ovation number two! I had shared 375 slides in fourteen minutes, which has come to be known as a Stephen Ritz Deep Breath. Diane had been right all along. "Sure, it's about growing plants and eating better," she told me, "but it's also about having a chance." That social justice message, backed by hard evidence, brought the audience to its feet and set off a social media frenzy.

Before my talk was over, Green Bronx Machine was lighting up Twitter. I was so clueless, I wondered what it was and how I could access this "Twitter" thing from my flip phone. I had no idea what it meant to trend. Thanks to those viewing parties, I heard from people across the country and beyond. I had no idea that would happen. What a great problem—figuring out how to keep the conversation going with people around the world. My students created our Green Bronx Machine Facebook page, and I eventually got around to setting up that Twitter account.

I didn't realize until later that Diane sent the edited video of my talk to TED.com, a curated platform that selects a handful of videos to showcase from the hundreds of locally organized events like TEDxManhattan. "You have to look at this talk," she had urged the producers, setting off more ripples of interest.

When my video was published on the main TED Web site, that set the stage for more collisions, connections, and co-learnings. By quickly racking up views, it became one of the top-ranked TED talks about education. Speaking invitations began to arrive by e-mail, generating unanticipated opportunities and new allies for Green Bronx Machine. When a TED talk goes viral, doors open. I was eager to step through if it meant that I could start to scale our work. To date, those fourteen minutes—a Stephen Ritz Deep Breath—have been viewed more than a million times and counting.

CHAPTER 11

GREEN BRONX MACHINE REVS UP

Spring 2012—Ever since my first group of Green Teens from Walton High School won the Golden Daffodil Award and were honored at a fancy dinner, I had been meaning to set up a formal organization. Several people in the audience that night had asked if they could donate to our nonprofit program. We didn't have one. For a long time, I didn't understand what it meant to be a nonprofit. I didn't have time to think about tax structures or organizational bylaws. We were too busy working from one project to the next. Our secret sauce wasn't our charitable status. It was passion, purpose, and hope.

Now Green Bronx Machine was revving up, but I continued to rely on my "I know a guy" strategy to solicit resources and get things done. Business plan? Clueless. Staff? Nonexistent. My wife and daughter contributed so many volunteer hours to our projects that we called ourselves Team Ritz.

As our efforts began to expand far beyond my own classroom, I recognized that we needed a formal organization to scale our efforts. Nonprofit status would enable partners and funders to support our work so that we wouldn't be dependent on limited school resources or my pocketbook. As I started the arduous paperwork required to set up a nonprofit organization, I laughed at the irony. A guy who had been broke his whole life was now starting a not-for-profit!

By early 2012, I was still teaching at Discovery High School and still experiencing friction with the principal, but anticipating my exit. I could sense that something bigger was coming, even though I struggled with questions about the best way to scale our work. The unexpected popularity of my TEDx talk had captured the media's attention. That brought more camera crews to our campus, further irking the principal, who already considered us a distraction. Too bad. My students knew that they were part of a story worth celebrating. The Monday after my TEDx talk, I got a hero's welcome. Every classroom that I walked past broke into cheers. Students had figured out how to watch the live stream of the event. We were onto something big. For once, the news was about something good happening in the Bronx.

Gradually we started building our brand, learning to leverage Twitter and Facebook like social media pros. We wore our Green Bronx Machine T-shirts and caps to every media appearance, including a widely viewed segment on the Cooking Channel. I added a bow tie and, later, green suede shoes. When I was invited to speak at a green schools conference in Wisconsin, I spotted a cheese hat in an airport gift shop and knew I had to have it. My students already called me the Big Cheese. That goofy hat became my instant trademark.

When my old mentor, Stan Zucker, saw a photo of me in my Green Bronx Machine getup, he chuckled, "You're like a cartoon character! But it's okay. When people see you coming, they associate you with something good."

The same month that I resigned from Discovery High School, fearing I would drop dead there otherwise, our tax-exempt status was approved. The pieces were falling into place. Green Bronx Machine was legit and ready to power up, what I prefer to call an impact-driven, for-purpose organization with 501(c)3 status. (Doesn't that sound better than nonprofit?)

Frankly, I refused to be defined by anything with a first syllable of *non* or *not*. We were CANS! Amer-I-Cans, African Amer-I-Cans, Domin-I-Cans, Mex-I-Cans, and Puerto Ri-Cans! I planned to get the organization revved up while continuing my teaching career.

Out of the blue, I received a speaking invitation from Joel Makower. As I was soon to discover, he's a well-connected guy in the sustainability world. The chairman and executive editor of the GreenBiz Group and a prolific author, Makower also produces high-profile events like GreenBiz and Verge that attract sustainability leaders, investors in the green economy, and leaders of corporate social responsibility efforts. Not your typical crowd to listen to a teacher who grows food with children in poor neighborhoods.

When he's planning the lineup for big, three-day speaking events, Makower tries for a mix of voices—known and unknown. He had learned about my outlier work via social media. As he explained, "I want to give the audience some percentage of what it wants and some percentage of what it doesn't know it wants." Clearly, I fell into the latter bucket.

Makower knew he was taking a chance by inviting me. I didn't look, sound, or think like the people who would be in the seats. I showed up for his event in a fancy Times Square hotel wearing my usual bow tie and cheese hat. Michaela was at my side. With my talk scheduled for ten minutes, I figured I would be in and out fast. I left her in the lobby with her math homework and headed inside the ballroom. One look at that crowd and I knew I was in over my head. What the hell was I doing in a room with all these power players? I was way out of my comfort zone. If TEDx Manhattan had been a leap into a warm, fuzzy community, this felt like a suicidal swan dive into deep corporate waters.

Shana Rappaport, one of Makower's staffers who looked barely older than my daughter, must have noticed my distress. She immediately came to my aid. "I'm so glad you're here," she told me. "Your work is so important." And then this hip-looking, tech-savvy twentysomething did the most amazing thing. She leaned in and gave me a hug. In the space of a moment, she made me feel like I belonged. That's exactly what I aspire to do for my students every day. That's the power of relationships. Then she looked me right in the eyes and said, "You're going to be fine." One deep breath later, I believed her.

Makower, meanwhile, was clearly at home in this milieu. In a sea of expensive-looking suits, he exuded confidence in his business-casual corduroy jacket and loafers. I watched him work the room, stopping every few steps to be drawn into another conversation.

When I began my talk, Makower watched the audience react, trying to figure out how much of my message was quirkiness, how much was substance. Later he reflected, "People quickly realize that you're both cattle and hat—literally the hat." To my surprise, Makower told me how his business-savvy audience had been disarmed by my message. "People are not sure what kind of defenses, if any, to put up, and before they realize it, they've just surrendered."

It turned out that our differences of wealth and status weren't barriers after all. I watched the audience warm up to my story about plants and my steady weight loss and life in the "ghetto." They responded to my focus on relationships as the most important bottom line. Innovation is always about people. That's true whether you're building a multimillion dollar company or building engagement in a classroom. Relationships are the game changers. A kind word or unexpected hug can move us from feeling apart *from* to being a part *of.* This was a story that people wanted to hear. It was the story I lived every day. Nine minutes fifty-two seconds and 275 slides later, people responded by giving me the first standing ovation in the thirteen-year history of GreenBiz. It had been another Stephen Ritz Deep Breath.

Before that talk was over, a banker in the audience was texting his office to ask if the company was supporting Green Bronx Machine. Makower was convinced that the financial support was there to expand and scale my program. All I had to do was ask.

Makower invited me to a second speaking gig. Verge, the Super Bowl of the green business world, took place at a posh resort in Phoenix. It was a return trip to the Arizona desert where, years before, I had done my student teaching. I should have known that I'd get schooled again.

Makower joined me onstage at the end of my speech. The crowd was on its feet. I was feeling particularly emotional about getting this warm reception in Arizona, the place that had shaped me as a young teacher. Makower offered his thanks as emcee, and then did something he had never done before or since at one of his events. In front of five hundred business titans, he asked me, "Stephen, what's your ask?"

When I heard that softball question, I stepped back and watched the ball float across the plate and sail into the catcher's mitt. Frankly, I was still stunned and quite humbled by the outpouring of support from this high-powered audience. I wasn't prepared to ask anybody for anything. I didn't think to ask for individual contributions or corporate support. I didn't invite any of these power players to come join the board of directors of our fledgling organization. I didn't even think to ask for the business advice that I so badly needed. The room was packed with people who launch and scale programs all around the world. What did I know, after a lifetime of making ends meet on a teacher's salary, about running a start-up organization?

All I could think to say was "Please like us on Facebook." My students managed our Facebook account and were eager for followers.

We all have moments we wish we could do over. That was one of them. As I thought about that encounter later, I realized that I needed to figure out my answer to Makower's favorite question: "What would it take?"

What would it take to lift up the lives of thousands more children and communities through the power of a plant? What would it take to put Green Bronx Machine on stable financial footing so that we could bring our solutions to many more communities? I was determined to figure that out, but finding the answers would take even more collisions, connections, and co-learnings. To date, we had accomplished everything with no money and with what I like to call sheer testicular fortitude.

What was my real ask? Capacity.

CHAPTER 12

LOCATION, LOCATION, LOCATION

Fall 2013—After leaving Discovery High School, I eventually became dean of students at Hyde Leadership Charter School. Hyde is a public K–12 charter school in my beloved stomping grounds of Hunts Point. Coming back to this neighborhood felt like a victory lap. The younger children knew about my earlier gardening projects via the Internet and word of mouth. Frankly, the work had become a local legend. They were so excited to have me join their school that they lobbied to have my title changed to Dean of Awesomeness.

Ironically, a national award that I had been given for my edible classroom at Discovery High School was just now catching up with me. A year after I had been forced to dismantle that program, I was recognized with the Chevrolet GREEN Educator Award by Earth Force and General Motors. I'll admit, being ahead of your time can get frustrating.

To figure out where we should hold the awards ceremony, I called the office of the Bronx borough president. His staff put me in touch with the Hunts Point Alliance for Children. When they suggested a location, I couldn't hold back a grin.

Back to the Bank Note!

They could not have picked a more iconic backdrop to tell my story. Returning to the Bank Note Building opened a flood of memories, going all the way back to my boyhood of Little Rascals adventures. Of course, this was also where an earlier crop of students had installed our garden in the sky. It's where I first met Majora Carter and found an ally working for social justice in the green economy. She, too, had moved on in her career by then.

The Bank Note Building, still a proud symbol of the Bronx, was also in transition with new owners and new tenants. One tenant was a second-opportunity high school called the John V. Lindsay Wildcat Academy Charter School, serving students who are overage and undercredited. I wasn't familiar with JVL, but I had spent my career working with the same demographic group served here. I was thrilled to learn that the school was part of the Hunts Point Alliance for Children, an organization serving all the children and schools in this community.

While I waited for the ceremony to get under way, I had a clear view into the JVL culinary program. I know a classroom when I see it, and this was a beautiful setup. Students were learning culinary skills in a commercial kitchen bathed in natural light from a skylight. I felt like I had come home. I had no idea yet who these young adults were but had met thousands just like them—many heavyset, heavily tattooed and pierced, wearing their anger like body armor. In fact, it was working with their peers that had earned me the award I was about to receive.

Watching these students in their kitchen whites, methodically dicing potatoes at individual workstations, I couldn't help but wonder where their produce was coming from. With all that light, this would be the perfect place to put an indoor farm. There was a big open space right next to the kitchen. My imagination took off.

I started picturing what it would mean to grow food *inside* the Bank Note, not just on top of it. My elementary children at Hyde Leadership had been hankering to do gardening projects, but we didn't have the space. If we could team up here, we wouldn't have to leave the community to find success. My elementary students could walk to JVL for gardening and cooking projects, unleashing that special magic that happens when big children and little kiddos learn together. I had been looking for the opportunity to give the edible classroom concept another try on a bigger scale so we could nourish the entire community.

Perhaps this was it. Maybe we could grow something even greater—intergenerational, intercultural, with public-private partnerships. How perfect to bring together all the means of production here in Hunts Point, which has always been an epicenter of distribution. This could be the whole enchilada, including value-added, hyperlocal products like Hunts Point salsa and JVL Wildcat hot sauce. On that day, though, my ideas didn't go beyond wishful thinking.

A week later, I got a call from a local company called FreshDirect, wanting to sponsor a hydroponic gardening program for education.

"Do you know a school that might be interested?" the caller asked. "We have some materials to donate." That was all I needed to hear. My brain went into overdrive.

I introduced myself to the principal of JVL Wildcat and shared some of my thinking. The more he told me about his students, the more we both liked the idea of teaching indoor gardening alongside culinary arts.

JVL is designed to serve students who have failed to thrive in traditional high school. Many students are already parents. Some are transitioning out of foster care or the juvenile justice system. When they arrive at JVL Wildcat, they collide with other students who are bringing their own issues, motivations, and agendas. The curriculum is hands-on and practical, designed to help these almost-adults master essential academic skills and get started on career paths with internships in businesses, hospitals, and elsewhere.

"I'll volunteer my time," I promised, "as long as my little ones get to come work with your big guys."

Game on.

Before my little farmers could get involved in the project, we had to construct a hydroponic system. I didn't get to handpick the fifteen or so JVL students who would work on the hydroponic project. I didn't even know their names yet, much less their dreams. But I had some ideas about how to connect with them.

"Hey everybody, I'm Mr. Ritz. Who's interested in earning some real money? Who wants a job where you don't have to work at a fry station or wear a fast-food uniform?"

That got a few students to stop staring at the floor and glance my way.

"Who wants to take a trip?"

That got a response. A few students even uncrossed their arms and raised a hand.

"Out of class for the day? I'm in," said a student who called himself Flim Flam. I never learned his given name but quickly realized that he was a guy who wouldn't pass up a good opportunity.

"Where we goin'?" Mario wanted to know.

"It's a garden, but not like anything you've seen before. You'll see tomorrow," I promised them, hoping to create some anticipation. "Field trip starts at ten in the morning. Bring a lunch."

There was a buzz of excitement the next morning when I stopped at the JVL classroom to collect my team. Everybody likes a field trip. But skepticism set in the moment we got downstairs and assembled curbside. A big yellow school bus pulled up to the curb and let out a hiss as it came to a stop. The students let out a collective groan. "Oh man, not the cheese bus!" Victoria said, speaking for everyone. "What are we, like kindergartners?"

For a young person on the cusp of adulthood, there's no dignity in riding a big yellow school bus.

Our destination: Greenpoint, Brooklyn. My wife and daughter, wearing Green Bronx Machine T-shirts, had come along. I leaned over to Lizette and whispered, "I hope this wasn't a mistake." I was flying blind in so many ways. I hadn't had time to build a relationship with these young people yet. I didn't know what they were bringing—or missing—when it came to motivations, abilities, or interests. I had never even seen the destination myself.

When the bus pulled up at the Wood Exchange Building in Greenpoint, I was sure I had made a colossal error. This two-story industrial warehouse had none of the architectural grandeur of the Bank Note. It was squat and ugly. Coming from Hunts Point, these students were used to gritty neighborhoods. Greenpoint looked even grittier, with none of the colorful street traffic that you see in Hunts Point. In fact, there were no people in sight anywhere. All the action was happening indoors, tucked inside these old warehouses that were getting repurposed to fuel a zillion-dollar start-up economy. The JVL students didn't have a clue about any of that. All they knew was that they had ridden a school bus for forty-five minutes through some ugly streets to get to a neighborhood more desolate than where they had started.

"How can there be a garden here?" Nona wondered, drawing more grumbling from her classmates. At street level, we couldn't see anything green.

The dissent only got louder as we trudged upstairs.

"Welcome, everyone," said the bubbly woman who greeted us on the second floor. She was very young and very white. "We need you to take off your shoes before you go inside."

Oh, boy. If there's one thing that's precious to these young people, it's their sneakers. And now they were being asked to check them at the door. I knew they felt disrespected. What were we in for? And then it got worse.

"Once your shoes are off, please put on some Crocs, and then step into the sanitizer and paper booties," our host said. Her cheerful politeness was the exact opposite of what I was reading on every participant's face.

"What the *fuck*? Take off our shoes? Put on ugly-ass Crocs?" It was practically a chorus.

I led the way, behaving as if it was no big deal to sanitize your Crocs and slip on a pair of paper booties. When the students saw Lizette and Michaela doing the same, they fell in behind us.

"This is some strange white-people shit," Duron muttered, but he stepped in and stepped forward nonetheless.

Once we were prepped, our guide led us through another set of doors and onto the rooftop. We stepped into what was then the largest urban greenhouse in the country. Rows of plants unfurled before us like a living carpet that covered fifteen thousand square feet. I had never seen so much green in my life. Bright lights intensified the color and added to the surreal feeling of the place.

The anger and distrust and grumbling that had been building up in the students all morning instantly dissipated into this tranquil sea of green. I watched everybody take deep breaths, inhaling the aroma that smelled so alive. I realized that I was doing the same thing, taking in the vegetable equivalent of a freshly mowed lawn.

Suddenly, the students erupted with questions.

"Who had this idea?"

"Who ever thought of doing this?"

"Can we do something like this?"

"Is this thing here full-time?"

"Yeah, where does it go in the winter?"

"Dude, it is winter. This is like summer at Christmas."

"How can we learn more about this?"

As if on cue, out walked Viraj Puri. Dressed in flannel shirt and jeans that were hip enough for my students to admire, he was a thirtysomething guy with dark hair framing his handsome, Indian American features. He unplugged from his earphones and music when he saw us. "Welcome to Gotham Greens," he said with a big smile.

From our e-mails and phone calls, I knew that he was the CEO and cofounder of this urban farming enterprise that aims to disrupt traditional agriculture by putting greenhouses on city rooftops. Greenpoint was the first location. Since it opened in 2011, it had quickly generated demand for hyperlocal, hyperfresh produce among New York City's top restaurants and gourmet grocers. Although Viraj is a proud New Yorker and graduate of Colgate University, he has worked on sustainable agriculture and alternative energy projects everywhere from India to Africa. From his first words, he came across as worldly and wise but also completely approachable.

As the students listened to him describe the origins of Gotham Greens, it dawned on them that they were meeting a new breed of farmer. Here was a twenty-first-century grower who was hip to technology and smart about saving resources. He had built something in New York that seemed as futuristic as Batman's Batcave, only bright green. And he had done it in plain sight, right on top of a warehouse, to bring produce closer to the people. Plus, the guy could control everything from his iPhone. The students marveled to see that he had apps for everything.

"Wait," said Mariano, taking a moment to process what he was learning. "You mean all this green stuff is . . . *food*?"

Even though these aspiring chefs were enrolled in a culinary program, they had little exposure to fresh produce and certainly not local produce. They knew how to cut and fry potatoes. They were learning how to blend sugar with butter and flour to make carb-heavy desserts. But they didn't know their way around the fresh vegetable aisle. They recognized tomatoes, carrots, and cucumbers. Beyond that, everything else in the veggie family was simply "salad." Eggplant? Purple salad.

Viraj gave them a tour of his favorite crops, pointing out verdant rows of basil, butterhead, bok choy, and more. Not only were these plants all grown from seed on-site, but they were harvested, packaged, and shipped under this same greenhouse roof. No pesticides. No soil. No long journey to market. By capturing and reusing water for hydroponics, the system was ten times more water efficient than traditional agriculture. Instead of cultivating acres of rural farmland, Gotham Greens was producing tons and tons of produce on a city rooftop that would otherwise sit empty. And no one got dirty!

Right away, Steven wanted answers: "How much do people get paid to work here?"

"Yeah, how do you get hired?" added Taja. "Do you need college?"

I could see the lightbulbs everywhere as students came to the same realization. There were good jobs up here!

The JVL students were curious about the employees they saw moving around in this big space. Some were checking on the plants, others tending to the technology, others preparing orders for delivery. Nobody was confined to a workstation. Even though everyone looked purposeful and on task, there was no boss barking orders. Signage posted in different areas and in different languages—Spanish, Arabic, Hindi—reflected the workforce diversity that we could see with our own eyes. Diagrams on some of the walls transcended language, explaining technical processes with graphics that looked like emojis. It wasn't hard for these young adults to imagine themselves working here someday.

"Mr. Ritz, can we eat lunch now? We're starving," Sheila said, shifting the focus to a more immediate concern.

"Yeah, can we eat up here? Like a picnic?" Maria added.

"Cool, a picnic at a farm!" Yolanda chimed in. Watching some of the boys and girls pairing off, I started worrying where rooftop romances might lead.

Everybody loved the idea of a picnic. Everyone, that is, except Viraj and our cheerful greeter. They explained their concerns about cross-contamination. For the same reasons that we had to leave our shoes behind and wear sterile booties, we had to keep our own food out of this pristine environment where every condition was carefully controlled.

Viraj got even more concerned when he saw what these visitors were carrying in their lunches. A typical meal was a can of soda, neon-colored bag of chips packed with salt and artificial flavorings, and maybe a day-old sandwich grabbed out of a bodega cooler. Worst of all were the sugary, packaged cakes—the perfect food to attract bugs! Those were the last ingredients he wanted to unleash into this greenhouse atmosphere, for so many reasons.

Cross-contamination was a new scientific concept to most of these students, but they quickly made sense of it through a cross-cultural lens.

"I get it. It's like my Muslim friends can't eat anything that touches pork."

"Jews keep milk and meat separate, don't they? Are you Jewish?" one of the bigger, bolder students asked Viraj, who shook his head.

He acknowledged the comparisons to halal and kosher, but then quickly pivoted. Viraj challenged students to think about what is "real" food and what's not. If they wanted to become chefs or maybe manage their own restaurants one day, didn't they want to serve food that provided good nutrition? He was clearly proud to be delivering products that were good for people and good for the planet. "You can do all that and make a profit, too," he explained, giving these young adults their first lesson in the triple-bottom line.

"Let's save lunch for the ride home," I suggested, drawing only a few groans this time. "We have plenty more to learn here first."

For me, that field trip opened windows into the JVL students' individual interests. I could see that several students were into technology in a big way. They peppered Viraj and his staff with questions about the solar panels that covered flat roof surfaces not being used for the greenhouses. Even though an urban greenhouse requires energy, a big, flat warehouse roof is great for capturing solar power.

I listened closely, too. I knew a little about green roofs from the Bank Note project but had never seen anything done at this scale. Viraj was clearly way ahead of his time. He was just the kind of guy we all wanted to know better.

Listening to him challenge the students about "real" food got me thinking about how much food marketing had changed since I started teaching. Back in the 1980s, there was good food and plenty of junk food, but it was easy to tell the difference. Sure, there used to be popular food brands and products, but now there was an official chip, an official cracker, an official cookie, an official ice cream, an official candy, an official hot dog, an official breath mint, an official beverage, even an official water, all tied to a specific celebrity, athlete, television show, movie, radio station, and anything else that affected children's lives. Packaging and marketing had become so much more sophisticated and well crafted. Sometimes it was subliminal, and sometimes it was in your face. One thing was certain: These messages were everywhere, and they were shaping our eating habits whether we realized it or not. It dawned on me that children were slowly but surely becoming little profit centers, programmed to generate income and opportunity for other people in far-off places. These children were at the bottom of the pecking order.

The hardest part of that day came when our tour ended. Nobody was eager to come down from that magical Greenpoint rooftop and climb back on the cheese bus. "Come on, you guys," I said. "Let's go build something great back at your school."

Hydroponic systems offer a reliable way to grow plants indoors by controlling all the conditions. In heavily industrialized Hunts Point, that meant we didn't have to worry about soil contamination or air pollution from diesel trucks. There is no soil in hydroponics. Roots are held in place by an inert material, such as rock wool or growing cubes, and nourished with a water-based solution that's enriched with nutrients. The solution gets pumped to the plant roots via long channels that fit into a suspended horizontal frame. In a high-tech way, it makes gardening sexy and the whole room beautiful.

For my students with a technical bent and for a natural tinkerer like myself, part of the fun of hydroponics was getting all those variables just right. We wanted a big system at JVL to supply enough food for the culinary training program. Once we got our system up and running, it filled a once-empty space with forty-foot rows of leaf lettuce, spinach, kale, sorrel, and more. We could measure the distance from farm to table in footsteps rather than miles. Aspiring farmers planted basil and learned to turn it into pesto three weeks later. The principal even hired a part-time staff member who had expertise in urban agriculture.

Our indoor farming program was humming along—until the first electric bills arrived.

The principal was shocked to see how much it cost to keep those big water pumps running to move plant nutrients through the system. The school's electric bill shot up by hundreds of dollars in just one month. I thought about those solar panels we had seen at Gotham Greens and realized how smart Viraj had been to harness the sun instead of the grid to power his greenhouses.

"Can you give us some more time?" I asked the principal. "I bet we can figure out how to increase efficiency. If nothing else, your students will get some valuable math experience by gathering and analyzing data."

"One more month," he agreed. We both understood that if the next electric bill didn't go down, it would be game over.

With the clock ticking, we had to innovate in a hurry. I challenged our techiest students to help me figure out how we could keep our system running on less power. One student had the bright idea to use gravity as our friend so that the system would be less dependent on running that big pump to move water. By studying how the ancient aqueducts had used gravity to move water, we modified the channels in our system to do the same. Another team experimented with diversifying the crops. Baby plants didn't need as much water as big ones. This meant less water flow and much less electricity. We changed the ratio to grow more microgreens and fewer mature plants. We kept tinkering until we found a combination that cut that power bill down to size while still producing bountiful crops.

A few months later, the JVL Wildcat team won the National Indoor Gardening Expo championship for coming up with a brilliant design for hydroponic gardening at a fraction of the typical operating cost.

"Students, pack your bags!" I told the JVL team. "We're going to California!"

The prize included a trip to an indoor gardening show in San Francisco. Actually, there wasn't enough prize money to bring students along. They didn't need to know that I secretly paid for their plane tickets out of my own paycheck. I wanted them all to feel like winners.

We flew across the country and walked into the convention center in San Francisco. I should have been suspicious before we ever stepped inside. I know what farmers look like—rugged, outdoorsy types with calloused hands. The convention center was filled with people wearing fancy eyeglasses, earrings, and piercings. No overalls or muddy boots in sight. These weren't farmers—they were hipsters!

We had walked right into an indoor grow show marketed heavily to the marijuana industry. The other chaperone I brought along was the straitlaced principal from JVL who had a haircut like a marine and a no-nonsense attitude to match. His father had been a Secret Service agent.

Before I could figure out what to do next, up walked a reporter from *High Times* magazine, eager to interview my students and me. I'm good at spin, but there was no way to report this story and keep us out of trouble. Yikers!

"Team meeting," I called out to my students, waving off the reporter. To myself I said, *What we have here is a teachable moment.*

I huddled with my students and went over the ground rules. No samples. No smuggling anything home. No selfies in the grow tents that would embarrass us later. I may have pleaded a bit when I said, "Please, everyone, help Mr. Ritz keep his job." I foresaw a return trip to the Rubber Room. At least I'd have the principal to keep me company.

The JVL Wildcat team flashed me big grins and said, "Don't worry, Mr. Ritz. We got your back." In that crowd, several people recognized me from my TEDx talk. My students marveled at that. "Mr. Ritz, you're like a celebrity!"

Under other circumstances, these young people might have been working the room for wholly different outcomes. But we all kept our promises, learned plenty, and came out with a good story to tell. Most importantly, we repped the South Bronx properly.

The eternal optimist in me decided to make the most of this dicey situation. What more could I learn here? I knew by then that indoor growers are natural innovators. Entrepreneurs like Viraj from Gotham Greens are ingenious at creating artificial growing conditions that mimic nature. Surely I could find some ideas to borrow. I wandered around the exhibits, chatting with eager vendors who said things like "I grow herbs, too, buddy."

Near a massive hydroponic setup that only the most successful pot growers could afford, I spotted a humble little product made of white plastic. It looked like a Lego toy dropped onto a high-tech factory floor. Called the Tower Garden, it was a cylinder standing about five feet tall with round openings on the exterior to insert twenty plants. A small pump circulated water fortified with nutrients; gravity pulled the water down through the tower to keep the plant roots moist. A sign explained that this technology, called aeroponics, required only one-tenth of the floor space and energy than similarly sized hydroponic systems.

The floor model was stuffed with fake plants, not real ones, but I was drawn to it like a pothead to a bong. Talk about a collision.

I spotted a short guy working the booth and waved him over. "I want this. We need this," I said in a rush, looking down at least a foot to make eye contact with him.

"Hold on," he countered, looking back up at me. "Who's 'we'?"

"I'm an educator from the Bronx," I told him, then started spewing ideas as fast as they popped into my head. Each detail I noticed on this little vertical garden offered a solution to a barrier I'd encountered as I tried to scale my green classroom. It was as if I was going down a requirements list and checking every box: "Wheels? Perfect. I can move it from class to class. Hard to set up? Doesn't look like it. Weight? Can't be more than fifteen pounds, right?" I glanced at the guy and saw him scratching his head. "Look," I explained, "I've tried green walls. Too much work for most teachers. Hydroponics can get expensive if they need a big pump, and they take up too much fixed real estate in a classroom." He barely had time to take that in before I was walking away again. "I'll be back in a few minutes," I promised.

I'm sure he figured he'd seen the last of me. He looked surprised to see me back at his booth ten minutes later with the JVL principal and students in tow. We started inspecting that Tower Garden as if we were checking out a luxury vehicle on a car lot.

"Look, I'm serious about connecting," I told him, grabbing his business card and noticing his name. Rich Downing. I promised him that I would e-mail some information about Green Bronx Machine. That was late Sunday afternoon.

On Monday, my phone call woke him up. "Dude, it's five thirty in the morning in California," he told me. "Where are you?"

After a night flight with the JVL team, I was back in the Bronx. I had barely slept, and not because of jet lag. My mind was buzzing with ideas about growing cylindrical gardens of plants inside the classroom.

"Guess you were serious," he said.

Two weeks after that early morning call, I was back on the phone with Rich. My JVL students and I were about to be featured in a national documentary called the Apron Project, sponsored by Progressive. When the filmmakers initially contacted me, they were interested in showcasing our hydroponic system. Now I suggested a better idea.

"I'm onto something bigger and better," I promised them. I wanted any teachers who were watching to see how easy it is to align the art and science of growing food indoors with academic outcomes across content areas. What could be easier than these vertical gardens that took up so little classroom real estate? Not only that, but the lifelong learner in me was itching for some hands-on learning with this new technology. The producers agreed to a budget to cover materials.

"Can you get fifteen Tower Gardens to New York?" I asked Rich. "And tons of plants of different sizes?" I even offered to fly him out to give us some technical support. That wasn't in the budget, but I didn't mind getting some skin in the game myself by covering his travel costs.

By this time, Rich had done his homework. He was convinced I was bona fide. What's more, he had a friend in the industry in Pennsylvania and thought he could convince him to drive a U-Haul full of plants to the Bronx.

Two weeks later, I recruited a work crew of JVL students to set up for the film shoot. "Who wants to be in a video?" I asked. Hands shot up.

"Let me be more specific," I added. "Who wants to be in a video about gardening?" Hands went right back down.

I kept promoting the idea, promising students that they could be Internet sensations even if they weren't making music or playing sports. The principal sweetened the deal by offering students extra credit for weekend work. Finally, I had enough volunteers for a Saturday work crew. Some had worked on the hydroponics project, but others were newcomers. Once again, we all had to get acquainted and learn to collaborate.

Our first step was to tear down the hydroponic system we had worked so hard to build.

"Why are we taking this down?" Hector wanted to know. "It's so cool."

"We're going to build something way cooler. Trust me," I promised, knowing that I was once again flying blind. To date, I had assembled exactly zero garden towers myself. Now I planned to fill a big room with them.

Rich Downing spent the morning working side by side with me and my volunteers to assemble our indoor farm. Thanks to his experiences at trade shows, he knew how to assemble a perfect-looking indoor gardening environment in a hurry. To my students' astonishment, I was happy to follow his lead. The students were used to me being in charge. Suddenly I was the one asking questions and taking directions from this stocky little white guy who huffed and puffed from the exertion of it all. I always like to model how to take direction.

Our indoor farm went up fast. Building the hydroponics system had taken us weeks of trial and error. These towers went from pieces in a box to full assembly in less than an hour. The students started timing themselves, getting faster on each unit, especially if they collaborated efficiently. There were important jobs for everybody. Some students sorted the screws and plastic components. Others assembled the wheel bases. The taller boys built towers on top of the units that the girls had put together. Students who were good with technology or mechanics got the pumps installed and working. Through teamwork, they experienced success over and over again, one tower after another. Once everything was assembled, we were ready to start planting.

"I get it," Steven said, stating the obvious as only a child can. "It's a tower *plus* a garden. These guys were smart to name it that."

Chuckling, I thought to myself, *Ya think?*

After lunch, Rich's buddy pulled up outside the Bank Note Building in a truck overflowing with seedlings. That was my introduction to Duane McCarthy, an impeccably dressed grower whom my students and I have come to know and love as the Gucci Farmer.

I brought some students down to help unload and carry materials back upstairs. "When you pick up a plant, pay attention to the roots," Rich cautioned them. "If you break off the roots, the plant will die." To demonstrate, he held up a head of bright green Buttercrunch lettuce with roots dangling down like tangled spaghetti noodles.

One of the older students, a tattooed twenty-one-year-old, recoiled as if he had seen a snake. "Dude, what is that?" he asked, pointing to the roots. "Is that, like, the inside of the plant?" Everybody crowded in for a closer look.

Once again, nature had blindsided my city kids. Just like the students who had been dazzled by a bunch of daffodils so many years before, these young people were held in thrall by something as simple as plant structure. Only it's not so simple if you've never seen it before with your own eyes.

"So if we mess up those roots, the plant dies?" the same boy asked, repeating what he had just heard. He took a minute to take that in before adding, "Guess it's on us to keep it alive."

In ways I could never have predicted, these fragile seedlings helped my students recognize the awesome responsibility that comes with caring for another life. It's on you. Even if it's just a plant. That's the power of a plant.

I gave us all a moment to think about that before I said, "Okay, everybody. Back to work!"

In the space of two productive workdays, we literally went from empty space to a fully functional indoor farm inside an oversize classroom. When they began, some of these young people frankly hated each other. A few were there just to get credit. Some wouldn't take out their earphones long enough to listen.

"Look, guys, you don't have to be best friends. But we have a tight schedule to get this done. And we need to do it right. It's not just the video. My little guys are counting on you," I told them, reminding them of the younger students at Hyde Leadership who were eager to come garden with them. That flipped a switch, especially for students who were parents themselves. Once they settled into the work and saw the results before their eyes, students realized that it didn't feel like a job. This was fun! They even recycled all the trash.

Most importantly, the project gave everyone an opportunity to set aside whatever else was going on in their lives and give themselves over to being nurturers. There wasn't much talking as students started to fill those towers with an array of plants. The vertical design brought them face-to-face with fuzzy mint leaves and spicy arugula. A great smell filled the room as if we were pumping life itself into the atmosphere. They tucked in tender seedlings as carefully as if they were putting their own children down for a nap.

Here was a benefit of tower gardening that I had not anticipated. It brought nature up close and made it personal. Our hydroponic system was cool, but it was fixed real estate. The long channel structure prevented you from walking between the rows. When our towers were finished, these big tough teenagers started playing hide-and-seek around the plants like farm kids in an Iowa cornfield. They wheeled the towers around and posed for photos next to their favorite plants as if they were celebrities. Move over, Beyoncé. The spotlight was now on arugula and sweet basil.

I learned and rejoiced right along with the students. Over the course of two days, I felt like I had shown them my life's work in time lapse. We all came away inspired.

Our success inspired others. When the Apron Project video went live, it became an Internet sensation. These students really did become film stars, watched by millions of viewers. Ripples of interest became huge waves. Suddenly, TNT came to film another piece, called *Dramatic Difference*, that was seen by millions and millions. Then Disney came calling, featuring our students in a series called *Pass the Plate* that was seen around the world.

All that visibility brought more visitors to the JVL classroom, including a US State Department contingent with dignitaries from forty countries. They were drawn by the same simple message that landed us in an Office Depot campaign and video: *Teachers Change Lives.*

And lo and behold, when the world's most famous food expert wanted to capture a scene of an innovative classroom farm, he brought his camera crew to Hunts Point. Michael Pollan's two-hour *In Defense of Food* documentary showcased my JVL students immersed in their indoor gardening and culinary training program. Millions watched the show the night it aired. In the most industrial part of the South Bronx, a place where no one expected to find green innovation, we had built something amazing.

The attention from Pollan and so many others helped me see how our work offers an antidote to so much that is ailing society. Like Pollan, I was fascinated with the intersection of nature and culture. For me, it centered on urban agriculture. It dawned on me: If you want to fix health care, look at food and farming. If you want to fix hunger and poverty, look at food and farming. If you want to reduce waste, look at food and farming. If you want to respond to climate change and make resource allocation more equitable, look at food and farming. If you want to have children involved in hands-on learning activities that engage them in school, look at food and farming.

As I watched those videos, I was equally amazed to see the transformation in myself. When I saw photos of my old self, I was shocked. Could that really have been me—all belly and no ass—stretching the limits of a XXL T-shirt? By 2013, I felt like a different person.

I had stuck with the healthier eating habits that I had adopted a couple years earlier. It took me seven months, but I managed to shed more than one hundred pounds and keep them off.

Simple changes added up quickly, especially given how much and what I had been eating previously. Everyone could see the changes daily as my weight started to drop. My immediate family, friends, and colleagues were all supportive, and that was reinforcing.

Once I got slim, however, keeping the weight off became its own challenge. Now I had to change old behaviors, adopt new strategies, and acquire a whole new understanding of cause and effect with food. I didn't want to celebrate my weight loss with bad decisions, like indulging in a big meal or calorie-laden dessert. As I got slimmer, I became even more active, which drove my appetite up in a different manner. I wanted a certain amount of volume and loved foods that crunched. Instead of reaching for salty snacks, I marveled that I could eat carrots, cucumbers, and colored peppers all day and feel satisfied, without gaining weight or feeling hyped up or lethargic. My energy level became more steady. Clearly, this beat the MESS (manufactured edible synthetic substances) that I used to consume. I needed a basic rule of thumb to live by, and someone told me about Michael Pollan's good advice: "If it is a plant, eat it; if it is made in a plant, don't eat it." This made a great deal of sense, and I started learning more about Pollan's work and sensible eating. My tastes changed along with my waistline, and I stuck with healthy habits to keep myself from ever getting too hungry or in a dangerous place.

Once I lost the weight, I noticed another set of consequences. Sure, my family, friends, and colleagues were supportive, but what I realized was how I was now perceived by folks who didn't even know me. Strangers treated me entirely differently than they did when I was heavy. I was deemed more competent and treated better, more expeditiously, and way more courteously. In retail shops, clerks were kinder, more attentive, and way more service oriented. Showing up as a thin person at a meeting, conference, or even for parent-teacher night afforded me an additional level of respect. It was all unspoken, but I could tell that people took me more seriously and treated me more professionally. I had uncovered a bias that society has against overweight people: They are definitely bullied, disrespected, perceived, and treated differently. Losing 110 pounds taught me that.

Given my personal epiphanies, was it any wonder that I wanted to introduce indoor vegetable gardening to as many schools as I could possibly reach? I wanted every child and every community facing a food-related health crisis to benefit from the power of a plant.

Steve Williams, director of the Tower Garden division for the parent company, Juice Plus+, fell in love with this technology for many of the same reasons that I did. He also envisioned getting Tower Gardens into schools and after-school programs but not at the scale that I had in mind. The first time we chatted by phone, he said, "Wow, you get it. And I get you."

In me, he and his colleagues found the champion they didn't know they had been looking for. I envisioned using these little vertical gardens to teach everything from math and science to language arts and career-technical skills. And, of course, healthy eating. It wasn't too long after those initial conversations and meetings that I would meet Jay Martin, the founder of the company. And wouldn't you know it—he had started his career as a teacher.

Although he went on to become a wildly successful entrepreneur and I stayed the course with teaching, Jay and I shared the common goal of inspiring healthy living. Jay explained to me that Juice Plus+ was doing very well on its own, and had been for nearly twenty years, but that he acquired Tower Gardens because he believed they could transform the way people think about, grow, and consume fruits and vegetables in their homes. I explained to him my vision for aligning Tower Gardens to curricula, and doing the same for children in schools. It was a natural fit.

I was thrilled to have the chance to use technology that would streamline my lesson plans and foster greater learning opportunities for my students. Jay's entrepreneurial spirit resonated with my desire for innovation. In turn, he was thrilled to have found someone with my energy and enthusiasm. That's how a fiftysomething guy from the Bronx and a seventy-year-old Georgia native developed a seemingly unlikely friendship, all because I accidentally took my students to an indoor marijuana convention.

Since that first collision at the indoor grow show, I've had opportunities to give lectures to Juice Plus+ and other audiences topping ten thousand attendees, sharing my passion for inspiring healthy living and healthy learning. At Hyde Leadership Charter School, surrounded by eager little children, I was determined to garden up a storm with Tower Gardens in classrooms. And the children loved it! Word spread like wildfire, and before I knew it, my little farmers and I starred in a video via Office Depot: *Teachers Change Lives*. This video highlighted how we gardened in school and learned about the power of a plant. Overnight, the video had several hundred thousand views and moved viewers to tears. Since that Office Depot video, more than five thousand schools have started indoor Tower Garden programs. Talk about *sí se puede*—that's the power of a plant. Of course, a vertical indoor farm isn't the only way to bring gardening into the curriculum. But it may be the most cost efficient and certainly the most replicable.

I've learned from experience that classroom real estate matters. Cost matters if a program is going to last. Convenience matters to teachers who are perpetually short on time. And impact—whether it's academic growth or better behavior or students learning to collaborate—matters most of all. All those qualities make this solution scalable with the potential to engage millions of children and adults alike. Here was a limitless possibility. I could see how everything I had done previously had gotten me to where I was right now. I was excited.

I knew that I had more work to do if I was going to get other teachers as excited as I was. I would have to come up with new lesson plans and classroom projects that would tie indoor gardening to the core curriculum and content area instruction. To get other teachers and administrators on board, I would have to show academic and behavioral benefits for my students in measurable ways.

All I needed was some more classroom real estate to keep building out my ideas and a school leader willing to give me room to innovate.

CHAPTER 13

GROWING A GLOBAL TEACHER IN THE PROJECTS

F **all 2014**—"Hello, handsome. Good morning, beautiful."

Wearing my cheese hat and bow tie, I struck a pose on the sidewalk in front of the garden at Community School 55 every morning, ready to greet each child personally. I was a new face at school that fall, but children and their parents quickly got to know me and our daily drill. We called it the Two-Five: two eyes, five fingers. It didn't take long for students to exceed the minimum requirements of eye contact and handshake. They soon started calling me Mr. Steve, Mr. Farmer Steve, even Father Nature. I soaked up all the smiles, hugs, and nicknames they wanted to throw my way.

Green Bronx Machine and I had found our new home.

For years, Principal Luis Torres had been trying to recruit me to teach at his elementary school. A Bronx native, Torres has a stocky build that harkens back to his days as a high school athlete. Now he's balding and wears a neatly trimmed beard. He has a warm, big, open smile, but behind his hip-looking glasses are eyes that have seen a lot of sadness. That's what comes from spending more than a decade serving one of the poorest schools in the South Bronx.

Community School 55 serves 730 children in a neighborhood called Claremont Village. This five-story schoolhouse with gracefully arched entrances was built more than a hundred years ago when the neighborhood was all single-family homes and farms. Today, every side of the school faces a towering brick housing project, each of which opens onto four more projects. Some buildings have windows that have been shot out and remain unfixed.

Just visiting is a challenge. The nearest subway is eighteen blocks away. The Metro North commuter train runs along one side of the school but never stops. If there were a train station in Claremont Village, it would be just six quick minutes to Manhattan, seventeen minutes to Westchester. Instead, all day long, rail commuters speed through this neighborhood bound for somewhere else. Street parking is a nightmare. Bus service is limited. Cabs are scarce and expensive. The forty-five thousand residents of this dense neighborhood are so cut off from the rest of New York, they might as well be living on their own island. If you grow up here, it's easy to imagine that you'll never find a job, never get out of the projects, never get a chance to change your luck. In the heart of New York, this place reminds me of my time and my students on the reservation in Arizona.

So why on earth would I want to bring my green curriculum, my passion, and every resource I could muster here to this "Never, Never, Neverland"? I knew when I arrived in Claremont Village that there could not be a more difficult place to work. This was going to be the heaviest lift yet for the Green Bronx Machine.

That supersize challenge fired me up. Imagine the impact if we could succeed.

"Steve, I have a big room on the fourth floor that needs a new purpose," Torres had told me a few months earlier. "It used to be the school library." Over the years, the space had become a dumping ground for everything that was outdated, underutilized, or badly in need of repair. It was the size of two classrooms. "If you want to redesign it as the home of the Green Bronx Machine," the principal offered, "it's all yours."

Torres knew that I needed a place to land. The previous spring, I thought I had worked out an agreement to move Green Bronx Machine to JVL Wildcat Academy Charter School and extend our reach with schools across Hunts Point. With a robust indoor gardening and culinary program there, I imagined connecting big kids, little kids, and the community for powerful learning experiences.

The plan seemed so solid, I resigned from my post at Hyde Leadership Charter School way in advance so I could make the transition. Only days before I was due to start, an unexpected organizational shift and brand-new leadership at JVL scuttled my game plan. Some surprise. Instead of moving into a new opportunity, I was out of a job.

Torres knew he could trust me. We had partnered in the past on a number of projects, and he saw how readily his students and teachers connected with me. Frankly, that was a shift from his first impression.

"I thought you were a crazy guy when I first met you," he confided. "I thought, who needs that much energy in the building? Why would I want to add to my workload by bringing you in?" When he saw how his students responded to my energy, though, he reconsidered. "You're like Disney. You can get children to do things and try things like nobody else."

By then, I knew Torres's backstory as well. He never set out to become a public school educator. The proud son of a hardworking community man, Luis joined the military right out of high school because a guidance counselor told him he wasn't cut out for college. My sense is that the person who gave that poor advice didn't live in his neighborhood or bother to ask him about his hopes and dreams. Under different circumstances, Principal Torres could have been one of my students back at South Bronx High School. He literally grew up in the backyard on the tough streets of Watson Avenue. After ten years of heroic military service, he decided to become a hero on the front line of children's lives. In Claremont Village, he took over one of the most troubled schools in all of New York City.

Years before, my high school students had built outdoor garden structures in front of Torres's school that became the talk of the community.

Garden boxes and park benches gave people from the neighboring housing projects a safe place to socialize, and their presence helped build community and deter neighborhood crime. Even the toughest gang banger will hesitate to draw a gun around a gaggle of grandmothers. Projects like this spoke to Torres's love of community and his desire for real impact.

Later, I came back with students from JVL Wildcat and Hyde Leadership to install indoor gardens on the first floor of the school. Torres noticed an improvement in his students' behavior as soon as the plants arrived. We had teamed up on media projects, too. First it was the Disney segment *Pass the Plate*, and then a TNT *Neighborhood Sessions* episode featuring Bronx-girl-made-good Jennifer Lopez. Our little ones stole the show with flowers in their hands and mud on their faces. The night that show aired, the projects in Claremont Village practically exploded with pride. You could hear everyone proclaiming, "Those are OUR kids!" Cheers went out across the South Bronx.

By the time I joined his staff, Torres was eager to get things moving in a more positive direction. "For a long time, we have just focused on getting our children to behave. That's not enough," he told me. "We need to help these students function at a higher level to accomplish what they want in life." He knew that I understood both pedagogy and engagement.

When I joined the staff, the school was still called PS (Public School) 55. The name changed to CS (Community School) 55 a year later, signaling our shift to a community school model. Just as Majora Carter and I had envisioned years earlier, schools were wising up to community partnerships that would leverage and embed local assets. Green Bronx Machine was as local as it gets.

Instead of assigning me to a regular classroom, the principal agreed to my proposal to have me work with the entire school. My big idea was to turn that unused library space into the first National Health, Wellness, and Learning Center in the country. I wanted to transform an outdated and underutilized library into a twenty-first-century learning center, retooled for the future, with hands-on learning for students and on-the-job professional development for teachers. It would be a living lab to benefit everyone.

Not only was Torres thrilled by these ideas, but I made him a financial offer that no visionary principal could refuse: "Just pay me for one day a week as if I am retired. I'll be here five more days a week as a volunteer." I promised to do all the fund-raising and construction myself for the new National Health, Wellness, and Learning Center. I just wasn't sure quite how.

After years of working with adolescents who had to be coaxed and cajoled into learning, in this new setting I was surrounded by little children who got excited if you offered them a smile and a handshake. They practically ran into class to find out what Mr. Farmer Steve was up to each day. They recognized me from the Disney special and from the J.Lo celebration. They expected excitement. Equally exciting for me, I got to be the oldest sixth grader in the Bronx in a school that only went up to the fifth grade. I may have acted like a big kid, but I could do long division in my head. I had a driver's license. And now I had my own master key to the building.

Our first task: Build our classroom farm. "This is a big project," I explained to the wide-eyed students. "I'm going to need everyone's help to put all these pieces together." Just as I had seen with older students at JVL, these little guys quickly found ways to contribute. Some sorted pieces, some assembled, and together we managed to get six Tower Gardens ready to plant.

"Now we're going to do something even bigger," I promised them. "We're going to create life." Little farmers eagerly pushed seeds into seedbeds and waited patiently for them to germinate under grow lights. While they waited, we learned about making predictions, fractions, and calculating percentages. Once the seeds sprouted into seedlings, we transplanted them into our towers. Students became scholars and sketched everything to help them understand the life cycle of plants.

Every day, there was a detailed lesson plan behind each adventure, carefully mapped to academic learning goals. Sometimes I crafted those lesson plans with other teachers, helping them with curriculum design. Some days, I modeled lessons while teachers observed. Other times, I'd be the one observing and coaching teachers on their craft. Every day was another chance for learning to happen across the curriculum and throughout the building.

More and more adventures unfolded almost daily. I ordered one thousand butterfly cocoons for our future butterfly garden and delivered a batch to each classroom to observe. "Butterfly delivery!" I would sing out when I walked into the room.

I ordered worms for our outdoor garden boxes and recruited a team of willing volunteers—led by the enthusiastic student I nicknamed Worm Girl—to care for them.

I started recruiting little engineers to test-drive spin bikes that I planned to use to power blenders for making smoothies.

When I noticed that children with attention challenges seemed to get calmer around our indoor farm, I invited them to come read to the plants. This generated important information to improve instruction. Students who struggle with reading typically hate to read aloud in class. That makes it hard to know why they're struggling. But the same students love reading to plants. While they read, I listened—and planned instructional moves accordingly.

Excitement spread from room to room as children—and teachers and even parents—wondered what in the world Mr. Ritz was up to next. I even kept a hidden stash of big plants. When students did a great job on a lesson, I would swap little plants for big ones and give my little farmers all the credit. "Look how the plants responded," I'd tell them after recess. "You're really helping them grow." And best of all, they believed me and came back to work even harder.

Our wellness center wasn't fully built yet, but it was already generating plenty of active learning and a positive, playful culture. When one of the boys called me Father Nature, the nickname stuck. When I praised the students for being science geeks, they responded with chants of "Geeks! Geeks! Geeks!" and "Nerd Power!"

Before we knew it, our little classroom farm was producing enough lettuce to supply salads for a weekly "lunch and learn" with the principal. Torres and a handful of children would arrive in my fourth-floor room each Friday. Many of those invited for these special events were the same children who used to be sent to the principal's office for getting into trouble. Now they were welcoming the principal to be their lunch guest and talk about things worth knowing. Passion, purpose, and hope were getting infused into the school culture.

"You know, people are starting to think differently about the children at this school," Torres told them. "We think you're going to do things that nobody expected of you."

"Like what?" one of the fifth graders asked.

"Like go to a great school like the Bronx High School of Science," the principal replied. "Who's ever heard of that school?"

Only a couple hands went up, but I quickly reminded students that they already knew a graduate of our borough's most esteemed secondary school. "Remember when you met my daughter, Michaela?" Heads nodded and smiles flashed across several faces. By now, Michaela was in college but still took part in Green Bronx Machine adventures when she was home on breaks. "That was her high school." In a community where only a small fraction of parents had completed high school, our children needed relatable role models to inspire their academic futures.

What else did they want to talk about? Health was a favorite topic. When I told them that I used to be fat—a full one hundred pounds heavier—they didn't believe me. I had to bring out photos and the XXL T-shirts that looked big enough to clothe two of me. That was good for laughs, but my example got us talking about the choices we all make about food, including the sugar in our diets and how our tastes are shaped by advertising.

"We hope that what you're learning here about being healthier, you'll teach your families at home," Torres told them. That prompted several students to talk about making dinner salads with the fresh produce that we were sending home to families each week.

Older students who had been attending this school for several years were quick to notice the changes happening all around them. From the addition of a salad bar in the cafeteria to the new features in my classroom, they noticed what was new—and wondered what was next.

"You guys have a lot of good ideas," I told them. "I bet some of your classmates do, too." That got heads nodding. "Principal Torres, what would you think of putting up some suggestion boxes?"

Not only did he support that idea, but he encouraged students to use their voice in other ways to help the school. That led to the launch of our first student government and a school-wide election to choose officers.

Whether it was over a shared lunch or a lesson in a classroom farm, food gave us a natural entry point for learning about all kinds of things that mattered. At CS 55, 100 percent of students are on free and reduced lunch. Across the community, 37.9 percent of residents are food insecure, lacking reliable access to affordable nutrition.

Hunger is the most noticeable symptom of problems that run much deeper. This borough leads the state in rates of adult diabetes, childhood diabetes, juvenile coronary disease, juvenile obesity, high blood pressure, and hypertension. In a cruel irony that affects many of our families, obesity is the new face of hunger. People fill up and fill out on cheap foods that are calorie dense but nutritionally bankrupt. I call it a MESS: manufactured edible synthetic substances. This community is filled with a MESS. While some people call this community a food desert, I call it a food swamp.

Tragically, children and parents who believe they are making good, healthy decisions are actually eating and drinking themselves fat and sick. Marketing disguises unhealthy choices as "natural" or "low-fat" (but still loaded with sugar). Fast-food outlets with ninety-nine-cent menus perch on street corners that children pass as they go to and from school.

Among all this branded and celebrity-endorsed junk, where was the "official healthy food" for children? How could we get back to healthier and simpler times? How could we make better decisions about building blocks of health? These questions ate at me.

Of course, hunger is also a symptom of joblessness and other issues. The immediate neighborhood around CS 55 has the highest rate of chronic unemployment, underemployment, second opportunity programs, homelessness, incarceration and crime rates, and children in shelters in the Bronx. A tremendous number of children are being raised by someone other than their parents or living in single-parent households. At any given moment, on any given day, in broad daylight, you will see scores of people congregating on Claremont Village sidewalks with seemingly nothing to do and nowhere to go. Liquor, lotto, and cigarettes are sold everywhere yet the community has neither a bank nor a public library. Instead, there are pawnshops and check-cashing counters on every block. Food pantries and food lines are everywhere. Despite being fully apprised of the data related to health disparities in the community, seeing it up close and daily continued to stun me and motivate me. In the heart of the hip-hop nation, looking at all these hungry people, I thought of Woody Guthrie's famous anthem and wondered, was this land made fairly for you and me?

I wanted the school to become a place for people to congregate for all the best reasons. And for a community that has limited means and limited access to healthy fresh food, I knew we could grow and provide it all year long, with learning experiences aligned to Common Core and Next Generation Science Standards.

While I was exploring ways to fund my vision for the center, Torres and I got busy on the fixes that were within easier reach. First came a lighting upgrade for the whole building. We got rid of outdated fluorescent lights that flickered and buzzed. The old lights also contained toxic mercury. In went high-efficiency lighting that bathed every room and hallway in a warm glow. The building felt better overnight. That was our first step out of the dark ages and into a bright new future.

To figure out what else was fixable, I started researching the relationship between the built environment and learning. I found architects willing to share their insights, including Jonathan Rose Companies and KSS Architects. I researched color schemes as they related to emotion and learning. I didn't want to overlook a single detail that might matter.

Although I wanted to fix everything overnight, change comes slowly to public schools. Blueprints were missing for a building this old. Electrical systems had to be overhauled. Feasibility studies were needed. Capital funding was limited, but that didn't stop me. I paid for many repairs out of my own pocket, even hand-delivering checks to the department of education to expedite the process. Even though I wanted to zip along like a speedboat, I knew I was riding in a large cruise ship docked in a tight pier. Nonetheless, every little change mattered.

"Steve, everything seems so much brighter. Even the walls look less dingy," one of the teachers told me. We put up new bulletin boards so that teachers could showcase student work and make good thinking visible throughout the building.

Principal Torres saw that I was true to my word, showing up daily from six a.m. to six p.m. or later, and always on Saturdays when I would spend time with parents and children, building community and becoming part of the fabric. When I offered to run a gardening club, I had sixty aspiring farmers show up daily after school. I worked with anybody and everybody in the building who was willing to team up, from parents and older siblings to custodians, cafeteria staff, and teachers. Best of all, everyone knew I didn't have the authority to write them up or pass judgment on their performance. Nor did I want to; I was only there to help.

As I worked with little ones, I noticed that most of the children getting sent to the office for disciplinary reasons were either overweight or were there because of a relationship or comment made to or from another obese or "body type"–insecure student. I didn't need a statistician to tell me that children who were overweight were being bullied or bullying, and issues around weight and body were often at the core of the problem. Obese children were not the ones picked for sports teams. They weren't part of the fashion show or dance team. They were never in the "in" crowd. I wanted no child to experience that pain, that shame, and the subsequent illness, discomfort, and dis-ease that would follow. I knew what it meant to be the "fat guy," but I understood even better how differently the world treated and perceived a slimmer, trimmer version of me. I wanted that life and reality for all my students.

When I had a chance to talk with children sent to the office, I would start with simple questions, nothing confrontational. "Did you have breakfast today?" I'd ask. "No," was a common answer. Beyond the no came some of the most shocking responses. For far too many, breakfast was soda, bags of cookies, candy, chocolate, energy drinks. What child really needs a sugar-sweetened energy drink? Why start the day with something that's nutritionally bankrupt and dense with sugar or loaded with high-fructose corn syrup? I began to think back on how many times, at how many different schools, I had seen children come to the dean's office and be bribed or pacified with snacks, chocolate, or candy.

I knew we were making progress when our new student council voted to remove chocolate milk from the lunchroom. Instead of being manipulated by jingles that encouraged them to "crave the wave," "obey their thirst," or "eat and be happy," our students were learning to make better choices for themselves. Principal Torres installed water jets in the cafeteria, and as a community we came to make and appreciate healthy decisions.

People from across the city and beyond began to take notice of our community school in the projects. We struck new partnerships and reconnected with organizations like Gotham Greens, which had been so helpful to my JVL students in the past. They provided us with seedlings to plant and nurture as well as freshly harvested vegetables to send home to families every week. I wanted our young farmers to see the seedlings and the harvest at the same time so they could envision where their efforts would lead.

Like butterflies in spring, people were attracted to our blossoming programs. Some of the most grateful parents were immigrants in our community. Many had arrived here with a taste for fresh produce from their home cultures, but they had no place to access it locally. Instead, they were finding out what it meant to be hungry. Many of these parents were also eager to get more involved with school. They valued education as their children's best hope for living the American dream.

In the summer, a crew of parent volunteers took over our outdoor school garden. We took advantage of the opportunity to offer classes to adults. Outdoors in the summer sun, surrounded by ripening strawberries and cucumbers that grew halfway up the school, parents came together to improve their own reading and math skills. Every day, there would be groups of parents and grandparents waiting at the garden.

It was easy to see that many parents were hungry for education themselves if it would prepare them for better jobs—or any jobs. Families struggled with rising rents, even in this part of the South Bronx, and often had to share housing to make ends meet. At the same time, I knew that New York City was experiencing a blossoming industry in hospitality and surging interest in food. There were good jobs waiting for people who were prepared. The more I got to know these families, the more I was convinced that we had fertile conditions at CS 55 to build something great.

Four stories above street level, the lights from our classroom farm made the school windows glow at night. The light reflected on construction scaffolding that has covered the sidewalk for years, protecting pedestrians from work that never gets done. School neighbors looked on with curiosity, wondering what on earth we were growing up there. I could only imagine their speculation.

Students' rapidly improving behavior made the whole school run more smoothly. Disciplinary issues dropped by more than 50 percent that first year. It didn't take a miracle to change behavior. Students would conduct themselves beautifully for the chance to make a smoothie or spend time in my room tending the plants. These little incentives were all they needed. Instead of the traditional disciplinary system of carrots and sticks, we focused on carrots. We had a new cheer to go with our SÍ SE PUEDE attitude as the children proclaimed, "Lettuce, turnip, the beet!"

In a school that had always struggled with a variety of staffing issues, we started getting résumés from talented educators who wanted to join us. Everyone needed to step up their performance. We went from a school where few new teachers wanted to work to one where teachers competed for spots. Many had heard about our ongoing professional development opportunities and the learning environment that invites innovation and collaboration.

Our results brought attention from far beyond the Bronx. My first year, we won a Best of Green Schools award, one of only ten given by the US Green Building Council. News travels fast. All the way across the Atlantic, a London journalist wrote about us in the *Guardian*. That article went viral. Then, catching me by complete surprise, someone who had seen the coverage nominated me for an award called the Global Teacher Prize, the equivalent of a Nobel Prize for education. I found out that I had to submit a detailed application to be considered as a nominee. Frankly, I thought it was a prank.

When I saw the required paperwork, I was initially shocked. But quickly thrilled. The essay questions weren't so daunting after all. They gave me the perfect prompts to fully describe and refine my vision. The answers came naturally. I luxuriated in that application. This wasn't labor; this was love! Here was a chance to reflect on all that I had learned by starting Green Bronx Machine and then lay out a road map of what I hoped to accomplish next with the National Health, Wellness, and Learning Center. So far, the completed center existed only on paper and in my imagination. Imagine what I could do with a million-dollar prize, or even a little slice of it.

When I learned that I had been named one of the top-fifty finalists, I was shocked all over again. I must be onto something. That recognition spurred me on to continue designing and refining our green classroom. Then things started to accelerate.

In January, I learned that I was a top-ten finalist, selected out of a pool of approximately eight thousand teachers from around the world. That brought an international film crew to the Bronx to capture the work. I insisted that the video focus on the entire school, not on me. It was filled with our children's voices and stories, filmed against a backdrop of beautiful green plants.

The Global Teacher Prize, sponsored by the Varkey Foundation, is part of a well-orchestrated international campaign to elevate the status of teachers around the world. Sharing compelling stories from the classroom is just the start. In February, as a result of that Global Teacher Prize video, I received an unexpected invitation. I was being summoned to the Vatican. From hope to the Pope, I was off to meet His Holiness to be part of a task force focusing on global education initiatives. I had always dreamed of seeing the garden at the Vatican. The thought of actually meeting Pope Francis face-to-face was beyond my wildest fantasies. I'm not Catholic, but this pope had been speaking to me, my community, and the wider world for months. His message of love, inclusivity, and care for the planet resonated with all that I did. His Holiness didn't know that I already had a picture of him in my classroom or that oppressed people across the South Bronx cheered his efforts to lift up the downtrodden. He truly was the People's Pope. I was eager to bring back his blessings and an autographed photo of the two of us.

As excited as I was, I couldn't speak a word to anyone about my upcoming trip to the Vatican. It was all hush-hush, under a nondisclosure agreement. I arrived at a hotel in Rome on a rainy night and looked for the two other teachers who were also there to represent the Global Teacher Prize.

Richard Spencer, a science teacher from England, looked as lost as I was. Daniele Manni, an Italian, greeted us with fresh loaves of bread practically warm from the oven. The three of us bonded immediately. None of us knew what to expect over the coming days.

Arriving at Vatican City the next morning was like stepping into a time machine. I struggled to imagine how many people had walked over these same brick pavers. How many carpenters had it taken to install the forty-foot-tall, carved wooden doors? We walked past one gilded library after another as we made our way to a meeting room where we spent the next two days with educators and experts from around the globe.

Our charge from the pope was to design a plan to serve the millions of children who are not currently in school. The numbers were so staggering— sixty-five million adolescents, fifty-nine million primary-age children—that I couldn't wrap my mind around the scale of the problem. I kept thinking back to Joel Makower at the Verge conference, challenging me, "What's your ask?" Somehow, we cobbled together a ten-page plan to present to His Holiness. Together with a team of twenty from the Varkey Foundation, my two teacher buddies and I sealed our pledge to serve the world's children with handprints. Mine were green.

Our big meeting with Pope Francis included a sea of dignitaries and conference calls with children around the world. In a packed room where everyone wanted his attention, His Holiness zeroed in on the children. His genuine concern for each child came through profoundly. By the time it was my turn for a brief face-to-face meeting and photograph, I was already emotional. When Pope Francis looked me in the eyes, I felt as if he was touching my very soul. When he leaned in to kiss my cheek, I cried. And then I kissed him right back and told him I loved him.

In March I was off again, this time to the Global Teacher Prize awards ceremony in Dubai. The thought of being in a room with the best teachers and change makers in the world was beyond thrilling. I watched each finalist's video in advance, learning about the incredible work happening in classrooms in Vietnam, Haiti, rural America, and every other corner of the world. I rooted for other finalists to win, not myself. I never went to compete but rather to complete a team. The premise or motto behind the Global Teacher Prize that screams *"teachers matter"* was near and dear to me. This was a movement I wanted to be a part of.

When I met Vikas Pota, CEO of the Varkey Foundation, he helped me understand the bigger goals of this initiative. "The best way of affording quality education to every child is to make sure there's a great teacher in the classroom. But today we have a crisis. Around the world, nobody wants to go into teaching. Everywhere, there is a struggle with recruiting and retaining teachers. We hope to change that by showing the magic that happens in the classroom," he said, and encouraging young people to pursue careers in education.

Apparently, the prize committee found that magic in my school. Pota was so intrigued by Green Bronx Machine, he traveled to the Bronx to see it for himself. "Here you are, working in New York, which is meant to be one of the leading cities in the world. Yet your school is so disadvantaged and isolated, it might as well be in Somalia," he told me. "The contradictions are so stark. And yet you are there by choice, bringing so much infectious energy to change children's lives."

Hearing this stark assessment from an outsider was shocking. Somalia? Really? I couldn't argue with the data about our community. Growing up in the South Bronx puts you on track for a higher chance of chronic disease and a shorter life. When an outsider could spot the inequality in those numbers, I became determined to work harder to change them.

I was humbled beyond words by the attention, but even more humbled by the colleagues I met in Dubai. Fostering collaboration among these esteemed teachers is another deliberate goal of the Global Teacher Prize. "We want to create a global community by bringing together the best teachers in the world," Pota explained. "How can we codify what you know? How can we make your strategies and resources available to every teacher in the world? We don't want to focus on lone heroes. We want to scale great teaching."

Scale. Replication. Community building. Networks. Everything I learned through the Global Teacher Prize experience inspired me to go home and extend the reach of Green Bronx Machine. As soon as I got back to the Bronx, I donated the entirety of my $25,000 in prize money—given in recognition of being a top-ten finalist—to start constructing the National Health, Wellness, and Learning Center that I had been imagining for months. I raised the rest of the budget with T-shirt sales, crowdfunding appeals, and other slow-drip fund-raising efforts. In a community of privilege, a fund-raising campaign like this would have happened overnight. Not here in Claremont Village. For us, every step forward required putting on the work gloves, getting down, and getting dirty.

On a May morning in 2016, our team of fourth and fifth graders were ready for action. This was their moment. Wearing Green Bronx Machine aprons, bow ties, and straw hats, these thirty ambassadors practiced their greeting: "Welcome to the National Health, Wellness, and Learning Center at CS 55!" In less than an hour, they would be the official greeters, demonstrators, celebrity photographers, and hors d'oeuvres servers at the grand opening of this sixty-eight-by-thirty-five-foot, state-of-the-art space, which had taken us eighteen months to complete. We were expecting a crowd.

Lizette and I had spent the previous day giving the room a final tune-up. In one corner, our six Tower Gardens were resplendent with bright green lettuces and fragrant herbs. We tested the stationary bikes, which send real-time data to an electronic dashboard to track workout time, calories burned, and energy generated to power the blenders. We checked the mobile kitchen, making sure we had the video camera attached at the right angle so that viewers could watch the chef's handiwork on the screen. Like a NASA engineering team, we did a final check of our rocket launcher, which we planned to set off just as Bronx Borough President Ruben Diaz Jr. cut the grand-opening green ribbon.

As we closed up late that evening, I took a moment to think about where this all began. A year and a half earlier, this space was jammed floor to ceiling with outdated materials and old encyclopedias, broken furniture, ancient report cards, cathode-ray monitors, rotary telephones, and more. Six months earlier, the children and I had given another TEDxManhattan talk, claiming we could change the way we live, eat, and learn and change outcomes for this and future generations. That had earned us a standing ovation but no wave of funding. Clearing out the old classroom had taken our immediate family—Team Ritz—plus more volunteers, Green Bronx Machine graduates, and custodial staff scores of trips up and down four flights of stairs on hot summer days.

Once the room was empty, we tackled the cracked plaster and ripped out ancient linoleum down to the asbestos floors, which had to be remediated by workers with masks. We took walls down to studs so that crews could install new electrical wiring, new plumbing, green floor tiles, and a dedicated Internet line. All that had to happen before we could furnish the room with flexible classroom furniture, an interactive smart board for teaching with multimedia content, and cabinets to store supplies for science experiments and cooking lessons. Everything reflected my research and experience in designing effective learning environments.

Even before construction was finished, the center started attracting attention. PBS heard about us and came to film a segment for *American Graduate*, a special project featuring community-based solutions to keep youth on track to earn high school diplomas. The crew had to do the shoot on a bare wooden floor because the center was still under construction. Our shiny, bright green flooring wasn't installed until weeks later. NPR did a radio show capturing the voices of our children proudly proclaiming, "Nerds! Nerds! Nerds!"

The morning of the open house, visitors began arriving well ahead of schedule; we had barely rolled out the green carpet and welcome sign. My student greeters were on the job early, politely inviting adults to step onto a square of green carpet and have a photograph taken. "Excuse me, but do you have a business card?" asked a girl named Elanny, who was determined to get every visitor's contact information. The cards quickly grew into a stack of potential partners and contacts from business, government, and nonprofits.

By the time New York State Education Chancellor Dr. Betty Rosa from the state Board of Regents arrived with a coterie of colleagues, the place was buzzing. Teams of students demonstrated each of the learning stations. Children challenged adults to race them on the spin bikes, which in turn powered the blenders to make fruit smoothies. Nearby, a crew of Green Bronx Machine hosts escorted guests to our mobile kitchen where Chef Roberto, a young man from the neighborhood, was whipping up hummus flavored with herbs from our classroom garden. Another team of students showed visitors how the Tower Gardens work.

Politicians worked the room, as well, including Bronx Borough President Ruben Diaz Jr., who went out of his way to acknowledge our own student council president. She beamed when he called her Madam President. He and Principal Torres, friends since their own Bronx boyhoods, share a deep commitment to lifting up the community. Local NYC Council Member Vanessa Gibson and Assemblyman Michael Blake, both frequent visitors to the school, were delighted to join us.

Like the visiting staff from Senator Rivera's office, these dignitaries all looked like grown-up versions of my students. Most were African American or Latino, and many had learned English as a second language before launching successful careers. By speaking with my students and asking them questions, these adults made students feel valued. Local leaders appreciate the need for specialized programs in communities like ours. They also know that engaged students today are registered voters tomorrow. They are my organically grown citizens. Together we screamed "*Sí se puede!*" for the video cameras and raised our fists in glorious celebration.

Talking to a video crew from MSNBC sent to profile our program for the Reverend Al Sharpton's show, Diaz insisted that the neighborhoods where today's children are growing up "are the safest Bronx the world has ever known. But they still face challenges, especially when it comes to health. Through their work with Green Bronx Machine, these young peo-ple are ambassadors. I'm happy to see them so excited and curious to learn. When they take this knowledge home to their families, they're becoming agents for change." On his show, the Reverend Al had proclaimed, "No justice, no peas!"

As I watched more than a hundred people interact with the dynamic features of our classroom, I spotted so many partners and community members who had helped us get to this point. Don Fernandez, a local guy made good, was the one who had donated the paint for our sky-blue walls. He was there, even though his mother had passed away just days earlier. A local business owner and carpenter, an immigrant-turned-entrepreneur named Alfredo Sosa, had installed our kitchen cabinets and counters. In the process, he said he loved helping to build a school where he would be proud to send his own children. There was Alan Sharkany from Ferguson Enterprises. He not only donated a refrigerator but delivered it four stories up in a building with no elevator. Our longtime friends from Gotham Greens not only showed up but also donated fresh greens to send home with our students as part of the celebration.

What everyone noticed most of all was how much fun the children were having. Students ran the equipment. They did the demonstrations. They provided the narration. They were the teachers. They made their thinking visible. It was a perfect celebration of all our collisions, connec-tions, and co-learnings.

CHAPTER 14

FROM CLASSROOM FARM TO CLASSROOM TABLE

Spring 2013—A year after my debut on the TEDxManhattan stage, Diane Hatz had invited me back to give an update. By then I was in much better physical shape. By following my own advice about healthy eating, I had lost weight and kept it off. I liked to hold up my old XXL T-shirt as a sight gag. Even I was amazed. This time around, I wasn't convalescing from surgery. I had my eyes wide open for possible collisions, connections, and co-learnings to help Green Bronx Machine reach even more schools and communities.

While I was roaming around backstage waiting for my turn to talk, a soft-spoken gentleman wearing titanium glasses and expensive-looking shoes walked up to me. Before we could even exchange names, he asked if my photographs were copyrighted.

"No, why?" I wondered.

"I plan to use them in my presentation," he said. "It's so great to finally meet the guy from the Bronx!"

I don't meet many gentlemen in my line of work. This guy was elegant, eloquent, and seemed to know all about me.

Then he introduced himself. "I'm Bill Yosses. I've been the White House executive pastry chef for the last two presidents. You know," he added, "everyone in the White House kitchen has enjoyed watching your last TED talk."

I was dumbfounded. This fellow was so unassuming, so cordial—and so connected. He worked at the White House—and he knew who I was! As we shook hands and exchanged pleasantries, I was thinking to myself, *What an awesome job! Who knew that the president has his own pastry chef?*

I had been so busy running my own program, I didn't realize that improving children's eating habits had become a top priority of First Lady Michelle Obama. Chef Yosses helped me understand that my Bronx students and I were part of something much bigger. He explained to me that the White House kitchen staff was very diverse, and everyone there appreciated our efforts to bring students of color into the healthier eating movement. In a heartbeat, I started to imagine what might happen if we could find a way to team up.

When it was the chef's turn to take the TEDx stage, his message about rising childhood obesity rates and Americans' poor eating habits clearly echoed my own concerns. But what a contrast when it came to presentation styles. While I was a whirling dervish onstage, his delivery was calm, thoughtful, almost reserved. He commanded the audience's attention with beautiful posture and well-chosen words. I was dressed in my usual Green Bronx Machine T-shirt and khakis. He was immaculately turned out in menswear that looked like it came from a European designer. And he was wearing the most beautiful pointy-toed leather shoes I'd ever seen. He advocated for what he called "a hedonistic culture of healthy eating." I was mesmerized.

Over the next few months, we stayed in touch by e-mail. I got myself more familiar with the First Lady's Let's Move initiative for children and learned about the White House vegetable garden planted under her direction. When Chef Yosses invited me to bring some students to visit the

White House the following spring, I told my farmers to get ready for an adventure.

Preparing for an overnight field trip took legwork, especially with young ones who had never left the Bronx let alone the state. I scrambled to raise funds and secure in-kind donations. We had to rent two vans to carry fifteen of our Green Bronx Machine ambassadors, plus adult chaperones. I hand-picked students of different ages, including older teens from JVL Wildcat Academy Charter School and some little guys from Hyde Leadership Charter School. They all had to jump through academic, behavioral, and attendance hoops to earn the privilege of coming along. Everybody needed a signed per-mission slip from home. Because they would be missing school days, I insisted that they keep a journal to capture their learnings from the experi-ence. Some already had pages of details before we left the parking lot.

The morning we pulled out of the South Bronx, we felt like explorers setting forth on an expedition. Even the big kids had their eyes glued to the windows as we left New York City behind and headed south toward Penn-sylvania. I was driving the lead vehicle; Lizette followed in a second van. As we headed over the George Washington Bridge, we made sure we had each other's cell numbers on speed dial.

First stop: Amish country.

"No traffic. No stores. No projects. Not even any streetlights. What is this place?" one of my teenage students said as he clambered out of the van. This wasn't just rural America—it was *Amish* America! That meant old-fashioned, labor-intensive farming with no modern technology or even electricity to make the work easier.

"People here live and work this way by choice," I explained to my stu-dents. "We live by our rules in the Bronx. The Amish have theirs."

"Man, they sure are doing it the hard way!" Giovanni said.

I let that sink in while thinking to myself, *Right, and you guys are always saying you wish life was easier.*

As excited as my students were to see horse-drawn buggies and old-fashioned farming equipment, they were equally amazed to see fields clothed in pure, white snow after a late storm. By early spring, any remaining snow in the South Bronx is the color of soot. Every last child—even the oldest teenagers (and the adult chaperones)—made snow angels.

To show my students that they have more in common with Amish farmers than they might guess, we stopped to see Farmer Sam. He is a legend, known throughout the agricultural industry for vertical farming. Abandoning ninety acres of pasture farming, he concentrates his business on a one-acre greenhouse where he uses hydroponics and aeroponics to grow produce year-round.

And make no mistake—this is a big business. Farmer Sam supplies companies like Whole Foods yet still manages to follow Amish tradition. He just subs out any work that involves technology.

"Cool. The dude keeps the faith," said Tito, one of the older boys.

The younger children were in love with the beauty of the place. They all clamored to feed the tilapia.

Dressed in black pants, suspenders, and black hat, Farmer Sam gave us a tour of the whole facility. As he talked about the science behind his greenhouse, my little farmers hung on his every word. "It works just like our Tower Gardens," said Armani, who was dwarfed by the rows of tomatoes that stretched to the ceiling. Imagine that—something we were doing in class also happened in the real world!

Then we were off to the nation's capital for the main event. A generous sponsor who had heard me speak at a social responsibility summit had lined up accommodations for us at the Ritz-Carlton in Arlington, Virginia, just across the Potomac River from the District. As we piled out of our vans with our luggage and backpacks, I watched my students' eyes widen. Bellhops and grand lobbies were things they had only glimpsed in Hollywood movies. A few children had never even seen carpeting before, let alone chandeliers and afternoon tea service. Lizette, eager to keep our young visitors on their best behavior, told students that the fountains and sprinklers were actually video cameras. Of course, they believed her.

I kept a careful eye on one of our youngest students. At a public event a few months earlier where we sold Green Bronx Machine T-shirts as a fund-raiser, Enrique had walked away with all the money in our cash box. This ten-year-old had smuggled out $1,000 by tucking it inside his stuffed animal. His plan was clever but not foolproof. When I showed up on his doorstop early on a Saturday morning and confronted him with my suspicions, he told me he only wanted the money to buy candy and comics. Thinking about my own Little Rascals capers when I was a kid, I decided Enrique deserved a second chance. How do you write off a ten-year-old child? He had been behaving like a model citizen ever since the attempted heist. And now he was about to visit the White House.

The next morning, Chef Yosses met us outside the White House gates. He was dressed in his pristine whites with an official White House monogram on his chef's coat. He led us on a VIP tour, sharing his favorite features and hidden treasures of the house and grounds. Even after more than a decade of working at the White House—first for President George W. Bush and then for President Obama—it was obvious that he took nothing for granted.

"Today's your chance to see American history close up. I always feel privileged to be here where so much began. It's the brilliance of this country," he told my spellbound students, "that a bunch of men who were self-taught came up with our system of government."

As much as my students loved the VIP tour of the house and grounds—including a glimpse of the vegetable garden and beehives—they really perked up when we arrived at the kitchen. It seemed so tiny. None of us could imagine how all the courses for an elaborate state dinner could come out of such a little space.

My students were full of questions, especially the older ones who had been in the culinary training program at JVL Wildcat Academy. Aspiring chefs themselves, they had technical questions about everything from making the perfect piecrust to estimating the right quantities to feed a crowd. They also wanted to know about Yosses's earlier work, reigning over some of New York's most notable restaurants. He took time to answer every question in detail. When my children starting calling our host Chef Bill, I could see that he had fallen in love with them.

The biggest takeaway for most of our children was how many people who looked just like them worked in the White House. They didn't have to sneak their way inside. They belonged here.

"How did they get hired?" Enrique wanted to know.

"They applied!" Chef Bill said simply. Children need to see it in order to be it.

Kind and patient as he was with my students, Chef Bill also gave us a glimpse of the demeanor that he brings to the job. He took us to the cake room, a special work area where his assistants were already working on a gingerbread replica of the White House that would be a crowd-pleasing decoration come holiday season. Work began a year in advance on some food projects. As soon as the chef arrived, his assistants snapped to attention. Without a word, he commanded their respect like a general. He could have been Washington crossing the Delaware. I noticed some of my older students studying the interactions, too, perhaps imagining themselves someday in the role of top chef.

When that magical tour ended, nobody wanted to say good-bye. We all invited Chef Bill to come visit us in the South Bronx. "Maybe I will," he said with a gentle smile. I don't think any of us imagined where that invitation would lead.

A few months later, Yosses was heading to Manhattan to do a cooking demonstration at a massively popular event sponsored by the *New York Times* called Taste of the World. People queued up by the thousands, many with children in tow, at the Javits Center for this annual event to learn about culinary trends and sample foods from around the globe. Participating in Taste of the World marked a career transition for Yosses. He had just announced that he was leaving the White House to launch his own organization. The man nicknamed "The Crustmaster" by President Obama was retiring his whisk, as the *New York Times* put it, to promote healthy eating. In particular, he wanted to focus on improving wellness and reducing obesity among America's youth.

"Do you have some students who would like to cook with me?" he asked me over the phone. When he paused for my response, I could picture him smiling.

As a dry run for the big event, Chef Bill came uptown to the Bronx. In advance of his visit, my elementary students and I had been growing the ingredients he wanted to use for making Tower Garden Tacos. We had planted six Tower Gardens with cilantro, scallions, lettuce, and all the other herbs the chef requested. Our plants looked luscious and smelled even better. We waited to harvest until he arrived so that everything would be as fresh as possible.

When the chef arrived, my sous chefs—ranging from grade three to high school—were ready and waiting in Green Bronx Machine aprons and scrubbed hands. Along with my usual all-ages participants from the South Bronx, we also happened to have some students visiting from Mexico. Everybody wanted a chance to cook with the White House chef. There was no stove or sink. We made do with a couple hot plates and some big tubs for cleaning vegetables. The results were a little messy but delicious.

The weekend of the event, our friend Farmer Duane, the Gucci Farmer, helped us haul our Tower Gardens to the Javits Center. Lizette and I brought two vanloads of students. The students took turns working in the demonstration kitchen, preparing their mouthwatering tacos and explaining how the Tower Garden worked. They were surrounded by some of the best-known chefs and top-selling cookbook authors in the country, including Chef Bobo, Victor Bongo, and SuperChefs founder Dr. Greg Chang. Among all those celebrities and the throngs of attendees, my students looked right at home. In fact, in their minds, they stole the show. And why not? They were personal friends with Chef Bill. They knew a guy.

With the cooking operations under control, I stepped away to wander through the exhibits and see what else I could learn. Perfect time for a collision! In a nearby demonstration area, I saw Greg Chang using what looked like a kitchen on wheels. I got just as excited as when I'd first seen the Tower Garden. With a few tweaks, this thing could transform any classroom into a place for culinary education and food science experiments. I squeezed through the crowd to get a closer view and jotted down the name of the vendor listed on the side of the kitchen unit.

As soon as the show was over and our children were safely home again, I started researching. By Monday, I had tracked down the vendor. Port Equip by Stephenson Custom Case Company happened to be based in Canada. The company's typical clients were arenas and sports stadiums with big budgets, not classrooms in poor neighborhoods. But my phone call piqued the curiosity of John and Debra Stephenson, husband-and-wife co-owners.

Maybe John was simply being a polite Canadian, but he didn't hang up when I launched into my pitch. "Do you realize what you have here?" I asked him. With each nerdy question I asked—about voltage, self-contained marine sink, locking wheels—the more interested he sounded. I felt like

Dr. Emmett Brown from *Back to the Future*, working out the specs for his flux capacitor. My goal wasn't time travel, but it felt almost as revolutionary.

"Do you realize the United States alone has more than one hundred thousand schools? What if they all had a kitchen on wheels that you could move from class to class and just plug into the wall? What if children didn't just grow healthy food but learned how to cook it, too?" I asked him.

Remodeling a school to incorporate a teaching kitchen could easily cost upwards of $150,000. Done right, a mobile unit would be a tiny fraction of that cost. I gave him a condensed version of everything I had been learning about healthy eating and childhood wellness. Didn't he want to be at the forefront of this movement? He soon brought his wife into the conversation. They both shared my enthusiasm for helping children live healthier lives.

Within a year, Port Equip had donated the prototype for what we have called the Green Bronx Machine Mobile Classroom Kitchen. It meets every safety and compliance regulation for school use across the United States and Canada and also represents a nifty bit of international collaboration. The components are manufactured in the States and assembled in Canada. All the tweaks to make it classroom friendly were tested right in the National Health, Learning, and Wellness Center in the South Bronx. Anything that's Bronx-tested is like having a gold seal for durability. It is a complete commercial kitchen, 100 percent portable and on wheels.

As excited as my students get about tending the plants and doing experiments with Mr. Farmer Steve, they're beyond thrilled when Chef Bill comes to school. Ever since we installed our first mobile kitchen, he's been volunteering to teach a culinary lesson every month.

Why would a guy who could work anywhere he wants come to the South Bronx? "The idea that healthy, fresh food is only for the wealthy is disgraceful," I overheard him tell a visiting reporter. "We're incurring a huge debt—a buildup of disease—if we don't change the way we eat."

He makes that change not only sensible but downright tantalizing.

"I'm passing around some things for you to identify," he told a class of fourth graders one morning. "What do you think these things have in common?"

Students crowded around to look into small cups that held an assortment of dried beans. One boy, proudly wearing his own chef hat, identified a lima bean. A girl pointed out a pinto bean. With that, Chef Bill launched right into a multisensory lesson about legumes and how they fix nitrogen.

Once he had explained the science of nitrogen fixation with stories and visuals that reinforced academic vocabulary, it was time to put this new knowledge to work. "Let's wash our hands and get ready to cook!" Nobody needed to be told that twice. The children sprang into action, lining up at our hand-washing station and donning Green Bronx Machine aprons.

Today's menu item: bright-green hummus made with edamame.

"That's a legume," Chef Bill reminded the class. "So what does it fix?"

"Nitrogen!" Everybody got it. They lined up to help flavor the hummus with herbs that they selected from our classroom garden.

From the back of the room, I watched this lesson unfold. My students were getting to learn scientific content and develop collaboration skills by touching, smelling, tasting, and enjoying fresh food together. They only had to travel about twenty steps to go from tower to table to tummy. And they had a sensory memory of the day to reinforce the learning.

These are the moments when my imagination takes off. I pictured homeless parents and families in transition—of whom we have many at CS 55—getting access to our kitchen after school to cook with their children. Or adults in need of job training coming in at night to learn culinary skills, using the produce that our students had grown during class time. From production to processing, we had it all right here.

After years of trial and error, all the pieces for true community-based learning were falling into place, right here in the heart of the projects. Outside the front steps of CS 55, we had outdoor gardening containers decorated with children's art and benches where people from the neighborhood could safely congregate among the greenery. Inside, the National Health,

Wellness, and Learning Center was fully equipped as a demonstration site for active learning across the curriculum. We welcomed a steady flow of visitors—from across New York and from around the world—eager to learn from our example.

Academic results, including the best improvements in science scores for elementary students in the city, showed the measurable benefits of learning in a green classroom. New teachers were applying in droves to join a school that had previously been dogged by a variety of staffing issues and poor morale. We had community partners like Gotham Greens donating fresh produce to send home to our families every week and amazing volunteers like Chef Bill interacting with our students and teachers. Along the way, he had recruited a protégé, Chef Roberto, a young man from the neighborhood. His mother had reached out to our school to connect her son with opportunities.

After years of telling my students to make their thinking visible, here was a real-world display of all our best ideas for improving schools and uplifting communities. It wasn't theory—it was action, and it was all happening right before our eyes. Each idea and innovation represented another seed that had germinated and taken root in the South Bronx. Green Bronx Machine wasn't about to slow down. We were poised to grow something even greater.

The eyes of the future are looking back at us and they are praying for us to see beyond our own time.

—TERRY TEMPEST WILLIAMS

PART III

SHARING THE HARVEST

CHAPTER 15

EVERY COMMUNITY WANTS HAPPIER, HEALTHIER CHILDREN

Fall 2015—Call it serendipity, timing, or just dumb luck, but sometimes you find yourself in the right place at the right time with the right people. You can't anticipate or engineer these moments. But you do need to be ready to jump when a good opportunity comes along.

One such opportunity unfolded the day when I was scheduled to speak at an event called the World of Business Ideas, or WOBI, at Lincoln Center in Manhattan. Movers and shakers pay $2,995 and up to hear inspiring talks from business gurus like Jim Collins, Richard Branson—and me.

My day had started at dawn at CS 55. Rain clouds threatened as Lizette and I hunted for a space to park our rented minivan. With forty-five thousand people living in an eight-block area that's full of one-way streets and no-parking zones, plus garbage trucks that use the place as their right-of-way, the neighborhood is a daily traffic mess. I finally eased the van into an open spot and handed Lizette the keys. As we stepped away, I made a silent prayer that the van would survive the day without a scratch, or worse.

I picked up the pace as we climbed the stairs to the fourth floor to get the day rolling in the National Health, Wellness, and Learning Center. Before the first bell, I had a quick huddle with the five students who were going to join me onstage later that day. The plan was for Lizette to bring them to Lincoln Center after school in that rented van. Sujeidy, a sweet fifth grader, leaned in for a good-bye hug for Mr. Farmer Steve, as she calls me. Not one of these children had ever set foot in Lincoln Center. Two had never been to Manhattan, just across the Harlem River from the South Bronx. One had arrived in this country four months earlier from Africa.

While the students were finishing their school day, I was having lunch at P.J. Clarke's, a landmark Manhattan restaurant lined with photos of actors, politicians, and other celebrity faces. A financial services company had reserved a private room for one hundred conference VIPs. I was their guest of honor, dressed for success in my bow tie made out of Scrabble tiles, my cheese hat, and my signature GBM T-shirt. My luncheon companions favored bespoke suits and silk neckties, designer dresses, and Manolo Blahnik heels. It had to be the highest number of Rolexes per capita I'd ever seen. Any one guest's net worth was more than what I and my entire student body will earn in our lifetimes. When the waiters delivered platters of beef that could have come from a Flintstones cartoon, I kept my polite smile in place. A younger, hungrier version of me would have swallowed it whole. By now, I had learned the self-discipline to control my intake and keep my weight down; I politely opted for a salad instead.

After lunch, I greeted my students and Lizette at the stage door and hustled them backstage. Their eyes were already wide from walking through what looked to them like a palace. Against the grandeur of gold-leaf ceilings and marble sculptures, my little farmers stood out in their humble school uniforms and Green Bronx Machine aprons. Fatima, the tiniest of the bunch, balanced a straw hat atop her headscarf. In our back-stage waiting room, I was proud to see Omar and Ernest reach for the fresh fruit and politely request water instead of soda. We played a quick round of a game I call "Who Can Behave the Best?" I declared them all winners. A final few words about logistics and then it was showtime.

I took a deep breath and pushed the button to start my slideshow. Gritty images of tired, time-worn buildings; trucks spewing diesel fumes;

and broken bottles tossed on cracked sidewalks filled the giant LED screen behind me. "Welcome to the poorest congressional district in America, my home, the South Bronx," I began.

I hurried through these opening images, wanting to get quickly to the shots that show the power of possibilities. After years of tinkering, I know that our Green Bronx Machine model is scalable, replicable, and adaptable to almost any community. If it works in the Bronx, where daily challenges can seem insurmountable, I'm convinced it can work anywhere.

Out in the audience, a woman named Angela Simo Brown heard those words and leaned forward with excitement. She had traveled to Manhattan from Toronto, Canada, in search of a big idea that she could present to her company to take corporate giving in a bold new direction.

A year earlier, Bryan Pearson, the CEO of a global brand customer loyalty company called LoyaltyOne, had launched Brown on a quest: "Go find *the thing*." The right thing would involve more than writing checks to charity. The right thing would drive sustainable change. The right thing would give LoyaltyOne employees a chance to contribute their talents and energies to improve their communities.

Brown had spent months studying, attending conferences, and talking to nonprofit leaders. She had seen some promising programs but nothing that rang all the right bells. "I needed something authentic—something so good, it tells its own story," she told me later. When she heard my talk at WOBI, she thought to herself, "This is *it*. Stephen has everything figured out. Now, how can we bring this program to Canada?"

I had no idea that a potential corporate partner was sitting in one of those plush velvet seats. Nor did I dream that our solutions from the gritty South Bronx would resonate with anyone from a beautiful city like Toronto.

I neared the end of my WOBI talk, glancing over at my little farmers poised in the wings to give them the special signal. This was their moment. Out they came, pushing onto the stage one of the Tower Gardens that we use to grow food right in our classrooms. The audience went berserk. The children cheered right back, blinking and smiling in the glare of what seemed like a galaxy of spotlights. Somewhere in that sea of faces, Angela Simo Brown was beaming. Here was *the thing*. Before leaving Lincoln Center, she started writing an e-mail to me. Determined to meet with me in person before returning to Toronto, she was ready to sit down any time, any place.

Little did she know, but another set of circumstances almost prevented me from getting to our meeting. When WOBI ended that evening, Lizette and I headed back uptown with our little farmers. The rain that had threatened all day started coming down hard as we loaded up the van, but nothing dampened our spirits. We promised the children we would stop for dinner on the way home. As I drove up Broadway, I heard them calling out the names of fast-food restaurants and corner stores where we could grab a bite. I had something else in mind. Instead of eating on the run, I wanted us to sit down with knives, forks, and napkins and share a proper meal. We found a family-style restaurant on the Upper West Side and gathered around a long table. The children were so sweet that other diners stopped to compliment them on their behavior.

Fifteen hours after we started our day, we were back on the same South Bronx streets, hunting for parking spots yet again. Lizette took the wheel so I could walk each child home. Fatima's public housing complex was our second-to-the-last stop. She was still wearing her straw hat. As we got off the elevator on the nineteenth floor, I smelled marijuana before I spotted a knot of teenage boys huddled in the stairwell. I glanced away but put a protective hand on Fatima's shoulder as I walked her around the corner to her apartment. She ran into her mother's waiting arms, chattering nonstop about our adventures. She was so happy! Her mother turned to hug me, then her father leaned in to shake my hand and offer his gratitude.

This is why I do what I do, I remember thinking as I walked back down the hall. I was soaking wet and exhausted, but exhilarated by seeing how our Green Bronx Machine lifts up families along with their children. And now my phone was ringing. Lizette. The police were telling her to move along. That minivan apparently looked suspicious, loitering at the curb with a woman and child inside. "Please hurry," she said.

As I rounded the corner to the elevator, I heard the *cli-click* before I saw the gun. "Yo," the young man growled. "Give me your sneakers. Your coat. Your iPhone." His two buddies stepped up, forming a tight knot around me.

"Guys, we don't have to do this," I started in. Before I could bargain, a child emerged from the stairwell and spoke up. "Hey, he's that *sí se puede* teacher, the guy with the cheese hat. Leave him alone, man." In that long moment, it struck me that every video we had made to date included the words SÍ SE PUEDE. Those three words rewarded and afforded me and my students the most incredible opportunities. Now, with a gun in my face, they even saved my life!

I didn't pause to ponder the irony. These guys were dead ringers for the young people I've been working with for decades. Under different circumstances, they could be learning and earning with Green Bronx Machine. Instead of smoking dope in a dingy stairwell, pissed off at the world that has failed them, they could be using their smarts and skills to rebuild their own community. They could be sharing their own stories onstage, helping others understand why every child deserves the chance to experience the opportunities that come with an education powered by plants and a living curriculum. Such reflections would have to wait. I took my opening and raced to the elevator, into the minivan, and back into the neighborhoods where there is so much work still waiting to be done.

Over coffee a couple mornings later, Angela Simo Brown opened my eyes to the challenges facing Toronto and LoyaltyOne's interest in making a difference. She had gotten my attention with a series of urgent e-mails. I still didn't know anything about her company or what her job was. But something in her messages convinced me that if I just showed up to talk with her, good things would happen. I suspected that we shared a taste for the same secret sauce—passion, purpose, and hope. But when we sat down for coffee, I still couldn't imagine what she wanted from me.

"We have our own version of the Bronx," she explained. "It's not as dire as where you work, but we have pockets. One in six children in Canada lives under the poverty line. Obesity affects one in four of our young people." She told me about children going to school hungry, about families squeezed out of apartments because of rising housing costs in the urban core, about food banks that can't keep up with demand.

I was shocked. Who knew that a beautiful city like Toronto, with all its vaunted social services, would have food deserts and many of the same challenges that we face in the South Bronx? "It's not who we think we are as Canadians," Brown admitted. "This issue has kind of snuck up on us."

Throughout my years of building Green Bronx Machine, I had been cobbling together the pieces one at a time. Brown came along and saw what we were doing as a whole system for improving childhood health and community well-being. She envisioned benefits in all kinds of neighborhoods, for all kinds of children, young adults, and families. And she used language that I understood. Although she was coming from the world of business, she made it clear that her bottom line was all about relationships. In her ideal workplace, "people can bring their whole self to work," she told me. That so resonated. It's been the story of my life.

When she explained LoyaltyOne's history, I realized what a compelling partnership we might make. Their corporate model is all about developing and reinforcing consumer shopping habits. When people shop at stores that are LoyaltyOne partners—gas stations, grocery stores, drugstores, and other retailers—they earn points that they can redeem for anything from air travel to appliances. "Our program is about changing behavior," Brown told me. "That's the expertise we own. When I look at your program, I see that you're changing behavior, too."

That resonated with me as well. My goal is always to change mind-sets and landscapes. I know that's critical in the South Bronx, but she got me thinking. What if harvesting hope turns out to be a universal goal?

Then she said something else that made me sit up and take notice. "Of course we want to help children develop healthy eating habits early in life by improving food literacy and access to healthy, fresh food. But when I look at Green Bronx Machine," Brown added, "I see all these other benefits. Reductions in behavior issues at school. Better attendance. Improved academic outcomes. Let's call it collateral positivity."

Listening to her outline how she could scale the program to as many as five hundred schools across Canada, I flashed back on my missed opportunity with Joel Makower at the GreenBiz conference two years earlier. I had been speechless when he challenged me to consider "What is your ask?" Here was my answer. I realized that I was exactly where I needed to be. Through strategic partnerships, our Green Bronx Machine could reach farther and scale faster than I had ever dared to imagine. Before our conversation was over, I was compelled to map out a new curriculum that teachers everywhere could use to get off to a fast start with their green programs. There was no need for them to start from scratch. I just needed to capture my own learnings and get ready to hand them off. Best of all, Brown had local partners ready to learn and deploy our model.

I came away from that meeting with a new game plan: Get ready, world, for some collateral positivity. Green Bronx Machine was gearing up to go global.

Dubai, a wealthy city in the United Arab Emirates known for its skyscrapers and luxury shopping malls, differs in just about every respect from the South Bronx. Street crime is rare. Poverty is invisible. When I visited Dubai with the Global Teacher Prize, I was stunned by the desert beauty—and the wealth.

Frankly, I was surprised when a representative from Dubai's education sector asked to come visit our program to see if she could find ideas to borrow. I told her that I was happy to host her visit but insisted that she and her colleagues take a cab directly to the school from Manhattan. Feeling protective, I added, "It might be a good idea to avoid wearing any traditional garb. You don't want to stand out too much."

Fida Slayman arrived at CS 55 on a sunny spring morning. It was her first trip to New York. I welcomed her with a Bronx breakfast of bagels and cream cheese and then gave her a quick tour of the neighborhood to help her get her bearings. Taking in the housing projects, liquor stores, and garbage trucks, she recognized at a glance that she was far from Dubai.

"Doesn't look so bad," she said tactfully, sidestepping parents who were walking their children to school. I learned that this charming, effervescent woman was originally from Lebanon. She had seen conflict zones up close in her home country. Our neighborhood didn't make her nervous.

"It's a little early for any trouble here," I assured her, only half in jest. The times when children are walking to school tend to be the safest hours of the day. There are some codes that everyone respects.

Then I asked the question I'd been wondering about since she first contacted me: "What can you possibly hope to learn from us?"

"I understand that you work with children coming from poverty," she told me. "We don't generally face that in Dubai. But we do face many of the same challenges you do. How can we motivate children to learn? How can we encourage them to be responsible for their own learning? How can we help our children grow up to lead happy, productive lives? That's what we all want for our children." I was shocked to hear about rising rates of obesity, diabetes, and other diet-related illnesses in Dubai, where fast-food chains from the West have built loyal followings.

In Dubai, I also learned, happiness is serious business. There's a government minister of happiness. There's also a minister of youth and the future, who ages out of the job at twenty-three years.

"Happiness is not just a nice word we bandy about," Fida explained. She and her colleagues at the Knowledge and Human Development Authority (KHDA), a government division that oversees private education, have been thinking hard about strategies and programs to promote happiness in schools.

When she explained the role of her agency, I was excited to hear about the emphasis on knowledge and human development. What awesome goals! This wasn't institutional thinking. This was evolutionary, maybe even revolutionary. For a guy whose previous "titles" included Prime Minister of Play and Dean of Awesomeness, I was thrilled to hear about Dubai's focus on positive psychology. Fida and her colleagues have even organized "happiness jams" to brainstorm ways to turn up the happiness factor in daily life. How cool was that?

"We've realized that you can't *make* anybody happy," she told me, "but you can enable environments that promote happiness."

That rang a bell. For years, I had been arguing—and demonstrating— that the built environment influences student behavior. Adding green plants, brighter lighting, and learning stations to a classroom can change mind-sets and improve how students and teachers interact. This wasn't untested theory; this was authentic learning. I'd seen it happen again and again, ever since my days at Walton High School. In our new space CS 55, I had applied research about color and mood to design our wonder world with a green and blue palette. Those earth-and-sky colors, so calming and inspirational, are rarely seen in this neighborhood.

An ecosystem for happiness—so that's what Fida was hoping to find at our National Health, Wellness, and Learning Center.

Judging by the dazzling smile on her face when Fida walked into our classroom, I could tell she wasn't disappointed.

"Students, let's welcome our special guest. Mrs. Slayman is visiting from Dubai in the United Arab Emirates. Who knows where that's located?" I asked a group of fifth graders, many of whom were special-needs students.

Little Omar, recently arrived from Africa, stepped up to our world map and pointed to the Middle East. "Do they speak Arabic there?" he wanted to know. "Because my family does, too."

Fatima, Mohammad, and several other Arabic-speaking students were delighted with Fida's gift of Arabic flash cards. And everybody got excited when our guest presented us with chocolates and a camel blanket. Is there anyone who doesn't love camels? How exotic!

After those preliminaries, we settled down to business as usual. Students took turns showing Fida our various learning stations. She gamely took part in a race on our spin bikes and was charmed by the Worm Girls, our all-girl team that tends the earthworms. When she saw our classroom tower farm, she told my students that Dubai plans to feed an entire community—called Sustainable City, the world's first net–zero energy city—with indoor agriculture just like this. When my students showed her the seeds they were sprouting under grow lights, she told them all about the seed library in Dubai that's temperature controlled and guarded by security.

As I listened, I thought, *Wow. They're thinking ahead for the next thousand years. In the South Bronx, we worry about survival day to day.*

Fida found plenty in our program to admire and emulate. We may not have an abundance of resources at CS 55, but scarcity has taught us to be überefficient. That carries over to academics. I'm always looking for ways to leverage whatever we have at hand to maximize learning. That's a strategy that resonates in rich schools and poor schools alike.

Before leaving, Fida shared her takeaways from the day's lessons. "Growing plants feeds right into learning about math, science, literacy. I can see that it's good for special-needs students—and for all students," she beamed. "Planting and growing food may seem like such a simple thing, but it accomplishes so much. And it's so joyful!"

Joy. Happiness. Laughter. Why do we American educators so often forget these essentials when we set our rigorous goals for school? We seem to assume that success—whether in academics, in college, or in careers—will automatically lead to happiness. I was intrigued by how Dubai has flipped the formula to emphasize optimism. Without that sense of possibility, without learning empathy and compassion, there can be no lasting success. What if children came to school to build a foundation of happiness strong enough to last a lifetime? What a difference that would make.

Next thing I knew, I was agreeing to come to Dubai to share Green Bronx Machine strategies with educators and to expand my own understanding of teaching for happiness. KHDA regularly hosts What Works conferences to encourage the spread of effective ideas. My talk—twenty-three minutes forty-nine seconds and 525 slides—was another Stephen Ritz Deep Breath. It earned the first standing ovation in the history of What Works.

When a gentleman named Tammam Abushakra heard me speak in Dubai about Green Bronx Machine, he realized that he had found a kindred spirit from halfway around the world. He is a key adviser to Esol Education, the world's largest network of American-style international schools. Headquartered in Dubai, Esol operates schools in Egypt, Hong Kong, and elsewhere, serving more than ten thousand students. "We're going to do great things together," Abushakra promised me.

On Esol's drawing board is a brand-new school for Sustainable City in Dubai, that futuristic community I had heard about from Fida Slayman. And guess what? The plan for a school focused on sustainability that Majora Carter and I failed to get off the ground in the Bronx so many years ago is going to inform the design of this remarkable school. In Dubai, a place that could not be more different from the Bronx when it comes to wealth and resources, the hope is to inspire a generation of young people who are committed to community service. Our collaboration should generate a fresh crop of organically grown citizens who have a deep commitment to everyone's well-being. A phrase I first heard from a colleague I met in Dubai has stayed with me ever since: "Instead of adding days to our lives, we can add life to our days." The wise gentleman who spoke those words, Dr. Abdulla Al Karam, is chairman of the board and director general of KHDA. When he shared that phrase with me, he was wearing my cheese hat!

As Green Bronx Machine sends out new shoots around the world, I'm seeing ideas that we have been fine-tuning for years take hold in every kind of community.

In the Colombian region of Antioquia, which includes Medellín, once best known for drug trafficking, young people are helping to reclaim their streets from gangs and cartels. Their strategy? Weekend dance parties that attract thousands of people to climb a mountaintop and celebrate their shared culture. Using art, advocacy, and aspiration, and spreading the word via social media, they are changing the way their community is seen by the world. Witnessing the outpouring of creative energy reminded me of the early days of hip-hop in the South Bronx.

In another part of Colombia, I sat down with teenagers in a quaint village that has always been home to skilled farmers and artisans. I found my way to the town of San Vicente Ferrer through a series of connections; it was "I know a guy" played out on a global scale. When village elders heard about the success of Green Bronx Machine, they invited me to help reengage their young people. Youth who spent their days plugged into video games and cell phones saw no good reason to stay in their community and become farmers or artisans. Many couldn't wait to move away to the big city that they had never even visited. Ironically, their community was just starting to enjoy a renaissance. Tourists who yearned to step back in time and experience a culture built on agriculture and artisanship were flocking there for the authenticity. Meanwhile, local youth were yearning to escape via virtual worlds. I sensed an opportunity.

"Tell me what's great about your community," I challenged the youth in my not-quite-perfect Spanish. "Better yet, show me."

That's all it took for these young people to take me on a treasure hunt through the winding, mazelike streets of San Vicente Ferrer. They pointed out their favorite artists, food vendors, musicians, and more. Together, we cooked up the idea of a video game app for cell phones that would appeal to tourists. The youth could identify all the local hot spots and drive visitor traffic via the game.

I, of course, knew nothing about making apps or producing digital games. "Teach me," I challenged the young people. "Explain it to me like I'm a second grader." That's a teaching strategy that works with children the world over.

Together we created a game and application called the Magic Marble. By following the digital marble through a virtual maze, tourists learn all about the agritourism and artisan attractions of the community. Creating and updating the content for the game made these young people realize just how many local assets they have to celebrate in a community that still respects the farmer, the artist, and the earth. Not only that, but they were able to earn income as app designers without ever leaving home. Even better, many are now making money as local tour guides. They are living the Magic Marble experience in a new economy built on apps and relationships. Best of all, they didn't have to leave their community to live, learn, and earn in a better one.

As more Green Bronx Machine partnerships emerge in far-flung locations, we're discovering that children from different parts of the world love to teach and inspire each other. Via Skype conferences, my students from the South Bronx will soon be tutoring their new friends in Toronto about indoor farming and healthy cooking. That's the kind of experience that turns sustainability education into global education, making our big world a little smaller and better connected.

Dr. Fernando Reimers, a Harvard education professor and global education expert, has helped me recognize the importance of building global citizenship into our program. We first met through the Global Teacher Prize and continue to cross paths. Becoming a global citizen, he explained, takes time and focused attention. "It doesn't happen with an annual festival or celebration. You have to set a high bar. You can't just check the box and say, 'Okay, we've done global.' Think about how we teach math, writing, science, or anything we care about," he challenged me. "If we're serious, we have to devote time to learning." Developing global citizenship requires the same steady practice. What could be more globally relevant than connecting students who are growing nutritious food in low-income communities, using 90 percent less water and resources and lessons aligned to college and career readiness?

Through ongoing collaborations with students around the world, I want my students in the Bronx to develop what all global citizens need: the ability to investigate the world, weigh perspectives, communicate with diverse audiences, and take action on issues that concern them. That's how local projects can have global impact.

By now, years after I started getting word out about our efforts in the Bronx, our Green Bronx Machine message has inspired and shaped programs in a wide range of communities and contexts. Students are learning by growing plants and growing healthier communities in St. Louis, Missouri; Medellín, Colombia; Toronto, Canada; and more sites spreading from Mexico to Egypt. In well-off suburbs and high-poverty urban centers, in schools and in Boys and Girls Clubs, during the school day and after school, communities are seizing on the opportunity to grow their own version of collateral positivity.

After years of feeling like an outlier in education, it turns out I'm smack in the middle of a movement. And a movement means a market. In marketing terms, green schools pay big dividends on the triple-bottom line. They're good for people, planet, and profits.

Dr. Jenny Seydel, executive director of a coalition called the Green Schools National Network, is another wise colleague. I've come to think of her as the godmother of green schools. While I've had to figure out what works through day-to-day experiences in the classroom, she brings an academic understanding of environmental education and a research-driven, evidence-based approach. I can see my students' excitement about learning when we grow, cook, and share healthy foods, and I can readily map the connections to academics. Jenny can watch the same scene unfold and see children connecting to something even greater—understanding the natural world and their part in it, based on their developmental readiness. She can map their understanding to academics and chart the impacts on performance.

For elementary students, she sees gardening projects bringing out our little kids' natural hunter-gatherer instincts. This can happen in an outdoor garden, in an indoor farm like ours at CS 55, or with milk cartons on a windowsill. Middle schoolers, meanwhile, are ripe for adventure. They like the mystery of looking deeper—at plants, insects, communities. Their questions push them to deeper understanding of the world. By high school, students are keen to explore questions of identity, fairness, and social justice. From preschool to graduate school, learning through plants creates entry points and lenses for everyone; the power of a plant with SÍ SE PUEDE moments for all along the way!

So when our paths cross at conferences, I always look forward to deep conversations with Jenny, along with some lighthearted moments. She was there the day I bought my first cheese hat at an airport gift shop in Madison, Wisconsin. When I came down the escalator wearing that goofy yellow hat, she broke into a grin and said, "Perfect, Steve!" For the rest of that trip, she snapped photos of me and the cheese hat everywhere we went. It quickly became part of my Green Bronx Machine identity. I've gone on to wear that cheese hat around the world, and children and adults everywhere line up to take pictures of me with it. I've used the cheese hat to inspire perfect attendance, random acts of kindness, and celebrate humanity around the world. This low-cost intervention has generated more goodwill than I ever imagined, and it continues to do so daily.

When I wanted to understand more about how Green Bronx Machine connects to global trends in education, I naturally turned to Jenny. "There are something like 133,000 schools in the United States alone," she told me. "Our hope is that every one of them will become a green, healthy, sustainable learning environment. What parent wouldn't want that for their children?"

The challenge, of course, is that every school has a unique personality and specific needs, influenced by local context. The goal of the Green Schools National Network is to offer schools a range of choices, sort of like a farmers' market where communities can shop for green education programs that fit their tastes. I like to say that green schools have the same soul but many different personalities.

"Some schools are ready for fully integrated, place-based curriculum. Others need to start with an emotional experience that will ignite the fire," she told me. Green Bronx Machine, she added, "has the potential to do both. Your work represents an example of those best practices that we need to share."

Who would have guessed that a program designed through one teacher's trial and error would emerge as a best practice? But here we are, Bronx proud and eager to share what we have learned and what we know.

Now that I've seen Green Bronx Machine inspire similar programs in communities around the world, I know that you need to start with a champion. Someone has to love this idea enough to bring it to life. Who's going to be so enthusiastic that others can't wait to join? Who's going to create the right culture so that the program can take root and thrive? Who's going to be the Dean of Awesomeness? There are plenty of other details that help programs grow, including the right equipment, curriculum, and professional development for teachers. But excitement about the learning experience—the sense of possibility—is what makes all those components add up to something greater. That's why I always encourage schools to take our model and add their own secret sauce of passion, purpose, and hope.

A champion is essential, but one person is not enough to keep green programs thriving. I like to say that Green Bronx Machine is about we, not me. How many teachers or parents have invested time and passion to start school gardens on their own, only to see them fall into disuse if others don't get equally invested? A team is what will sustain programs for the long run.

This is a challenge I've discussed at length with David Hyman, a long-time educator friend. He is the director of sustainability at the Calhoun

School, an elite private school in Manhattan's Upper West Side. We have been friends for years, ever since his random visit to my classroom; collisions, connections, and co-learnings. Our students could not be more different when it comes to socioeconomic status, but they collaborate like champions when we get them together for gardening, cooking, or design projects. They even spent a weekend together in the Calhoun woodshop to build the signage for one of my TEDx talks. The Calhoun School, an early advocate of healthy eating and sustainability, also uses Tower Gardens to grow food. The school's response to all these green projects is positive. The educational and social benefits to students are so profound, he says, "they go way beyond making pesto. This approach deserves a place right in the center of learning."

It also helps to be absolutely fearless about failure. I'm one of the best experts at failing that you'll ever meet. I couldn't have been more disappointed when I failed to convince the board of education to approve any of our new school proposals for the Bronx. Majora Carter and I had three strikeouts, each proposal better than the last. Now we're dusting off the best plan and bringing it to life in Dubai. Being ahead of your time can make you feel like a failure—until the world catches up. I might not be quite as great at failing as Thomas Edison or Steve Jobs, but I've come damn close. Like those guys, I never let setbacks stop me from learning. That's a lesson I try to teach by example every day.

Since my earliest days in the classroom, I've been figuring out what works through experimentation, trial and error, and iteration. I've sought to be transparent, making my own thinking visible and asking my students to do the same. For decades, that made me an outlier in education. I wasn't willing to stick with canned curriculum that didn't meet my students' needs. I always thought all children, and especially the most marginalized, deserve to see how math, science, and other subjects connect to the real world.

And guess what? I was just a little ahead of my time. My natural inclination to learn by tinkering and making stuff has put me in the vanguard of a movement that is inspiring new learning experiences all around the globe. ZIP code and skin color should not determine outcomes in life; access to quality education is the answer! I'm not willing to accept the things I cannot change, I'm going to change the things I cannot accept. This all starts with a seed: the power of a plant.

CHAPTER 16

FULL STEAM AHEAD TO LEAVE A BETTER PLACE BEHIND

WHAT AN EXTRAORDINARY TIME TO BE ALIVE. WE ARE THE FIRST
PEOPLE ON OUR PLANET TO HAVE REAL CHOICE: WE CAN CONTINUE
KILLING EACH OTHER, WIPING OUT SPECIES, SPOILING OUR NEST. YET
ON EVERY CONTINENT A REVOLUTION IN HUMAN DIGNITY IS EMERGING.
IT IS RE-KNITTING COMMUNITY AND TIES TO THE EARTH. SO WE
DO HAVE A CHOICE. WE CAN CHOOSE DEATH; OR WE CAN CHOOSE LIFE.

—FRANCES MOORE LAPPÉ

January 2016—When the White House throws an event to inspire student interest in the high-demand fields of science, technology, engineering, and math (also known as STEM), you can expect to see some cool stuff on display. President Obama's State of STEM showcase did not disappoint. The National Institutes of Health wowed more than one hundred young visitors with a two-foot model of DNA and 3-D–printed molecular cells that they could hold in their hands. Students got to test-drive NASA's Mars Rover. I even volunteered to let participants drive it right over me!

National Oceanic and Atmospheric Administration scientists demonstrated the high-tech rain gauges used in the White House garden and elsewhere. What an honor that our elementary school was one of seven in the whole country invited to bring an exhibit to share alongside these cutting-edge demonstrations.

The scene-stealer of the day might have been Ernest, my ten-year-old student from CS 55. Standing next to our Tower Garden that was bursting with leafy greens, he fielded questions like a seasoned pro. He didn't care if he was talking to the presidential adviser for science and technology, a CNN reporter, or brilliant high school scientists who had been handpicked to attend the event. Everyone got to hear Ernest's sage advice about growing food in our classroom to promote health across our community.

"When you grow your own food, that just makes you want to eat it," he explained to one adult visitor. "I take vegetables home to share. My whole family is eating better."

Chef Bill Yosses, a beloved personality at the White House and a regular visitor to CS 55, was also on hand to demonstrate how we go from seed to tower to table right in our classroom. Visitors could see at a glance how our program brings together all the STEM subjects—and more—in interactive, meaningful ways.

I watched visitors respond the same way my students do. Vertical farms are a novelty; they instantly turn heads. When people see plants growing up instead of out, they get curious. They want to get up close, take a whiff, get a taste. That initial sensory experience leads to deeper questions about light, water use, growing cycles, nutrition, and more. In a room packed with high-tech wizardry, our humble display of living plants fired up everyone's imagination.

After that White House event, we were invited to put a living replica of our classroom in the US Botanic Garden for a six-month exhibition. For a decade, I'd been saying that the Bronx was ready and willing to export our talent, grit, and diversity. Once again, I was invited back to the nation's capital to be part of a teach-in about our transformative way of teaching and learning. I was awed to think that our classroom was impactful enough to showcase.

Through word of mouth, Sherry Huss, cocreator of Maker Faire and a celebrity within the burgeoning maker movement, heard about Green Bronx Machine. She was so intrigued that she came to visit our National Health, Wellness, and Learning Center in the Bronx. And when she fell in love with our classroom program, that led to more collisions and connections. Next thing I knew, Green Bronx Machine was being featured at one major Maker Faire after another.

The National Maker Faire in New York City was a weekend-long show-and-tell event that attracted the most incredible gathering of nerds. There were fashion nerds who invent wearable technologies, energy nerds who combine solar and wind energy to power homes and communities, transportation nerds demonstrating vehicles that look like they're from *The Jetsons*. There were amateur roboticists, rocketeers, and drone designers whose inventions promise to change how we live, work, and play. Folks who hadn't seen the light of day in months emerged from their basements to share their inventions in broad daylight. Maker Faire brings out one hundred thousand of these creative types, including educators who are keenly interested in the learning that happens in "makerspaces." Fittingly, the New York fair was kicked off by Carmen Fariña, chancellor of the New York City Department of Education. I met her face-to-face and had the honor of handing her a personal copy of the video about our program.

Wandering among the exhibits on a rainy fall day, I saw and heard technology everywhere. People gathered around 3-D printers the way they used to gather around campfires. They geeked out together over electronic music and rode around in vehicles powered by biofuels and who knows what else. Back at our Green Bronx Machine exhibit, I had to chuckle. At this national nerd fest, I'm sure I was the only guy who still used an AOL account and couldn't figure out how to track changes in a Word document.

Yet our exhibit—a pop-up vertical farm that we assembled on the spot—attracted more visitors than I could count. I must have exchanged fifty thousand handshakes and high-fives. When people saw me and three elementary schoolchildren in straw hats assembling the plastic towers and planting them on the spot, and then taking them apart so we could do it all over again, they crowded in to get a closer look. We had a line to see our display that lasted for hours. People wanted to take selfies with the plants and listen to the soothing sound of the water circulating. They asked a zillion questions about how the technology worked. Surely this was some space-age stuff?

"No, it's actually pretty simple," I explained over and over again. "My junior farmers take care of everything. It all starts with seeds."

"But is it real food?" they wondered.

"Of course it is! We grow enough fresh produce right in our classroom to serve lunch to seven hundred hungry children, teachers, and families. None of it comes out of a test tube or 3-D printer."

When it was time for my keynote speech, I was frankly a little intimidated. Who in this audience would want to hear from a food guy? A plant guy? A soil guy? Surely there were cooler things to hear about. But after twenty-five minutes, 525 slides, and two standing ovations—another Stephen Ritz deep breath—I realized I had struck a nerve by talking about hacking the food system with twenty-first-century technology.

Even in this crowd of tech-loving nerds, food gets people's attention. It's a nonnegotiable. Everybody eats. And as Ernest and his classmates explained to the throngs, eating better just makes good sense. The Maker Faire crowd loved that we were hacking the food system and doing it in an affordable way that's simple enough for a child to explain.

"You know, you can change the way you feel if you change your diet," Ernest told a group of high school students. He pointed to the soda cans and energy drinks they were all clutching and gave them some tough love. "Do you know how much sugar and caffeine one can holds? What your body really needs is more water."

The big kids laughed, but they listened. And when we found out that they were from the Bronx, too, we all celebrated our shared roots.

"Tell you what. If you guys come back at the end of the day, we'll give you a tower to take back to your school," I promised. They were as excited as if they had won a flying robot.

When I learned that these students attended the Bronx Academy for Software Engineering, I realized what a wonderful collision this could be. These were students with serious technical chops. They planned to go full nerd with their new tower and analyze every aspect of it like engineers. Not only that, they offered to help my students learn about coding and data analytics to track the outcomes of our indoor farm. Our two schools were within walking distance. Once again, I was picturing the magic of big children and little children learning side by side in our own neighborhood. And what brought them together? The power of a plant.

We came away from Maker Faire with the Best in Class prize and four Editors' Choice awards. Lizette and I were wearing so many medals, we looked like we had won a marathon. Better yet, we found ourselves right at home in a community that's all about making change through shared creativity and collaboration.

Much as I love the energy and excitement of showcase events like Maker Faire and State of STEM, I'm convinced that technology alone will not solve the world's problems. For that, we need people.

If our Green Bronx Machine approach can make farming simple but sexy with low-cost, portable, scalable technology, we're onto something big. Even better if we can connect more people to the natural world through their senses. And if something as simple as gardening can get children to be more curious about how the world works and how they can improve it? That's downright revolutionary. As I've always said, if we change the way children eat, change the way they live, and change the way they learn, we can change outcomes for this and future generations. And all while being kinder to the planet.

I've discovered that employers who depend on technology for their bottom line tend to share my belief in people power as the foundation for STEM success. One of the biggest names in the indoor agriculture industry is a Florida entrepreneur named David Smiles. Farmer Dave, as he's known in the business, operates an amazing indoor ag operation in Tampa, Florida, called Uriah's Urban Farms. We met on a television set when we were both being interviewed about innovations in agriculture and have been friends ever since. His story is remarkable. His oldest son, whom Farmer Dave named his company in honor of, was born with a rare metabolic disorder; the treatment consists of a diet of fibrous vegetables and fats. In a miraculous twist, Farmer Dave invented a system for growing healthy plants that provide the precise healing nourishment his son needed. In a converted warehouse rising from a formerly abandoned building in a cement parking lot in a marginalized and forlorn area, Farmer Dave grows some of the most nutritious, gorgeous, and high-quality produce in the world. The very food he grew to help his son is now served by some of the world's most preeminent chefs. Farmer Dave is a global sensation; talk about the power of a plant!

In my Green Bronx Machine students, Farmer Dave saw evidence of the very success skills that he looks for in employees. "Every day, what my employees and I do is problem solving, data collection, analysis, and critical thinking to come up with creative solutions. Stephen has made those same skills readily teachable and engaging." As indoor agriculture continues to innovate, his employees need to be adept at mastering new technologies and solving new problems. "Those are things that traditional schooling doesn't teach," he told me, "but your program does."

At the high-poverty schools where I've spent my career, we never get the latest and greatest classroom technology. We make do with the leftovers and the castoffs. My students tend to be eager consumers of technology, coveting the latest cell phone the same way they consume fashion. But they're seldom empowered by it.

During my years at Walton High School, I used to say that a technology upgrade would be drinking fountains that worked, urinals that flushed, and doors on the bathroom stalls. I wasn't joking. To date, in the Bronx, the most impactful technology giveaway I ever witnessed at school wasn't laptops. It was toothbrushes. And trust me, I've given away plenty of stuff. We gave away a thousand toothbrushes and then had to go get more because the children asked if they could have extras for their families.

Our demonstration classroom at CS 55 regularly attracts education experts looking for ideas to encourage more students to pursue technical studies and fill the STEM pipeline. They're especially eager to attract more students of color who are sorely underrepresented in the tech world and scientific sector. These visitors naturally get excited when they see my diverse students calculating the energy they generate on spin bikes or graphing the germination rates of different seeds. They love to hear students like Ernest make their thinking visible and offer evidence to support their scientific conclusions.

When our students excel on standardized tests in science, it's undeniable proof that what we're doing has academic value and is preparing all students for twenty-first-century success. In 2016, when we saw a 45 percent increase on passing rates for all students, including special-needs and English learners, on the New York State science exam, this shattered data in our school and across our district. For teachers, classroom technology lets us examine data and understand our students' individual strengths and weaknesses so that we can better support them as learners.

That's all good stuff, but it's not why I do what I do. STEM is not my holy grail. (That's an understatement. At home, my VCR still flashes 12:00.) I think we do our children and our communities a disservice if we focus only on STEM and forget to add an A for STEAM. That A is critical. It's about art, aspirations, and advocacy. STEM is about career readiness. It's about technical know-how, which we'll have to keep updating and relearning with every reboot or new product release. STEAM is about heart and soul; human expression; passion, purpose, and hope. It taps into who we are as a thinking, compassionate, evolving species living in complex and challenging ecosystems. STEAM is what will make our lives better.

Years ago, Chardyna and other students from one of my after-school programs took part in a teen design challenge with Cooper Hewitt, Smithsonian Design Museum. Redesign Your Hood challenged students to think like designers to reimagine a community resource. My students came up with an idea for a one-stop homeless shelter that was revolutionary at the time. Instead of having to chase services all over town, clients would get everything they needed in one efficient place. Students were thinking like engineers, making systems work better for everyone. They wanted clients to be able to get food stamps, insurance cards, and medical checkups under the same roof, with no waiting in long lines. And of course, with arty students like Chardyna involved, the architectural design looked cool, too. It was warm and welcoming, anything but institutional. It was a building that invited you in. They called their prizewinning project GRACE because that was what they wanted clients to feel. For my students, the project was about design and problem solving, but most of all it was about dignity. That's the kind of thinking that STEAM makes possible.

If we want our children to be curious and adept at solving problems, we have to offer them environments that invite big, important questions. Then we have to give them room to try out their own solutions. It's not so complicated. It always starts with a question.

"Mr. Ritz, what are you doing there?"

"I'm starting a fish tank."

"Can I help?"

That's how a seventh grader named Miguel became a tireless problem solver in my middle school biodiversity center. He wanted to help set up an aquarium.

"Mr. Ritz, what are you doing there?"

"I'm starting a garden."

"Can I help?"

That's all it took for a high school student named Calvin, who didn't want to get his hands dirty, to pick up a shovel and start beautifying his community. He wanted to help plant some flowers.

"Mr. Ritz, what are you doing there?"

"I'm trying to work out a budget to make my teacher's paycheck last to the end of the month."

"Can I help?"

That's all it took for a tough teenager named Vanessa to demonstrate her understanding of mathematics and real-world problem solving.

Whenever I hear those three magic words—*Can I help?*—I know I've done my job to spark students' curiosity. Then I've got them! And that's just the first spark. I always want to be ready for their next questions to take learning deeper. *How? How can I get involved? How can I help fix this thing or solve this problem? How can I make my life better?*

If I have an insight to transform STEM/STEAM education, it's simply to focus on passion, purpose, and hope. Start with the assumption that children are yearning to engage and then give them reasons to do so. Remember that every single thing we do in the classroom has a major impact on a child's life. It's our job, as educators, to invite students to be involved in solving interesting problems that relate to their world. That's what will move them from being apart from their community to being a part of it. That's what will inspire them to keep asking questions until they arrive at the understanding that's required to get to good solutions.

There's something irresistible about the invitation to do real things. This doesn't surprise me. My whole life has been one long maker experience. I've been hacking my life since I was a kid in the Bronx. Back when I started teaching, I tried to stay one lesson ahead of my students. Three decades later, I'm still learning right along with them. Tackling one hard question after another has made me a better teacher. I've always lived in beta mode, constantly working toward better.

I see the same resourcefulness in many of my students. These children know how to make toys out of paper because that's all they have to play with. When their cupboards are empty, they make sandwiches out of bread and air. They make something out of nothing but grit and hope because that's what they have to work with.

As I've seen again and again, an invitation to solve real problems will ignite students' curiosity. Almost always, those problems have a local solution. Guide students to interesting problems right under their noses and provide them with the support they need to succeed, and then stand back and watch what happens. The answers are right in front of us. That is the beauty of authentic learning.

"Mr. Ritz, what are you doing there?"

"I'm trying to grow food for hungry people."

"Can I help? I'm hungry, too."

By changing the way we eat, we've changed the way we live and learn in our community. Every community has access to the resources it needs to grow something greater. This work is social nutrition rooted in a biological imperative. What could be more impactful? All it takes is the willingness to pick up a shovel, plant a seed, and welcome others to pitch in with you. A seed well planted will give you a crop of epic proportions. In the words of businessperson and activist Judy Wicks, "I'm helping to create an economic system that will respect and protect the earth—one which would replace corporate globalization with a global network of local, living economies. Business is beautiful when it is a vehicle for serving the common good."

CHAPTER 17

THE PROBLEM IS THE SOLUTION

**LET US BE GRATEFUL TO PEOPLE WHO MAKE US HAPPY.
THEY ARE THE CHARMING GARDENERS WHO MAKE
OUR SOULS BLOSSOM.**

—MARCEL PROUST

Fall 2016—South Bronx High School, where I was a rookie teacher so many years ago, now exists only in memory. The four-story building on St. Ann's Avenue has been renovated and remodeled to house smaller and more humane high schools. These days, it's an actual campus with playing fields, computer labs, college prep programs, school gardens with thirty raised beds, and an environment that exudes happiness and health instead of chaos and danger.

A stroll around the neighborhood takes me past affordable housing that didn't exist when I was teaching there. There are community gardens blossoming on streets that once were burnt and barren. St. Mary's Park is safe enough that children can play and teenagers can try out their moves on the basketball courts. More renovations are happening everywhere. Along the Grand Concourse, Art Deco beauties are being restored to their original grandeur. Each spring, a forty-mile cycling event called the Tour de Bronx attracts thousands to explore our borough.

Progress brings new concerns. As developers from Manhattan start to build market-rate housing on this side of the Harlem River, just two subway stops away from the Upper East Side, some longtime Bronx residents worry about getting squeezed out by rising rents. In a community that's always had its own gritty sense of style, people worry about hipsters coming in and gentrifying the place.

Don't get me wrong. Our community still faces plenty of challenges. On too many blocks, the only thriving businesses are fast-food outlets and dialysis centers. Instead of emphasizing education and preventive self-care, we keep putting the problem and temporary solutions within a hundred feet of each other. Real change requires more than Band-Aids. We can't solve poverty or chronic disease if we keep cultivating businesses that feed on the poor. We can't rebuild the middle class if we keep losing our young people to the school-to-prison pipeline. We need to foster inclusivity instead of division.

But as Bronx Borough President Ruben Diaz likes to say, this is the best Bronx the world has ever seen. Crime is down to a fifty-year low. Employment rates are up. One story at a time, you can see a better future taking shape here.

Speaking of shape, this is the best Stephen Ritz the world has ever seen. At the Global Teacher Prize ceremony, I happened to meet President Bill Clinton because he was attracted to my bow tie and cheese hat. We bonded over our weight-loss stories. A year later, he invited me to speak at the Clinton Global Initiative and share my message of going from Impossible to I'm Possible in marginalized communities. I closed with the words SÍ SE PUEDE! From pre-K to the president, everybody loves a happy, healthy person in a cheese hat and bow tie. Everybody loves to scream SÍ SE PUEDE!

My longtime ally Majora Carter isn't worried about the Bronx losing its soul to progress. She recently opened a hip new coffeehouse in Hunts

Point. The Boogie Down Grind Café has brought this industrial neighborhood its first taste of espresso and pastries in a locally owned space with exposed brick walls and tables that invite lingering. Majora imagines the place doubling as business incubator, bringing together creative people who can conjure more ideas to reinvigorate the Bronx. No banks were willing to bet on such an enterprise in this neighborhood, so Majora put together the deal herself. It's a perfect example of what she calls "self-gentrification." By bringing people together around food and relationships, she is creating the perfect ecosystem for collisions, connections, and co-learnings. Everything is hyperlocal, hyperconnected, and niche-specific. The coffee is amazing, too!

Of course, every hyperlocal solution we figure out in the Bronx has the potential to make life better for people all around the world. That's something I've learned from my new friends and allies working for food justice. I grew up in a world where we loved people and used things—instead of loving things and using people. My friends and colleagues are helping us grow that garden mind-set.

Danielle Nierenberg, president and founder of a global think tank called Food Tank, scans the world for practical solutions to bring healthy nutrition to the people who need it most. She worries that the good food movement appeals mostly to the wealthy and well educated, "people who can shop at farmers' markets and feel good about themselves on a personal level. That's awesome," she acknowledges, but not enough to address deep social challenges. "You need the same healthy, nutritious food whether you're a child in the Bronx or in sub-Saharan Africa. Healthy food gets you where you need to go in life," she insists. Nierenberg realizes that my students may not all grow up to be farmers, but with a healthy start in life, "they might become doctors or government officials. Food is a vehicle to educate and move people in a way that nothing else can." She speaks of treating farmers, communities, and soil with respect; the same way I see and treat my students and my community. She, like I, is concerned for this and future generations ahead as well as the planet.

In her comments to me about Green Bronx Machine, Nierenberg says she sees "a lifetime approach to learning differently. It's not about just filling people up, but nourishing them. These practices will live on. That's what we want from any innovation."

Even the connections that we formed so many years ago in our middle school biodiversity center continue to generate benefits. Way back when I was teaching in the Creston corridor, my curiosity drew me into a neighborhood pet shop. Oscar, the general manager, became a lifelong friend. Over the years, Oscar has hired more of my former students than I can count. Good jobs have enabled them to build good lives. When Oscar told me that he had a son with special needs, I got him into a high school program where I could work with him. That young man is now an independent, successful adult. As the pet store business has thrived and expanded, some of my former students have grown into management positions. And why? All because two guys from the Bronx took time to get acquainted and support each other's success. We both knew a guy.

As I've been telling my students for decades, our problems and our solutions are inherently intertwined. How do we address poverty? Teach students the skills they need to be self-supporting and introduce them to relatable role models. I always say that students need to see it in order to be it. How do we improve health outcomes in a community with limited means and poor access to fresh, affordable food? Grow it ourselves and sell the excess. How do we reengage children and young adults on the margins? Give them good reasons to connect. How do we build sustainable programs? Leverage untapped local resources, imbed the solutions into education, think self-care and proactively, not health care and reactively.

Organically grown change takes time, but it doesn't have to be complicated. Another longtime colleague of mine, David Ross, directs an organization called P21, the Partnership for 21st Century Learning. His work in the education field has taken him all over the world to connect like-minded people working to improve schools and prepare students for twenty-first-century success. Ever since he visited us at Green Bronx Machine a few years ago, he has been eager to see our program scale. "There are extraordinary opportunities for a program like this," he told me, both in the United States and across the developing world. "What you're doing doesn't take millions of dollars. It's powered by people. All you need to replicate it are drive and passion, along with the vision to recognize the resources that are already available in your community. What you're doing isn't just a good idea," he told me. "It's a moral imperative that we do this work."

Once change takes root, it sends out new shoots.

As for the children, I love them all like I love my own, with the same passion and commitment, and I stay in touch with so many of them to this day. They also stay in touch with me. I've moved on to my second and even third generation of students. They endeavor to pay it forward, to thank me, to share good news, and remind me that we are a family. All the data point to the single fact that having consistent access to one kind, caring adult will propel a child to success in life. I am forever determined and committed to being that adult for as many children as possible. You will never go broke giving love, and the return on the investment is phenomenal.

On a recent afternoon, I stopped at a substance abuse counseling center in a neighborhood that's still pretty tough. I smiled to see the middle-aged woman who came out to greet me. Here was Vanessa, from my very first class at South Bronx High School. Still short, stocky, and full of energy, she's no longer furious with the world. In fact, she exudes calm. Many of her clients are teenagers trying to break from the grasp of gangs and drugs. She doesn't hesitate to tell them her story. Her own son couldn't be farther from the gang life. He's a proud science and math nerd. In the home that Vanessa owns, she and her son love to cook together. Now that she's no longer stressed out, she loves to geek out. Still good at math, she enjoys playing sudoku with her son. "I keep it real," she told me. "I found my way out, didn't I?" She did indeed. Now she comes to work every day "wanting to stretch some more hearts." Thirty-two years after Vanessa called me Gringo, I am proud be called the Green-Go all around the world.

Another day, I stopped at a Manhattan skyscraper in the heart of Times Square to catch up with Miguel. When Lizette was working in the financial services field, she recommended him for a mailroom job. His current title is flow coordinator for a Fortune 50 accounting firm. "If people need help with their computers, documents copied, meetings set up, or packages delivered, I take care of everything," he explained to me. He attends to the daily needs of three hundred coworkers spread over four floors with the same careful attention he used to tend to our biodiversity center. "I'm solving problems all day long. No two days are ever the same. I like that."

In many ways, Miguel has been proving himself ever since he was labeled special ed because he couldn't read English. After he finished middle school in the Creston corridor, I helped him get into one of the better high schools in the Bronx. "From there, my life changed," he told me. "I expanded my mind." He put in extra class time during summers to make sure he graduated with a regular diploma, not a special ed diploma. Miguel recently teamed up with his sister and her husband to buy a house in a relatively quiet Bronx neighborhood. "I'm so happy there. I don't have to step over dog poop to get to my door. There's no elevator where people are fighting. I don't have to worry about some crackhead jumping me when I walk around the corner. It's a better place than I've ever lived. And we own it."

Then there's Chardyna. She entered the shelter system when she was a teenager and faced more hardships than any human being should have to endure. Her father attempted suicide by jumping out of a building. He broke both legs but somehow survived. Her mother lost an eye to diabetes and suffered complications that kept her hospitalized for weeks. Her recovery was brief. At twenty, Chardyna had to take out a loan to pay for her mother's cremation.

Through it all, she never lost her passion for art. "I like to make art that brings people together," she told me when we had a chance to meet for lunch. Her exuberant hat designs have become a fashion sensation, featured in magazines and sold in boutiques. "People go crazy when I say I made them myself. They're very authentic." She still lives in the Bronx, just down the street from the high school where we first crossed paths. She lives with the dignity that she always wanted for others. When she designed a one-stop service center for the homeless for an after-school project, she wanted to call it Grace. That's exactly what she has found in her own life. "Everything I went through, that was just preparing me for the future," she told me. "I live to inspire others."

These young people continue to inspire me. Calvin, the kid who didn't want to get his hands dirty at Walton High School, now does landscaping and maintenance for public schools in the Bronx. He, too, owns his own home—impeccably landscaped! He works with teens after school, teaching them gardening skills that may lead to paying jobs. He leaves behind a cleaner, nicer place every day. Not a week goes by when we don't connect by phone.

Nadje, the former foster care ward, earns a good living as a butcher for Whole Foods. He lives in the Bronx and is an advocate for food justice. He continues to team up with me on Green Bronx Machine projects, including our newest efforts in Canada.

Alberto, once a struggling middle school student with the technical skills to hardwire his own school building, now enjoys a successful IT career, just as I always promised him. He owns a home and even rental property in the Bronx. He bought his dad a mechanic shop in Hunts Point and has been a longtime financial contributor to Green Bronx Machine.

Another former student is a counselor for a group foster home. Two work for local green suppliers; some at Hunts Point Market. Still others work for GrowNYC, ensuring that fresh, healthy food gets to the people who need it most. On my regular rounds throughout and across the South Bronx, I bump into former students and their parents practically every day and hear uplifting stories about their lives. I've celebrated more weddings, graduations, and other milestones than I can remember.

Michaela is about to graduate from college with a dual degree in geology and environmental science. She has a world of opportunities awaiting her. In 2014, *The Root* magazine honored her with a Young Futurist award, predicting big things ahead. She has literally grown up around Green Bronx Machine, contributing to Team Ritz right alongside Lizette and me. "I treasure every minute of it," she told me recently. "What other kid ever got to spend so much time with her parents? Who ever thought we would create something together that's become such a force of nature?"

What's more, a whole cohort of my first official Green Bronx Machine students are graduating college at the same time as my daughter. I always said I wanted to treat my students the same way I wanted my own child treated. All of these beautiful young people are on a path to become whatever they choose, not what society chooses for them because of the color of their skin or the ZIP code of their birthplace.

These are just a few of my organically grown citizens. They have all figured out how to make good lives for themselves without turning their backs on the Bronx. They are homeowners, taxpayers, and voters. Each day, they all leave the world a little better than they found it. When they have good news to share, I'm one of their first calls. I'm honored to have them call me Dad, Mista, Steve, Yo Ritz, Farmer Steve, or Mr. Ritz. To date, I haven't lost a single basketball game to a student although I am now picking my opponents more strategically. I am determined to finish my career undefeated!

And me? I'm back in elementary school with a whole new cast of Little Rascals; the biggest kid in the school, with a master key no less. I march to the mantra: "It is easier to raise healthy children than to fix broken men!" With each and every challenge I face, I ask if it is incompetence or noncompliance, and I am determined to teach to both. I am hell-bent on leaving the world and each life I encounter better than I found it. On a daily basis, the best ideas continue to come from within, working together to solve problems.

As I told my students years ago at South Bronx High School, social justice depends on all of us doing our part. Who brings about justice? Just us.

CHAPTER 18

MAKE
EPIC
HAPPEN

On a dreary winter morning, I stood in my usual spot on the front steps of CS 55, greeting each student with the Two-Five. Up walked Christian, a fourth grader who's usually chatty and happy to see me. Not that day. He was practically dragging himself toward the school entrance. I noticed at first glance that he was not wearing his school uniform.

"What's wrong, handsome?" I asked him.

"Oh man, Mr. Ritz. It's my birthday and I have to spend it in school. I'm ten today, can you believe it?"

"Don't worry, buddy. It's going to turn out okay," I promised him. "Chef Bill's going to cook with your class today, remember? See you later this morning."

As I watched him head up the stairs with a little more pep in his step, I started to come up with a game plan. I was reminded of the wisdom of First

Lady Michelle Obama, who once said, "How we treat our children is indicative of who we are as a society."

An hour before lunch, Christian and his classmates filed into my classroom for a lesson with Chef Bill and his assistant, Chef Roberto. Hungry students could smell the delicious aroma of roasting chicken as soon as they arrived. It wasn't time to eat just yet. First, they needed to take part in a science lesson about yeast and bacteria. They attached balloons to water bottles filled with a yeasty solution and watched them expand with gas. Leave it to Christian to observe, "Cool. The water is farting." The chefs artfully redirected students' attention to their next lesson: preparing vegetables we grew in class to complete their delicious meal.

I watched Christian do his best to behave himself. Sitting still was a daily challenge for this little guy. Even at the ripe old age of ten, he was still smaller than many of the other boys in his grade. That made him a bit of an outlier. It didn't help that he seemed confused and often silly. His teachers knew that he could also be a little defiant, pushing back against rules that he didn't like.

Frankly, he reminded me of a younger version of myself. What would my old mentor, Stan Zucker, make of this student? Was he struggling because he was incompetent or noncompliant? In either case, I knew that my job was to teach. My job was to love. Christian soaked up any kind words I offered him. So that morning, when he showed up in a leopard print T-shirt instead of his school uniform, I let it slide. After all, it was his birthday.

Whenever we have a special lesson, we have the video camera rolling. The camera captured the children finishing their lesson and settling down to enjoy a meal they had helped cook. The chefs had picked Christian to assist in preparing a special sauce for the chicken, and he was savoring every bite. At my signal, we all broke into song, regaling Christian with a rousing rendition of "Happy Birthday."

The look of pure delight on his face thrilled all of us—Chef Bill, Chef Roberto, Lizette, the other teachers, the students, and, most of all, me. "Mr. Ritz, this is the best birthday I've ever had. And I'm in school!" he called out. "This is EPIC!"

Epic. What a fantastic word! It took a child to remind me of a lesson that is way too easy to overlook. We can make epic happen every day! When you see a smile spreading across the face of a child who thought he was having the worst day ever, that's epic! When you see children and adults building relationships by sharing a healthy meal, that's epic! One epic moment sends out ripples of goodwill, touching everyone in the community.

The great joy of my work is getting to see those ripples day after day. Last summer, Lizette and I ran a summer camp for children from CS 55. Unlike traditional summer schools, our program wasn't about remediation. It was about empowerment and enrichment. Every day was epic. Our students got to meet people working in interesting food careers, from hospital chefs to supermarket butchers to makers of hand-churned organic ice cream. They spent every morning in our outdoor school garden and gave away vegetables by the armload. They built a farm at the Bronx Zoo. They rode horses and escalators—both equally novel modes of transportation for these children. More children knew about horses than about escalators. Of the eighteen students, twelve had never set food outside the Bronx until that camp. In the process, we logged more than three million steps, which we calibrated on pedometers!

Every family that sent a child to our summer camp received a weekly box of fresh produce through a community-supported agriculture program of GrowNYC called Fresh Food Box. Everything was locally sourced to support nearby farmers. Our children took home recipes and cooking insights to turn those raw ingredients into wholesome family meals. When summer ended, families were able to continue the program by using food stamps. The benefits have been epic for the whole community.

Epic is taking children to the White House! Epic is having kids do TED talks and traveling with me around the world! But epic starts with *please, thank you, have a nice day, good morning, good afternoon,* and *thank you for correcting me.* Epic is having hundreds of children wear a cheese hat to celebrate perfect attendance and hundreds of acts of random kindness; but epic starts with the decision to wear that cheese hat at school and make it a daily practice. Epic is writing a book, but epic starts with the first word. A seed and an idea, much like the power of a plant. Remember this: Epic is a reflection and result of daily practice, bringing your A game daily.

Recently, I learned that since 2014 and the Office Depot video, there are now more than five thousand US schools with Tower Gardens. Imagine if Rich Downing and I never stopped to talk? Recently, I learned that the children who starred in that Office Depot video, my first little Tower Gardeners, were inducted into the National Junior Honor Society. Recently, there was a replica of my classroom installed at the US Botanic Gardens. We were even invited to the South by South Lawn festival and put a Tower Garden on the White House lawn for the event. I've reconnected with the artist Robert Shetterly only to learn that he has been following my career since 2007 and wants to paint and add my portrait to his collection of Americans Who Tell the Truth.

Simply put, my life has put my dreams to shame. So now it is time to dream bigger, dream smarter, and dream more inclusively and abundantly, and to dream and live for others; all in testimonial to the power of a plant.

When I have opportunities to share my odyssey with audiences, I offer them this challenge: *What will you do to make epic happen?* It doesn't matter whether I'm talking with teachers, business leaders, foodies, or social justice activists. It doesn't matter if we're in the Bronx, in Dubai, in Canada, or in the mountains of Colombia. We all need to take this on as our call to action.

Every night before I go to bed, I look out my windows and see lights on. That tells me someone is working, someone is doing something, and I find that inspiring. I keep all hours—not office hours—and every day, every moment, every minute is an opportunity to do something great. Each and every moment affords us an opportunity to do better, to get better, to inch forward, and to grow. The time that is most important to me is constantly *right now*—each and every second. I look at calendars and datebooks frequently. I notice the days of the weeks and dates of the month; not one of them is named "someday" or "tomorrow." I don't like somedays or tomor-

rows. I like todays. Here and now, this and every moment matters, and if you are not speaking specifically, you're simply fantasizing.

Our story and technology, featured in schools, textbooks, media, homes, and communities across the globe, serve as an example of what is possible: the power of a plant. It teaches us to MAKE EPIC HAPPEN! We scream SÍ SE PUEDE! Martin Luther King Jr. said it best: "The time is always right to do what is right."

Moving forward, I try to always live in solutions, driven by outcome and impact; I always want to pay it forward. Even this book is solutions oriented and will pay it forward; proceeds are going to fund Green Bronx Machine and the work, to create new and additional opportunities—and for that, I thank you, I appreciate you and am forever grateful. I encourage all of you to live your lives with dignity and respect as well as impact and purpose so that together we can all prosper and grow something greater. I've been blessed to travel around the world and meet incredible people—to scream SÍ SE PUEDE and wear my cheese hat on mountaintops—but my favorite place to be is in a classroom full of children and plants and standing outside a schoolhouse at seven o'clock every morning, right next to the garden, meeting and greeting every child, parent, and colleague.

On a daily basis, I bump into students from five years ago, ten years ago, fifteen years ago, twenty years ago. They all remind me of something that I did for them. Every day, I am stopped in the street and thanked by someone for what I did, whether it was wiping their nose, celebrating their birthday, sending a postcard, saying please or thank you, walking them home, sharing my lunch, or singing a song. Much as students liked my lessons, they most remember how I made them feel. How we treat people is key to how we motivate, educate, and inspire. I am forever reminded of the Maya Angelou quote: "I've learned that people will forget what you said, people will forget what you did, but people will never forget how you made them feel."

I've launched a curriculum so no teacher will ever have to experience what I did my first day, my first week, my first year of teaching. And while that curriculum is driven by my passion for health, wellness, nutrition, and gardening, it is grounded in what I have learned about effective, engaging instruction and the use of data, assessment, student voice and choice, and constructive self-assessment and feedback that helps all students and all teachers succeed. I'm not out to put gardens in schools; I'm determined to wrap schools, content, and subject-area instruction and the entire academic experience around project-based learning and deep, authentic learning experiences that inspire healthy living in line with people, planet, and twenty-first-century opportunities. I am and remain an equity warrior and strive to be a voice for the voiceless until they learn to speak for themselves. I am determined to end hunger, poverty, and educational inequity in this lifetime—win, win, win—SÍ SE PUEDE!

Not too long ago, I received an amazing e-mail. It was from my former principal at Discovery High School congratulating me on my successes since. He went on to apologize for the way things unfolded between us. For that, I am forever grateful. It meant and still means the world to me. It also teaches that it is never too late to learn or mend broken fences, and that we can always get to yes and thank others for correcting us.

I approach every day with the energy and excitement of the first day of school. Every day is an opportunity to do something great, to make epic happen, to pay it forward, and to grow something greater. The reality is, we are living in a world of abundance. We should not settle for life as it is nor life as it could be, but rather live life as it should be—lived elegantly, eloquently, respectfully and in line with a greater global good.

My wife, Lizette, is a perfect example. She enjoyed a very successful career in Manhattan's financial sector, rising to the rank of vice president for a major investment firm. Her salary and benefits gave our family stabil-

ity, allowing me to take career risks and eventually scale the work of Green Bronx Machine. Lizette has always been central to our success, spending her weekends and evenings with us on gardening projects and escorting children on field trips.

Eventually, she chose to become even more involved. She quit her finance career to join me as a full-time volunteer at CS 55. "This is our legacy," she told me when she came to that decision. "It's about the people we impact." Now she gets to make epic happen every day, even on days that feel Herculean. She spends her days surrounded by children who adore her. In fact, she has a tribe. Being so closely involved in our programs has convinced her that whatever successes we achieve "are about the power of perseverance. That's the story of Team Ritz," she told me at the end of one particularly long day. "We'll always do double-duty if that's what it takes to get things right." This isn't just what we do; it's who we are.

"In the end, nothing is more important than the health and well-being of our children," Michelle Obama reminded us all shortly before she ended her term as the First Lady of the United States. Like my friend David Ross says, connecting children with the power of a plant "is our moral imperative!"

Sometimes epic involves a big decision, like changing careers or launching an innovative program to transform education. Sometimes it's as simple as choosing to celebrate a child's birthday with a song. Either way, it's about taking responsibility, taking ownership, and working tirelessly and relentlessly to make things right.

Regardless, the choice is on you: MAKE EPIC HAPPEN! *Sí se puede!*

APPENDIX

The Power of a Plant Around the World

By Dr. Abdulla Al Karam, director general of the Knowledge and Human Development Authority (KHDA), Government of Dubai

The first thing I noticed about Stephen Ritz was not his height or his smile or even his unique bow tie, but his heart. "I farm in the South Bronx," he joked, "but I'm certainly not a farmer." He doesn't just grow vegetables, but citizens. He doesn't just nurture plants, but hearts and minds. And he doesn't just provide his students with healthy food, but a healthy future.

Dubai and the South Bronx are at opposite ends of the world and in many ways worlds apart. Each city has its own culture and history and faces its own teaching and learning challenges. Yet here in Dubai, we share with Stephen a belief in the goodness of the human spirit and our children's capacity to create a happier world.

Stephen's work in building and enabling happy communities reflects the vision of Dubai put forward by the ruler of Dubai and prime minister of the United Arab Emirates, Sheikh Mohammed bin Rashid Al Maktoum. Like Stephen, we believe that by connecting minds, by nurturing hearts, and by empowering students, parents, and teachers to bring out the best from within themselves, we will help to create a happier society in which all residents have opportunities, options, and hope for the future.

We had the privilege of visiting Stephen's school in South Bronx in early 2015, when his space was little more than an underused classroom and a dream. Electrical cables snaked around the floor; tables were scattered throughout the room; paint was peeling off the walls.

"Can you believe that this room is the National Health, Wellness and Learning Center?" he asked. "Over here," he said, enthusiastically pointing at an empty corner of the room, "we've got bikes that kids ride to generate electricity to keep the Tower Gardens running. And over here," he said, pointing to two lonely Tower Gardens, "is a food forest." As we listened to his descriptions and took in his energy and enthusiasm, Stephen's vision came alive. We started to see what he saw.

In January 2016, Stephen came to Dubai as a guest speaker at What Works, a regular collaborative learning event for 600 teachers and school leaders. The educators who listened to his story were more than impressed—they were inspired. Stephen's talk was not about himself nor even his students. Rather, it was about the audience—the teachers—and *their* students. They came away confident in the belief that they, too, could make positive change in their schools and in the lives of their students through the power of a plant. The urban gardening movement in Dubai's schools had begun. Many educators immediately started making plans for their own school gardens.

The long-term impact has been palpable. Schools that had already established vegetable gardens have begun to integrate the learning they offer into their curricula. In some schools, students are not just growing vegetables, but also learning to cook with them. They hold "market days" where they sell vegetables to school families, educating them about the transformative educational power of growing food and raising money for charitable causes at the same time.

In other Dubai schools, students have taken the lead. They have pooled their communities' resources to start their own gardens, with teachers taking on support roles. With students in charge, they become emotionally invested in the success of their projects. They have organized themselves into teams responsible for soil quality, water, and pest control, to name a few.

For each of these students in all of these schools, vegetables are certainly not the only fruit of their labor. As well, extending their knowledge in core subjects such as science, math, literacy, and business, they (together with their parents and teachers) learn many of the "survival skills" that will enable them to thrive in their lives: communication, teamwork, analytical thinking, problem solving, resilience, grit, and creativity.

KHDA is responsible for the quality and growth of private education in Dubai, including 183 schools offering 17 different curricula to 265,000 students from 190 nationalities. KHDA also oversees private universities, early learning centers, and training institutes in Dubai.

The Glue Trap

Being in special education is like being stuck on a glue trap. Once you're on it you are not getting off. It's like people can put us here for any reason they like. Kind of like throwing out garbage. People do not understand unless they know.

Most kids in special education do not belong here. They got on some teacher's nerve so they just throw you away. We are not stupid. These are the worst teachers. They don't come to school when it rains. They don't come to school when it snows. They invent holidays that students can't pronounce. Some pretend that they are down for you, but they are not. They come to school late and leave early. They talk and talk and talk. Yak, yak, yak. They are boring. Worst of all, they are cheap.

They tell us stories about when they were young and hopped to school on one leg in hurricanes carrying books. They lie. They talk about the good old days, but they helped make the problems we have today. But they really don't want to be here. They are afraid of us. They don't want to live with us or near us. They wouldn't put their kids in special education. Even ones from the Bronx send their kids to private school. We are not the problem, they are.

Mr. Ritz is different. He seems like he wants to put special education out of business. He wants us in regular education. What would he do without us? At least he makes us feel important, not like we are bad or rejects. People hate special education students. They make fun of you. They talk bad about you. In lunch we sit with all special education. That is wack.

Some people need help. Some people can't read or write or walk or see or hear. They need help. The rest of us need a break. People need to change their attitudes and lots of people should be fired. Glue traps are nasty. When you step on one, it always leaves a stain no matter what. So does special education.

"The Glue Trap," written by a middle-school student known as TJ, was published in our collection of stories called *The League of Distinguished Gentlemen*.

Letter from Student

Dear Office of New Schools:

I am thrilled to learn that my teacher and mentor, Mr. Ritz, is trying to open his own school. I am thrilled and honored to write you informing you how much he deserves it and what a difference it will make. I met Mr. Ritz 3½ years ago at Walton HS. I was 17 years old at the time and had just started YABC. I was behind academically and was assigned to work with Mr. Ritz in the Dean's Office. From day one I was amazed at how he handled the most difficult students; he had a way about him. In many ways, he literally controlled the school.

At that time, like most students, I was concerned about my hair, my sneakers and girls. Although I had a job through YABC, I was going nowhere. Mr. Ritz took an interest in me. He signed me up for private tutoring, encouraged me to read, to learn and to do things I never thought of. He shared with me his experiences of growing up in the Bronx and offered me hope. Most of all, he worked with me. He found a way to make me want to graduate because he tied it to working. He got me extra hours with him when he became Dean at Discovery HS as long as I performed in school. It always amazed me how he knew everyone's name and took the time to work with kids most people couldn't or wouldn't work with; gang kids, kids on and selling drugs. He was like a father to so many. He was tough but he was fair and most of all, he gave you a chance. His Green Teen Program was amazing, kids from all campus schools wanted to join.

All along he stuck with me, encouraging me to take extra classes, computer classes and he kept motivating me with talk of a job. Along the way, Mr. Ritz got many kids jobs so I knew he was for real. Thanks to Mr. Ritz, I graduated. Then, the work began. He encouraged me to see beyond my block, the park and "hood" so to speak and opened my eyes up to possibilities of a better life; one I could have never imagined. After encouraging me to get a haircut and increase my vocabulary, he got me an interview at Williams Lea, a facilities management/reprographic outsourcing company. Through him, I got a job as a messenger at Morgan Stanley. There I met many past students of his who were doing incredible things. Mr. Ritz made sure I went to every onsite training offered and continued his involvement in my career. I say career because today I am a Reprographics Operator/Client Service Representative. My W-2 for calendar year 2007 reflects earnings in excess of $34,000. I have complete benefits, a 401 K plan and am opening up a brokerage account with my year-end bonus. I never knew about any of these things.

At 21 years of age I have more than I ever imagined however now, in many ways, my life is still unfolding. This spring, I will have earned my Associates Degree and am working with Mr. Ritz to apply to either Fordham or NYU. I plan on going into accounting or finance. Best of all, my company offers tuition reimbursement/assistance programs. When I look to my left and right at work, I also see students like me, who Mr. Ritz has helped. When I go home to the Bronx I see stores filled with students Mr. Ritz has gotten jobs for and I look at parks that he and his students have built and renovated. You can see the love he has for students and the love they have for him. He is a guy who has changed lives in a big way.

I cannot say enough about Mr. Ritz and his family. I know how he can and will change lives. Kids today need the support and discipline he can offer. The fact that he carries this respect where we live counts for something. The fact that he has made us want more and different things that we could have never imagined is incredible. When he says something, he means it and we know it will be true. He is a person of his word. Our community needs him and the school he wants to build. I would be proud to send anyone I know to a school he ran.

This letter was written in 2008 by a former Walton High School student in support of our proposal to start a new public high school in the Bronx with a focus on sustainability. That school proposal was never approved. Instead, the same concept is being used to design a new school as part of Sustainable City in Dubai.

GREEN BRONX MA

1. Children should not have to leave their neighborhood to live, learn, and earn in a better one.

2. Every day that you put your feet on the ground, pull air into your lungs, and extend your head toward the sun sets the stage for spectacular.

3. Our job is to love children until they learn to love themselves.

4. It is easier to raise healthy children than to fix broken men.

5. We are living in a world of abundance. We should not settle for life as it is nor life as it could be, but rather life as it should be: lived elegantly, eloquently, respectfully, and in line with a greater global good—with dignity for all.

6. When we teach children about nature, we teach them to nurture, and when we teach children to nurture, we as a society collectively embrace our better nature.

7. Having consistent access to one kind, caring adult will propel a child to success in life. Commit to being that adult for as many children as possible.

8. Schools should not be content with educating children. They need to uplift and empower families and communities.

9. We need to understand that every single thing we do, say, and think in a classroom—every decision made—impacts our children.

10. Teaching children to count is cool, but teaching them what counts is far more critical and important.

SÍ SE PUEDE!

:HINE MANIFESTO

11. Teaching happens in classrooms, but learning happens in the real world.

12. ZIP code and skin color should not determine outcomes in life. Quality education should.

13. Children can't be well read if they are not well fed.

14. What you eat can determine your destiny.

15. Eating across the rainbow is not a bag of Skittles, dammit!

16. We need to refresh and respect our soil and communities like our precious laptops and computer screens.

17. Unconditional love and goodwill are free. No one will go broke giving love and goodwill.

18. If you're not pissing people off, you're not working hard enough.

19. Keep falling up the ladder of success.

20. If you don't stick to your values when they and you are being tested, they're not values; they're simply best wishes and a part-time hobby.

21. Fall in love with doing something and fall so hard that it stands the chance to kill you; therein lies the potential for impact.

22. Refuse to accept the things you cannot change and change the things you cannot accept.

23. Asking for permission is begging for denial.

24. How we walk with the wounded speaks far greater than how we sit with the great.

MAKE EPIC HAPPEN!

THE POWER OF A PLANT TOOL KIT

Mr. Ritz's Favorite Vegetables to Grow with Children (of All Ages)

1. Bibb or romaine lettuce. Children of all ages are willing to nibble on lettuce. It's not a stretch for anybody's taste buds. I like Bibb and romaine because the leaves are big and crunchy. The plants are visually appealing. You can plant red and green varieties in a candy-stripe pattern, incorporating art. Plus, these plants are fun to handle. Children can spread a big leaf of romaine with hummus and roll it up into a satisfying snack. Spring mix lettuces are harder to grow and keep alive, so avoid those seed varieties until your gardeners are more proficient farmers.

2. Bok choy. I haven't met a person yet who doesn't like Chinese food. Bok choy, also known as Chinese cabbage, is a common ingredient. To harvest, pull leaves from the outside, and more leaves will keep coming. Some children like the crunchy white stems; others prefer the dark green leaf. When sunlight hits a big bok choy plant at just the right angle, it looks like it's glowing. You have a photography lesson or art activity in the making. Bok choy is a little more sophisticated than leaf lettuce. It has more bite than Bibb, but it's not as spicy as arugula. You can eat it raw or stir-fry it with other vegetables. And the name itself is intriguing. A little mystery goes a long way to keep your students engaged.

3. Radishes. Radishes grow fast. Little farmers find them amazing. They'll watch the green shoots come up and wonder, where's the radish? That opens a conversation about what's happening underground and how the leaves feed the roots. When little ones see a radish come out of the soil for the first time, they are astounded. Children are surprised to learn that radishes come in a rainbow of colors, not just red and white. They're easy to grow in a window box or even a milk carton. Unlike some of our other garden favorites, radishes don't attract bugs.

4. Carrots (tricolored). We've all been conditioned to think orange when it comes to carrots. That's why I like to plant the tricolored varieties. Something as simple as a purple or yellow carrot can open a conversation about diversity and inclusion (not to mention genetics). Like radishes, carrots are among the "unders"—root vegetables—that make good use of garden space. And like radishes, they're bug-free.

5. Cucumbers. These humble vegetables offer a wealth of lessons. I like the Marketmore varieties, which produce big cukes on vines that are easy to train—right up the classroom wall or around a windowsill. They're also easy to pollinate. Teach students how to recognize male and female flowers, and then show them how to pollinate using a feather or small paintbrush. In the process, students will be building their scientific vocabulary. (Older students will quickly catch on that this is a sex ed lesson.) Cucumbers are ideal for beginning pollinators because the flowers are hardy enough to withstand some roughhousing. They're also useful for teaching students to be good observers. If your scientists look closely, they'll see the tiny cucumber forming behind the flower. As the cukes get bigger—which happens fast—you can start talking pickles. Ask your students, "What's better, cukes or pickles?" I guarantee you'll have a debate on your hands, which you can use to teach about effective argumentation. And now you've set the stage to make pickles, which opens new lessons about food preservation and kitchen chemistry.

6. Collards. If you want to grow something with a high success rate, plant collards. They grow outdoors in colder climates from early spring until early winter. In warm climates, collards will grow outdoors all year long. These hardy greens not only grow readily but will regenerate if you cut the leaves back but leave the roots. Keep plucking and they'll keep producing. Many students love to eat greens. Do a cooking demonstration with collards and you have set the stage for an inquiry lesson. A big pile of greens shrinks to a fraction of its volume when cooked. Expect inquisitive children to ask, "Where did they all go?" I like to harvest greens in fifty-five-gallon sacks and then cook them down with students watching. It's an ideal lesson for teaching about water content. Your students may have heard that their bodies are 70 percent water, but many will have trouble grasping that concept. You can't cook a child, but you can cook a pile of collards!

If your students aren't crazy about eating collards, you can use the greens to feed classroom pets like tortoises or rabbits (and teach about the food chain). If you're growing outdoors, your students may notice insects around the collard plants. Ladybugs love to hang out on these big green leaves. They offer more lessons about beneficial insects versus pests.

In culturally diverse classrooms, collards give students from around the world a chance to connect what they're learning to their families and home traditions. Immigrant students from Africa and Mexico can compare family collard recipes with African American children. In the Bronx, my farmer-chefs can go block by block and collect a world of recipes.

Don't overlook the health lessons that humble collards offer. In a region of Mexico, doctors have eradicated childhood eye disease caused by vitamin A deficiency by encouraging families to grow, cook, and eat collards.

7. Tomatoes. Is there a cuisine in the world that doesn't include tomatoes? Students from every culture are familiar with the flavor, color, and smell of tomatoes. My favorite varieties to grow are San Marzano, Celebrity, Big Beef, Brandywine, Green Zebra, plus some "uglies" (also known as heirlooms). San Marzano plants grow to a manageable size. Green Zebras, one of the heirloom varieties, produce spectacular striped fruit. Celebrity and Big Beef produce beefsteak tomatoes that are as meaty as a steak. Choosing which variety to grow with children involves some decision making. If you grow cherry tomatoes, you'll get hundreds of ripe fruits all at once. That means every farmer gets to pick a handful. The downside is, once all that fruit ripens, you need to pick fast or you'll have a bug problem. I prefer to grow the larger varieties that require children to share.

Tomatoes have to be pollinated. Outdoors, insects will do that work for you. Indoors, you can hand-pollinate, but this requires a delicate touch. This requires precise and well-trained little hands. The

cultural and cooking lessons you can teach via tomatoes are practically endless. Pizza, anyone?

8. Eggplant. Take your pick. The slender Japanese varieties are easier and faster to grow than the Black Beauties, but the big ones are a sight to behold. Eggplants require pollination, but the flowers are big and reasonably durable for beginners to pollinate by hand. Like tomatoes, eggplants are found around the world. From eggplant lasagna to tempura, baba ghanoush to ratatouille, many children will have encountered eggplant around a family table. They can interview family members to gather recipes and raw material to inspire their writing. The joy of cultural celebration comes from comparing uses and favorite flavors.

9. Peppers. As you consider the enormous variety of peppers you might grow, keep a few pointers in mind. Many students love hot peppers, but the oil can get on their hands and into their eyes. That can turn a happy gardening lesson into an eye-watering nightmare. Experience has taught me to avoid growing the hottest ones, especially with younger taste buds. Peppers are tricky to pollinate; you're best to leave this to nature rather than trying to do it by hand. Like so many other vegetables, peppers come in rainbow of colors and are used in a wide range of cuisines. Teach your students the health benefits of eating across the rainbow.

10. Basil. This fragrant herb grows fast but draws mixed reactions. Some students love the smell, others hate it. Too much basil in the classroom can even make some children irritable. So start with small doses—a pot or desktop container of basil—until you know whether your students will tolerate it. Once you're good to go, explore all the colors and species of basil. You can plant a pattern of purple Thai basil alternating with Genovese green basil. Students who find fresh basil too strong for their taste might enjoy tasting pesto. Basil also makes a tasty *agua fresca*. Mix cold water with sliced cucumbers and basil leaves, let it sit, and you have a sugar-free soda alternative. Students who have an entrepreneurial bent will appreciate learning that basil is a high-value cash crop. Not only does it draw a handsome price by the pound, but the plant will keep producing if you pinch back the blossoms.

11. Arugula. This green leafy plant, also called salad rocket, packs a surprising punch. It smells sweet but fires up the mouth. Most of my students like the flavor, which reminds them of hot Takis Fuego chips but without all the salt and chemicals. Arugula plants keep producing for a long time but can grow in tight spaces. If you only have room for a Dixie cup garden, you have room to grow arugula. These plants are great for developing your students' vocabulary. I'll ask children for five adjectives to describe the flavor—and they can't use vague words like "good" or "nice" that belong in what we call the word cemetery. Arugula will guarantee a reaction, inspiring descriptions like spicy, sharp, overwhelming. I've even had students launch into raps about arugula. To surprise them, offer a taste of an arugula flower. They'll expect it to be sweet, like a Skittle. Surprise! When they taste the peppery flower, you can help them understand how they have been conditioned to make associations that aren't necessarily true. Lemons don't taste like lemon candy. And arugula flowers don't taste like sugary nectar.

12. Peas. You can't go wrong with sugar snap peas. These vines grow quickly, and the entire pod is edible. Foraging farmers like to open up the pods and find the peas inside.

13. Green beans. These are some of the best-behaved plants you can grow. Whether you plant the bush variety or the vines, beans will follow any prompt you give them. Unlike your excitable students, beans always behave themselves. Just by growing (and fixing nitrogen), they improve the soil for everybody else.

This is just a starter list. As you make your own planting list with your students, think about your reasons for choosing certain vegetables as well as the space you have available. You'll want plants that have different growing habits—over, under, vining, leafing, creeping, crawling. And you'll want plants that will ignite your students' curiosity. Be sure to plant what you like, too.

You might decide to mix in herbs like lavender, which brings a calming, peaceful scent to your classroom. Greek oregano is a robust, impossible-to-kill herb that you can start with cuttings in water. Chocolate mint is guaranteed to surprise students with its cocoa flavor.

You may notice that I've left out one of the most popular backyard garden plants. Zucchini has no place in my school garden. Why? As I tell my students, he's a bully! He spreads out, demanding to be in the front. He gets too big too fast, pushing everyone else around. And then when he's done, he keels over like he's had enough fun. Want to end school garden bullying? Don't plant zucchini (or its close cousin, butternut squash—another school garden bully!).

How to Grow a Green Vocabulary and Mind-Set

School gardens and green classrooms are ideal ecosystems for growing your students' academic vocabulary and thinking skills. Here are some key terms, concepts, big ideas, and little nuggets to introduce and build on across grade levels. They're equally applicable in classrooms, in community gardening programs, or at home.

DIRT VERSUS SOIL. "What's the difference between dirt and soil?" That question stumps many children at first, but my veteran gardeners know the difference: "Dirt is what's behind your ears. Soil is what we plant in." Soil is a living thing. It's a community. Dirt is a liability. Soil is the greatest asset in the world; it provides a medium to grow.

Expect your new gardeners to be surprised to learn that soil is a living, breathing material. Challenge their assumption that it's "just dirt" by having them investigate healthy soil using all their senses. Using an inexpensive handheld magnifying glass, they can get a close-up look at soil samples. Teach them to roll a pinch of soil between thumb and fingers to see if it forms a ball—a way to check for clay content. What do they notice when they close their eyes and smell a handful of soil?

Their observations lead naturally to descriptive writing activities.

In outdoor gardens and container gardens, soil is what holds plant roots in place and delivers nutrients and water essential for healthy plant growth. Soil contains millions of living microorganisms; it is an ecosystem unto itself.

Academic language will blossom along with scientific understanding as students learn to identify organic and inorganic materials. Encourage questions about what they can do to improve soil quality. Earthworms, anyone? Good questions open the door to scientific investigations along with profound conversations about how we can improve our own environment.

THINK (AND FAIL) LIKE A SCIENTIST. A green classroom invites students to think like scientists every day. I keep a visual reminder of the scientific method posted on the wall of our National Health, Wellness, and Learning Center and refer students to it regularly. I want to power up their thinking by using the active verbs that scientists use: *ask, wonder, inquire, question, test, measure, observe, evaluate, analyze.* And *fail.* Fail often. All scientists need to know that failure is part of the scientific method. Failure is data. It tells us when we're wrong and need to try a different approach. Understanding what doesn't work is a step toward success. In a classroom filled with growing things, you have the perfect opportunity to remind students that nature succeeds by adapting to failure. The strong survive. Students will thrive when they understand that failure gives us all the opportunity to learn and grow.

MAKE YOUR THINKING VISIBLE. I want to honor my students' thinking, but I'm not a mind reader. That's why I constantly ask them to make their thinking visible. Once you know what's on their minds, then you can follow up to go deeper. Some of my favorite questions to uncover students' thinking: *Why do you say that? Why you think that way? How can you defend what you're saying with evidence?* There's never a one-word answer to why or how.

If it turns out that students are basing their thinking on incomplete information or misunderstandings, then you can correctively instruct. What's the thinking behind their mistakes? They need to feel safe in answering that question. One of my favorite strategies is to say, "Talk to me like I'm a two-year-old. Help me understand." That flips the script, and now a struggling student gets to teach you what he or she is thinking. From there, I always build on the positive. It's not about what you can't do but what you *can.* "No" shuts down learning. Instead, build on "yes."

GENETIC POTENTIAL. Seeds are amazing little metaphors to help students understand the world—and themselves. Every tiny seed comes packed with genetic potential. It's a promise, and promises really matter to children. Promises are about the future. Show a child a picture on a seed packet and they get it: A carrot seed promises to grow into a carrot. Every seed is another story waiting to happen, but the story can't begin until the conditions are right. The same is true of children. Each one is filled with potential. Every child has a story to tell. Our job as educators and nurturers is to create fertile conditions so that all children can achieve their potential. When you make a promise to a child, be sure you can fulfill it.

RAIN FOREST VERSUS OASIS. I used to be flattered when people called my green classroom an oasis. Not anymore. An oasis may seem wonderful while you're hanging out there, but it's not a sustainable environment. It's isolated from what's around it. In contrast, a healthy ecosystem puts out roots and shoots. It's hyperconnected and regenerative. It's more like

THE POWER OF A PLANT TOOL KIT

a rain forest. That's the ecosystem I'm striving for in my green classroom.

In fact, I think it's time to challenge the current focus on sustainability. Sustainability is about maintaining the status quo, keeping things going. That's barely a starting point. I want us to aim for transformation. How can we grow something greater? How can we restore and regenerate our communities? That's what rainforest thinking will help us achieve.

JOYFUL LEARNING. When you walk into a green classroom, you can't help but feel happy and alive. That's how I want my students and fellow teachers to feel every day. The learning we do together addresses important academic concepts, but it's not about skill-and-drill or memorization. There's room for joy and laughter along with the serious business of learning. That's refreshing for everyone—children and adults alike.

My story has been an odyssey, but I still walk into school every day with a smile on my face. I can't wait to show up and figure out what's next. If you're not having fun yet, and if your students aren't enjoying the journey, then there's something wrong. Focus on joy and you'll be amazed by what you can accomplish together.

How School Leaders Can Help Grow Green Programs

During my three decades in education, I've worked with all kinds of school leaders. The best ones inspired me to become a better teacher and advocate for children. Some gave me room to innovate in the classroom—as long as I could show that using approaches like indoor gardening to teach across the curriculum was good for children.

Here are key leadership lessons I've learned from experience, both as a teacher and as a leader myself. Bottom line: Green school programs can't thrive without supportive leaders.

1. Everyone's watching. School leaders are highly visible. They're the face of the school. Simple things like knowing your students (and teachers) by name help build a positive school culture. So do frequent classroom visits—and not just when it's time to evaluate teachers. Leaders who support green programs show up often. They show an interest in what students are growing and learning. They ask questions that prompt students to reveal their thinking. Sometimes they even get their hands dirty. They taste and sample everything. They always ask "Why?" Leaders need to be seen doing work.

2. Share the game plan. Effective leaders communicate the vision that guides their decision making. This shouldn't be a secret. A shared vision means that everyone's pulling in the same direction. If the leader is transparent about the vision, then teachers who want to introduce a green curriculum or gardening program will know from the outset whether and how this aligns with the school's vision. Sharing is service. Service is a great form of leadership.

3. Lead by listening. Good leaders are good listeners. That's one way they build community and demonstrate respect. They understand that school success is about "we," not "me." They're open to fresh ideas, knowing that they'll get better results if everyone works together.

4. Be selfless. Effective leaders acknowledge others (even if they did much of the heavy lifting themselves). They catch people doing positive work and celebrate those efforts. That recognition is equally important for students, teachers, parents, and community volunteers who are supporting gardening projects.

5. Welcome attention. Green school programs are still so novel that they attract public interest. Wise leaders don't fear media attention; they welcome it. They know how to use social media strategically to communicate success.

6. Invite (the right) partners. Schools don't thrive in isolation. Like any organism, they do best when they are part of a healthy ecosystem and are encouraged to evolve. Connections with community partners build and strengthen that ecosystem, creating access to expanded resources and increased opportunities for student and community success. Visionary leaders are strategic when it comes to forming partnerships to grow green programs. The right partnerships add value to both sides, just like a balanced math equation. When considering a collaboration, leaders need to look beyond a potential partner's Web site or glossy brochure. They must be wary of being used as a photo opportunity to support a partner's

fund-raising efforts. Effective leaders also know that they can't say yes to everything that comes along or they will overwhelm their staff.

Asking the right questions will help leaders build strong partner relationships. Understanding who will be doing the actual work is critical. Here are my opening questions to ask potential partners: *What will our combined effort look like— how can we make sure one plus one equals more than two? Where else have you worked with schools? Which partnerships didn't work out? Why? How often are you committed to being here at our school? How do you screen and/or train your volunteers and staff? What data do you plan to collect? How flexible are you willing to be to meet our unique needs?*

Once they have done their due diligence about partners, wise leaders need to make the call by asking themselves: *Will this partnership help us achieve our vision for our students? Will it support and inspire our teachers, or overwhelm them? Who's excited about moving forward, and why?*

ACKNOWLEDGMENTS

With dreams begin responsibilities. I hope this book makes you hug a child; thank a teacher; kiss a parent, grandparent, auntie, or uncle; and inspires you to do one kind act. I hope you remember that behind every success story, there is a teacher, a mentor, and someone who cared; acknowledge them, please.

Without a doubt, I stand on the shoulders of giants. I am forever grateful to my parents, principals, supervisors, fellow teachers, classroom aides, mentors, and students who have spent time with me teaching me that relationships and honesty are at the core of all we do. These are the people who remain a part of my life and my students' lives to this very day. For those who have always believed in me and supported me, I am forever grateful. Each and every day is an opportunity to pay that faith forward by investing in my students and colleagues. I appreciate the congratulatory notes and kind words from all—friends old and new. I thank each of you for helping us to grow, including those long removed and apart from any of the work we are doing today. We are the ones we are waiting for! The Bronx is no longer burning. We are blooming!

For my beloved Borough of the Bronx, my city of neighborhoods, home to the people and life that I love, your grit, resilience, fortitude, passion, dignity, and humility—against all odds—continue to amaze me daily. From the Grand Concourse to Hunts Point Avenue, from Jerome Avenue to Southern Boulevard, from Gun Hill Road to Bruckner Boulevard, from Boston Road to Sedgwick Avenue, from Port Morris to Fieldston, from east to west and north to south and all points in between, each and every scene is the essence of my being. From the walls I have written on to the doors I have knocked upon and run through and back—again and again. From the rivers and beaches I have swum in and canoed upon, to the trains I have ridden and been conductor on; looking back, never whack, across miles of track, always going somewhere and dreaming big. From girls, babies, and grandmas kissed to XXL opportunities missed, from the roof of the Bank Note to love letters wrote, from the war on drugs to the never-ending hugs, friends old and new everywhere, this is a mad and torrid love affair.

From the basketball courts and bodegas I have played in, to the synagogues, churches, and mosques I have prayed in, to the soil, roofs, and farms I have tended with your cool, forgiving wind on my back and brow, thank you for being the lifeblood that pumps through my heart and veins, here and now. I have lived a thousand lives on our streets, danced with so many of you, and am proud to call you my home. You have helped me find my place and will forever be my sacred space. You are my endless energy and eternal optimism. Play hard, praise God, avoid drama, love mama, and forever shoot the three. Plan to win, run from sin, turn the volume up. Grand funk, slam dunk, always play good D. Beat box, run blocks, dance, dance, dance. From abandoned lots to number spots, train yards to boulevards, from hip-hop to barbershop, shattered crumbling glass en route to Sunday mass, we have a rhythm and song that are all our own; seeds forever sown and internationally known. We are the phoenix forever rising. Bronx rock, planet rock—soul sonic force! Can't stop! Won't stop! *No pares, SIGUE, SIGUE!*

To Stan Zucker, who gave me a chance by betting on my future and giving me a chance when no other person would: thank you. To my students past, present, and future, and their parents: thank you for trusting me, for believing in me, for listening to me! I LOVE YOU ALL. Thank you for coming to school each and every day, for braving snowstorms and rainstorms, for riding buses and trains, for coming early and staying late, for walking me home at night and bringing me breakfast, for doing your homework and saying please and thank you; and of course, for eating your vegetables. Our collective successes are reflective of the belief that together, we can grow something greater. This moment teaches us many things and points to the future with one singular message: THE BEST IS YET TO COME!

To Marisa Vigilante and the team at Rodale; Lynn Johnston, who called me one day with an idea for a book and planted this seed; my manager, Jared Shahid; and my cowriter, Suzie Boss, and her husband, Bruce Rubin: Thank you for your support, your belief, and for enduring a cavalcade of e-mails and edits; collisions, connections and co-learnings. We made epic happen! To my colleagues and all who gave me that special opportunity, provided a quote, a blurb, a hug, or a shoulder to cry on, either long ago or recently, I will work never-endingly and relentlessly in appreciation, determined to be the change we all believe in. This is for all of us; no justice, just us!

I know that my father, my son, my grandparents, and far too many more in heaven are smiling right now. I miss them all and hope to honor them everlastingly. In particular, I want to thank my wife, Lizette, and my daughter, Michaela, who have given selflessly and tirelessly through the years and who are at the heart and core of our extended Bronx, national, and international families. Without you, I am lost. Team Ritz never quits; I love you dearly! SÍ SE PUEDE!

Utah Phillips wrote, "The degree to which you resist injustice is the degree to which you are free." It is time to get back to work! Inspired by Samuel Gompers, my cry is a simple one: more schools and less jails, more books and less guns, more learning and less vice, more leisure and less greed, more justice and less revenge! More opportunities to embrace our better nature! Together, we can do this! One student at a time, one teacher at a time, one classroom at a time, one school at a time, one community at a time! Today and forever forward, we plant our stake in the ground; lettuce, turnip, the beet! MAKE EPIC HAPPEN!

INDEX

GREEN BRONX MACHINE: JOIN THE MOVEMENT!

To learn more about Green Bronx Machine, visit our Web site at www.greenbronxmachine.org.

For information about ordering our curriculum, including green classroom lessons and authentic learning experiences mapped to academic content standards, visit www.greenbronxmachine.org.

Connect with Green Bronx Machine on social media:

To learn more about Stephen Ritz or inquire about speaking engagements, visit www.stephenritz.com.

Follow Stephen on social media:

Green Bronx Machine is a 501(c)3 organization. We appreciate your support!